ARTIFICIAL INTELLIGENCE AND CONTEMPORARY MEDIA

Editors:
Dr. Moon Jana and Dr. Shourini Banerjee

notionpress.com
INDIA · SINGAPORE · MALAYSIA

ISBN
Paperback 979-8-89744-597-4
Hardcase 979-8-89929-952-0

Dedicated to

Moon Jana's Grandmother - Renuka

Shourini Banerjee's Grandmother - Maya

Contents

About the Editors

Dr. Moon Jana is working as an Assistant Professor in the Department of Journalism and Mass Communication, Asutosh College under the University of Calcutta. Dr. Jana has completed her Graduation and Post-Graduation from Siliguri College, Siliguri, and Visva Bharati (Central University). She is UGC NET scholar and has completed her PhD on Environment Reporting of Print Media from Visva Bharati, Santiniketan. She has published several research papers in national and international peer reviewed journals and contributed book chapters published nationally. In her short career, she has worked with multiple reputed colleges and universities including University of Kalyani, Jadavpur University. She is also a member of the Under Graduation and Post-Graduation Board of Studies of several reputed institutions in the field of Journalism and Mass Communication. Prior to her present status as an Assistant Professor, she was associated with All India Radio for more than 15 years. She has been working closely with nature and environment conservation organizations to promote desirable change with regard to environmental awareness and literacy. Beside academic writings, she also has published many non-academic environment literacy-based articles in reputed journals. Her main area of research is environment reporting, climate literacy, media literacy, community radio etc.

Dr. Shourini Banerjee is currently an Assistant Professor in the Department of Visual Communication, The American College, Madurai. She is the Head of The Dept of Costume Design and Fashion and Co-Ordinator of BVoc/MVoc Media Technology, The American College, Madurai. She is also a Visiting faculty for Jain University Online and is associated with Xaviers Institute of Management, Odisha as an Adjunct Faculty.

She has over 10 years of experience as a media academician. She completed her Ph.D. research on "Gender and Masculinity in Television Commercials- A Critical Study" in 2019. She has presented 25 papers at national and international conferences and has 47 publications which includes Scopus indexed articles. Besides to her credit, she has 2 co-edited books on "A Panoramic View on Women and Films in India" and "Regional Media-Emerging Trends & Prospects". Her area of specialisation is Communication and Media Research, Media Literacy, Advertisements, and Gender Studies. She is also an active member of the Book Guild of Madurai.

She has delivered lectures on different topics in various colleges across the country. She is a certified trainer from FACTSHALA which is a news and information literacy initiative launched by Internews in collaboration with DataLEADS with support from Google.org. and has conducted 32 Factshala workshops across the country.

Preface

All India Council for Technical Education (AICTE) has announced 2025 as "The Year of Artificial Intelligence". Artificial Intelligence has totally transformed not just the IT industries but all the sectors around the world. Artificial Intelligence has even been diffused in the educational sector with the Ministry of Education emphasising it to be a part of the curriculum. Artificial Intelligence being the buzz word has transformed the media industry. This book aims at analysing and delving into the aspects of Artificial Intelligence's influence in the media industry.

The rapid advancement of Artificial Intelligence (AI) is reshaping contemporary media in profound ways. From content creation and journalism to audience engagement and ethical considerations, AI's influence is undeniable. This edited volume, **"Artificial Intelligence and Contemporary Media"**, brings together diverse perspectives from scholars, practitioners, and industry experts to explore the intersection of AI and modern media landscapes.

We dedicate this book to our beloved grandmothers, Smt. Renuka Pal and Smt. Maya Mukherjee whose love, wisdom, and unwavering support have been a guiding force in our life. Though she is no longer with us, her memory continues to inspire us, and this work is a tribute to her enduring influence. This journey would not have been possible without the unwavering support of our families. We are deeply grateful to our parents and spouse whose encouragement, belief in my aspirations, and constant motivation have helped me bring this project to fruition. Their presence has been a source of strength throughout this endeavor.

I profusely thank our reviewer Dr. M. Muthukumar, Assistant Professor, Department of Visual Communication, The American College, Madurai for his meticulous review of each chapter and invaluable suggestions. I sincerely thank our authors for bringing out unique chapters delving into different aspects of Artificial Intelligence and Media. I also thank our esteemed professors Dr. Onkaragouda Kakade and Dr. G.Kannabiran for their warm feedback and input regarding the book.

I also extend my sincere appreciation to the contributors who have shared their expertise and insights, enriching this volume with their knowledge. Their contributions have made this book a meaningful exploration of AI's role in contemporary media.

I hope this book serves as a valuable resource for researchers, media professionals, and anyone interested in understanding the evolving relationship between AI and media.

This book is a dedication to all the scholars, students and academicians interested in Artificial Intelligence and the work of media.

Foreword

In an era where artificial intelligence (AI) has seamlessly woven itself into the fabric of modern society, its profound impact on the media landscape cannot be overlooked. AI has revolutionized how information is produced, consumed, and disseminated, transforming journalism, entertainment, governance, and even the cultural and emotional dimensions of human interaction. It is with great enthusiasm that I present this remarkable compilation, Artificial Intelligence and Contemporary Media, edited by the scholars Dr.Moon Jana and Dr.Shourini Banerjee.

This book stands as a crucial academic intervention at a time when AI continues to disrupt traditional media structures while opening up new frontiers of possibilities. The editors have meticulously curated a collection of insightful chapters that explore AI's multifaceted influence on media, covering its technological advancements, ethical implications, and socio-cultural consequences. By bringing together eminent scholars and experts, they provide a well-rounded perspective that enriches our understanding of this dynamic intersection. The chapters in this volume traverse a broad spectrum of themes, from AI's role in journalism, art, filmmaking, and digital literacy to its implications for democratic integrity, cyber terrorism, and emotional well-being. Discussions on algorithmic governance, the amalgamation of languages with AI, and the impact of AI on socio-cultural-economic constructs make this book not just a technological exploration but also a philosophical and ethical inquiry into the future of media. Particularly relevant is the chapter on ChatGPT in Indian newsrooms, which highlights how generative AI tools are reshaping journalistic practices, raising concerns about credibility, authenticity, and creative autonomy.

Dr. Moon Jana and Dr. Shourini Banerjee deserve commendation for their vision and dedication in compiling such a timely and thought-provoking volume. Their editorial expertise is evident in the diverse yet interconnected themes explored within this book. They have succeeded in fostering an interdisciplinary dialogue that bridges technology, communication studies, and social sciences, making this book an invaluable resource for scholars, media professionals, policymakers, and anyone interested in understanding AI's evolving role in contemporary media.

As AI continues to redefine our media landscapes, this book serves as a guiding beacon, shedding light on both opportunities and challenges. It compels us to critically engage with AI's implications, ensuring that media remains a space for truth, inclusivity, and ethical storytelling. I am confident that Artificial Intelligence and Contemporary Media will spark meaningful discussions and inspire further research in this ever-evolving field.

With deep appreciation for the editors and contributors, I wholeheartedly recommend this book to readers eager to navigate the complex yet fascinating relationship between AI and contemporary media.

Prof. Onkaragouda Kakade

Senior Professor and Head,

Department of Journalism and Mass Communication,

Karnataka State Akkamahadevi Women's University,

Vijayapura, Karnataka

Foreword

It is heartening to note that Dr. Moon Jana and Dr. Shourini Banerjee are bringing out a volume on Artificial Intelligence and Media. This scholastic work is a testament to their commitment to academic excellence and dedication in addressing contemporary challenges.

In the ever-evolving landscape of technology especially in Media, Artificial Intelligence (AI) has a profound impact on society. As both educators and consumers, we find ourselves at the intersection of these two powerful forces. Media, in all its forms — print, broadcast, digital and Social media has always been a pivotal force in shaping public discourse and influencing societal trends. The media acts as both a disseminator of information and a platform for the dissemination of ideas, opinions and narratives surrounding this transformative technology.

AI, with its complex algorithms and capabilities, often feels like an abstract and distant concept. It is the media that makes these ideas accessible and relatable to the general public by breaking down technical jargon and presenting it in a way that is understandable to the wider audience. For example, films like The Matrix, Ex Machina, Irah (Hindi), Ra. One (Hindi), Wandering Earth, Enthiran (Tamil) introduces themes surrounding AI. While these fictional portrayals are often sensationalized for dramatic effect, they still raise important questions about the role AI will play in shaping future societies.

Media is also a powerful tool for promoting AI applications, particularly in industries like advertising, entertainment, journalism, communication, etc. AI algorithms now power much of the content we consume daily. Recommendation systems that are used by Netflix, YouTube or Spotify use AI to suggest videos, shows and music based on our preferences. Social media platforms use AI to curate news feeds, target advertisements and even identify patterns in user behavior. While these algorithms are often invisible to users, their influence on shaping opinions, behaviors and even political ideologies cannot be understated.

The portrayal of AI in the media often swings between utopian visions of AI-powered utopias and dystopian nightmares where machines overpower humans. These extremes can lead to fear or unrealistic expectations, and in both cases, hinder a balanced, informed discourse on the ethical and practical implications of AI. Thus, it becomes crucial for media outlets to navigate their role as information agent with a sense of responsibility, ensuring that their coverage of AI fosters a thoughtful, nuanced conversation rather than contributing to sensationalism.

The compilation of articles highlights the role of Artificial Intelligence (AI) in shaping media, needless to say that it encompasses almost all the important aspects of art, journalism, film marketing, cyber terrorism, emotional health, opportunities and threats that impacts on socio- cultural and economic fabric of the society. This book seeks to explore the critical role that media plays in shaping our understanding of AI and shape a future where AI and media coexist that benefits all.

Dr. G Kannabiran

Associate Professor and Head,

Department of Economics

The American College (Autonomous)

Madurai, Tamil Nadu.

AI in Art: Analysing Dall-E'S Interpretation of Fauvism, Surrealism, Pointillism, Impressionism, Expressionism through Postcards

Ms Mouli Priya PC,Research scholar, Department of Journalism and Communication, Madras University, Chennai. Email: Moulipriya1023@gmail.com

Dr. T. Jaisakthivel, Assistant Professor, Department of Journalism and Communication, Madras University, Chennai. Email:bbcsakthi@gmail.com

Introduction

Artificial Intelligence has intruded in a host of realms, and the gifted creators are turning a new leaf in creativity and artistry. It transforms the creative industry by automation of repeated operations. It generates new concepts of design and makes rounded designs with ease, bringing efficiency and creativity into the profession. (Mustafa, 2023) In its very essence, at the core of this technological renaissance, is AI-generated artworks, which use very complex internal algorithms to devise vivid visual artwork. This research paper will focus on the details of AI-generated artworks while shadowing four of the most distinguished art movements, including Fauvism, Surrealism, Pointillism, Impressionism, and Expressionism. Artificial Intelligence has intruded into a host of realms, and gifted creators are turning a new leaf in creativity and artistry. It transforms the creative industry by automating repetitive operations, generating new concepts, and enhancing efficiency in the design process. At its core, AI-generated artworks rely on complex algorithms to devise vivid and unique visual outputs. The use of AI in art raises fascinating questions about its ability to replicate human creativity and artistic intent. While AI tools like DALL-E can generate impressive images, the nuances of human artistry—such as cultural, emotional, and philosophical underpinnings—pose significant challenges for these systems. This brings us to an important question: How well can AI capture the essence of art movements that are deeply rooted in specific cultural and emotional contexts?

To explore this, the research shifts its focus to four distinguished art movements—Fauvism, Surrealism, Pointillism, and Expressionism—each with unique stylistic and philosophical characteristics. These movements were chosen for their diversity in technique and interpretation, offering a rich framework to evaluate the capabilities and limitations of DALL-E's outputs. As a result, these two movements, in itself, significantly diverse from the other, in their philosophical and aesthetic underpinnings alike, are a platform for the explanation of the abilities and disabilities of AI in replicating human artistic expressions. (Shi, Y. 2024) These four art styles are each very different in approach to visual representation and therefore uniquely challenging for AI to be coded to replicate. More specifically, this paper explores how an AI model, DALL-E, interprets artworks in those four styles. DALL-E has demonstrated a remarkable ability to emulate the visual styles of major art movements, capturing the boldness of Fauvism, the intricate detail of Pointillism, and the dreamlike qualities of Surrealism. Its technical proficiency in synthesizing these artistic features highlights the creative potential of AI to innovate and expand the boundaries of traditional art.

However, while DALL-E excels at mimicking surface-level stylistic elements, it falls short in grasping the deeper cultural and emotional nuances that define these movements. For instance, art movements like Expressionism and Impressionism are rooted in the subjective experiences and emotional responses of the artist, elements that an AI system, reliant on pattern recognition, cannot genuinely replicate. Additionally, DALL-E often overlooks culturally specific motifs and symbols, resulting in outputs that feel generic or detached from their intended cultural contexts.

This bias toward emphasizing visual aesthetics over meaning raises questions about the authenticity of AI-generated art. While DALL-E can 'perform' styles convincingly, it lacks the human insight and lived experience required to imbue the art with context, emotion, or philosophical depth. To fully integrate AI into the creative process, there must be a conscious effort to address these limitations, ensuring that AI systems are not only tools for innovation but also respectful interpreters of cultural and artistic traditions.

Dall-E

The intersection of artificial intelligence and art has led to a new era of creativity and innovation. One of the greatest developments in this field is DALL-E, which is an AI model that can turn a sentence into an image; it is State of the Art in Text-to-Image modeling. (Liu, Zhang, 2021). The fact that DALL-E can restyle images to include stylistic nuances of famous art styles raises intriguing questions regarding art and the artist himself. On the other hand, the process of designing artwork with artificial intelligence has been described as 'autolography'- derived from Greek phrases 'automatos + logos + graphos' literally self + word + drawing (Chesher, 2022). This has transformed the conventional ways in most industries, and art is another interesting element. AI technologies such as machine learning algorithms, generative models, and neural networks are increasingly applied to augment and automate the creative process (Brown & Singer, 2020). This dissertation explores the current trend in which AI is found to broadly dominate the art world, and the discussion focuses on the means with which AI systems operate and the impact this has on the art community.

There have been quite substantial developments on the use of AI in works of art. In the olden times, AI was mainly applied only for automation purposes such as in content creation and literature writings. The advancements in machine learning algorithms and generative models made the abilities of AI in assisting, and even sometimes alone, create creative visual contents (Sculley et al., 2015). The efficiency, creativity, and possibilities of developing multiple forms of art characterize the advantages of AI in the process of producing art. AI provides the designers with a chance to think more abstractly due to the automation of mundane activities and new ideas for innovation on higher levels (Chen et al., 2018). This research seeks to explore the capabilities of DALL-E in reproducing and reinterpreting the released postcards by the developing media platform called Postally Hut run by students as young communications learners, where the mission is to bring to life an almost-lost art in writing letters through this digital century by the creation of fresh interest in tangible forms of communication, such as postcards, among the youth.

Postcards have been the manifestation of national phenomena, changes in printing technology, developments of postal regulations, modes of communication, and popular culture in one. Lear,2008 It was always able to hold within the small physical form memories, emotions, and expressions. There were postcards recognized as feting or recording nations' cultures and celebrations. (Kearns,1997) Hence the research paper will look at the various forms of art, including fauvism, surrealism, impressionism, pointillism, and expressionism through the reproduction of postcards on the theme of postal communication produced by the postcards used as references for creating the art produced by Postally hut.

The purpose of this research is to get an understanding of the possible and impossible for a model of this type, such as DALL-E, which can represent the art world by understanding how DALL-E understands these specific art forms. This chapter is on the theme of postal communication-the reason it was chosen is in its historical and cultural significance as an expression and a means of connection. Postcards are a rare combination of visual art and communication, capturing a moment in personal sentiment and cultural representation. Through the lens of postal communication, we may study how art movements connect with everyday life, cultural identity, and the exchange of ideas across time and space. In addition, as a physical medium of communication, postcards are well suited to explore how AI understands artistic styles in terms of close, communicative imagery, capturing the aesthetic and narrative qualities defining every movement.

This paper will describe the nature of these art movements, illustrate examples of DALL-E's renderings, and compare these AI-created works to the traditional counterparts, for an all-inclusive assessment of the interaction between artificial intelligence and artistic heritage.Therefore, in addition to bringing attention to the technological advances made by DALL-E, this study contributes to the ongoing discussion about the dynamic between technology and art. With AI constantly advancing, it is important to understand its impact on creative fields, which can give insights into future possibilities and ethical considerations. On the contrary, the paper describes how the adaptation is cross over different forms of art and is manageable and replicable of any artistic style that speaks about the possibility of DALL-E by producing images in the theme of postal communication. This paper attempts to know all the strengths and weaknesses of this model in reproducing various nuances of any style of art which shall add further dimensions to the growing discourse of technology and art.

The AI-driven generation of images has traveled a long way through the development of models according to OpenAI, DALL-E, capable of generating images according to a given textual description. From DALL-E 1 to DALL-E 3, one can realize the developments made in terms of image quality, fidelity, and complicated prompt understanding. (Baker, Gonzalez, Carter, & Turner, 2024) The early methods of image synthesis were based on paired datasets; however, the high cost and impracticability of collecting such data instigated interest in unsupervised methods. Models like Cycle GAN have made it possible to perform robust image-to-image translation without paired data. Supervised approaches, mostly based on conditional GANs, have combined adversarial loss with L1 regularization to generate realistic images. These, in turn, have not only helped in supporting the betterment of artistic creation but also implicated applications in marketing, design, education, and healthcare. AI's ability to generate great quality imagery that is relevant in context within seconds underlines the transformative potential across various industries. Ethical and logical considerations, however, are huge in responsible development and deployment regarding AI, particularly in the processes associated with keeping it from misapplication to generate deep fakes.

The other paper, "Applications of Artificial Intelligence in Graphic Design," contributes to the understanding of how AI technologies change the perception of graphic design. The study grounded its research on descriptive content for the sake of getting knowledge about the way AI finds space within this domain and the influences it has on creativity and efficiency during the design process. (Al-Dulaimi, 2023) The research focused on the possibility of AI automating routine tasks to give the designers more room to pay attention to the creative sections while performing their duties. AI explains that besides giving a competitive advantage, it stimulates innovation and new design methodologies. Therefore, the research covers the preliminary challenges that were faced when adopting AI, especially the creative awareness required for proper integration. However, it posits that these are not permanent challenges and that AI is soon going to turn out to be a much-needed tool in the graphic design industry in terms of enhancing productivity, improving creativity, and raising innovative output.

"The Work of Art in the Age of AI Image Generation"(Coeckelbergh, 2023) is a paper on AI image generators like DALL-E 2 and their changes impact on art. The discussion centers on whether AI-generated images would be considered art and who would be accorded the title of artist. The author criticizes the traditional definition of art, showing that AI can indeed create art; however, for this, a shift in one's understanding is needed toward process and performance. In this context, ethical and legal issues about AI art creation are, inter alia, questions of authorship, copyright, and possible biases. On this basis, the author argues for a dynamic understanding of human–technology relations in art creation, where the act of creation by a human or an AI signals a co-creative process with important contributions from both. This relational view brings to the fore the roles of the artist and the artwork as not intrinsically fixed, but rather as emerging in interactions and performances between humans and technology. Therein lies a holistic view of the role of AI in art—a move beyond the rigid definitions to encapsulate modern complexities of technological contributions in creative processes.

Method of Analysis

Relevance of Semiotic Analysis in AI Art Evaluation

Understanding AI-generated art requires more than just evaluating its technical proficiency or visual appeal—it demands a deeper examination of how these works convey meaning and whether they capture the essence of human creativity. Semiotic analysis, a framework pioneered by Ferdinand de Saussure, provides a structured approach to deconstructing the elements of AI-generated art.

By differentiating between the "signifier" (the physical form of the generated image) and the "signified" (the conceptual meaning or cultural essence behind it), semiotics help us evaluate whether AI effectively captures the stylistic and cultural nuances of traditional art movements. This approach is particularly relevant in assessing AI's ability to replicate movements like

Fauvism, Surrealism, and Pointillism, which are not just defined by their visual styles but also by their emotional and philosophical underpinnings.

Semiotic analysis allows researchers to systematically evaluate the relationship between AI-generated images and their intended artistic inspirations, highlighting gaps in cultural authenticity, stylistic fidelity, and emotional depth. This paper employs Saussure's semiotic model to dissect the effectiveness of DALL-E's outputs in reimagining these distinct art movements.

The primary objective of this research is to investigate the artworks generated by DALL-E and examine the art style employed by the system. Through qualitative research methods and semiotic analysis and adapting art style, the study aims to provide a comprehensive understanding of the evolving landscape of DALL-E meeting its abilities to create artwork.

The semiotic application, as created by Ferdinand de Saussure, in the analysis of AI art gives a structured way within which the examination of just how close the artificial intelligence systems, such as OpenAI's DALL-E, are capable of emulating and re-imagining styles of important artistic movements, among them Fauvism, Surrealism, Pointillism, and Impressionism. In this simple structure, the basic premise is Saussure's theory of differentiating between the form of a sign, the signifier, and the concept a sign carries meaning to, the signified, upon which any attempt at analysis of the linkage, or otherwise, the chain between AI-generated visual elements and their corresponding related cultural and stylistic meanings.

Based on the semiotic model of Saussure, the binary connection stands as Signifier: The physical form of a sign. In the context of art created by AI, this will be the output image generated by DALL·E. This includes the formal elements: line, color, texture, composition, and others that are evident to the eye. Signified: The concept or idea to which the signified relates. Artistically, these are thematic and stylistic essences within which each art movement resides.

Analysis

Trek from DALL-E 1 to DALL-E 3: Into the Quantum Leap in Image Synthesis

Art and AI technologies, such as machine learning algorithms, generative models, and neural networks, are increasingly being integrated to support and automate the creative process. For example, DALL-E is a transformer-based neural network that is one of the deep learning models good at sequential data processing, like text. In this model, the two-step process is applied: first, it encodes textual descriptions into a latent space representation, linking words to abstract visual concepts. Second, it translates this representation into an image with a generative adversarial network or a diffusion model, refining the output iteratively for increased realism and stylistic consistency.

To reproduce particular styles, DALL-E uses massive training on datasets that consist of paired images with their corresponding textual prompts. It thus learns to associate descriptive words ("bright colors," "brushstrokes wide enough") with visual features typical of these styles. For instance, to create a Fauvist image, DALL-E leverages its knowledge of the bold color palette and expressive brushstrokes. Yet, while the system can emulate surface-level stylistic features, it often cannot replicate the nuanced emotional and cultural underpinnings of human-created artworks. DALL-E uses a transformer-based neural network to process sequential data. The use of a generative adversarial network (GAN) then helps create a visual output after encoding textual prompts as vectors. Having a training dataset that holds millions of text-image pairs lets DALL-E associate linguistic cues with stylistic features to mimic different styles of art. OpenAI keeps on creating new benchmarks in the arena of artificial intelligence. They gained a new revolution with the arrival of DALL-E 3, an AI model generating images based on long-form textual descriptions — a robust base having developed earlier through ChatGPT. This advanced image synthesizer drew a lot of attention in the tech world. We analyze in great depth the complex features of DALL-E 3 and its possible repercussions in this paper, also explaining why this development in AI technology is such a big deal.

The journey of OpenAI with DALL-E 3 began with the innovation of the pioneering release of DALL-E 1, an image generator that could create visuals from textual descriptions. Every step along the way with each new release, DALL-E has been a huge leap forward; DALL-E 3 is really representative of the improvements that have been made. The latest iteration weaves in the advanced linguistic abilities of ChatGPT and significantly enhances its synthesizing capability with images of high quality and rich in detail. This represents a huge step up in terms of image resolution and quality, improved handling of more complex details, and reduced visual artifacts from DALL-E 1 to DALL-E 2. DALL-E 3 will take it a step further with state-of-the-art linguistic models imported from ChatGPT, enabling the system to understand and execute even more complex prompts with incredible accuracy.

DALL-E 3, at its core, relies on complex neural networks trained on a large dataset to learn text-to-image translation. The combination of linguistic analysis and art creation is enabled by transformers and masters in the processing of sequential data such as text. First, it starts with encoding text prompts, and then there is the creation of an image, where the model orchestrates pixel after pixel to make sure the fidelity remains to the descriptive nuances captured in the prompt. In essence, DALL-E 3 is trained on unfathomable text-image pairs that are aimed at making the association of some words with visual elements easy. Such extensive training allows it to take on all kinds of subjects and styles, thereby making its application even more versatile.

Artistic Implications of DALL-E 3

One of the most alluring aspects of DALL-E 3 is its ability to turn textual descriptions into striking visual art. What it creates is stretching imaginative and sometimes quite surreal in nature, well beyond the bounds of what is usually classified as creative. For an artist or designer, it will be a new facility that can help open many new possibilities for trying out styles in art to conceptualize and visualize something that was not so easy earlier. This is a feature that allows the realization of just about any piece of art directly from the text, allowing the creation of unique and original forms of artistic expression like never before. This moving feature of DALL-E 3 will redefine the crossover between technology, art, and creation, showcasing the model as a creative and independent partner for the art generation. Further analyses of the artworks generated by DALL-E verify its capabilities by creating art around the theme of postal communication, namely postcards, postmen, and letter-boxes, in each of those four art forms.

Fauvism

The Fauves used pure, brilliant colors, aggressively applied straight from the paint tubes, to create the effect of an explosion on the canvas. As with the Impressionists before them, the Fauves painted directly from nature but charged their works with an effective emotional reaction to the subjects shown. The first avant-garde movement that flourished in France at the beginning of the 20th century was Fauvism. This was a remarkable break away from the Impressionism of the older generation and more traditional ways of perceiving. Fauve painters translated their spontaneous, often subjective response to nature with undisguised bold strokes and high-keyed, vibrant colors applied directly from the tube. Such style resulted in pictures that were emotionally intense and immediate, thus making Fauvism a very vital movement in the development of art throughout the twentieth century.

This AI-created postcard is vibrant and strong coloration with lively strokes capturing the liveliness synonymous with the Fauvist genre. But

the true style of fauvism has faded. For instance, comparing the artwork of Henri Matisse's *The Green Stripe*—a quintessential example of Fauvism—highlights how DALL-E attempts to replicate the bold, vibrant colors characteristic of the movement but fails to capture the spontaneity and emotional intensity of Fauvist brushstrokes.

Thematically, though all elements are there, with the red postbox, the white cats, and the birds being as they were in the basic design. Maintained are the color values of Fauvism, yet it misses some of the cultural connotations that a piece in an Indian style would contain. This actually makes it miss some local architecture, traditional patterns, and cultural motifs that seriously deplete the authenticity and relatability of an Indian setting. The applied AI is quite plain and tends to a style far less characteristically of the colonial United Kingdom, sans the flair of India from the original. For example, the flowers in the postcard AI were a lot less abstract, non culturally succinct, and detailed compared to the originals.

Further, the peeling off of depth and richness develops into an opening up of the scene. In that Further, the peeling off of depth and richness develops into an opening up of the scene. In that process of simplification, the light, frivolous, fancy atmosphere of the original goes lost, enriched by minute expressions of the cats and specific postures for the birds. The AI replica comes with text positioned to read "Happy Postcrossing," missing this stylistic element of Fauvism with regard to placement and font styling, so fluid and solid. On some more macro levels, the postcard indeed mirrors the vibrancy of Fauvism in that it doesn't share deeper—some theories are put here—unconscious contexts of culture and nuanced brushwork to blow life and motion into an original piece of art. This means a scarcity of the job, deep down reminding us that AI should not just mimic a fleshy color scheme but rather a stroke of culture: very intricate textures that give charm and character to the original.

This style of traditional Indian art sometimes consists of intricate floral work, geometric motifs or simply iconography and folkloric aspects.

The lack of such markings can be seen in the use of postcard design by means of lacking rangoli-type floral motif designs or Mughal-type floral motifs that result in the lack of an essentially Indian visual discourse for its content.

Pointillism

Pointillism cropped up in the mid-1880s as a kind of scientific protest against the subjectivism of Impressionism. In this innovative technique, dots of pure and unmixed colors were applied very attentively to the canvas, causing the eye of the viewer to blend the colors and create images that were full of brilliance and vividness. Inspired by the work of French chemist Michel Eugène Chevreul on color harmony, the Pointillists applied the theories of complementary colors in order to increase the optical effect of their paintings. The term "Pointillism" was coined by the art critic Félix Fénéon, although Seurat himself preferred the terms "Divisionism" or "Chromoluminarism." Because of its methodical and scientific procedure for applying paint, rather than the more fluid and immediate process typical of Impressionism, Pointillism is removed even one step further from Impressionism than Impressionism is from Realism. A musical metaphor was often used to describe the process that was involved in the Pointillist technique, comparing the effort of arranging colors to, say, fitting together a symphony. Bold color combinations in pointillism led to great influence on the movement that succeeded it - Fauvist movement.

Seurat's **"A Sunday Afternoon on the Island of La Grande Jatte"** is a meticulous depiction of 19th-century Parisian bourgeois life, where static human figures, leisure activities, and a balanced composition reflect societal order and class distinction. The Pointillist technique enhances the vibrancy and depth, making it a social commentary on urban life and modernity.

In contrast, the AI-generated postcard, while visually engaging with its red postbox, doves, and cats, lacks the emotional and cultural depth found in Seurat's work. Its absence of human presence and reliance on generic symbols of communication render it more decorative than narrative-driven. Furthermore, it lacks cultural specificity, offering no connection to a particular tradition or context, thereby reducing its ability to convey layered meaning or social critique. This retains very well the positioning and key elements in the scene, like the red post-box, white cats, and flying doves. For example, the fine Indian cultural markers, as well as the originality found in the source image, are lost in the AI. In comparison with the reference image, it lacks some form of cultural inscription or design characteristic of the latter.

The flowers here have been very abstracted and undetailed within the postcard, hence losing aesthetic value and cultural worth. Although spirit-laden with the Pointillism treatment, the background lacks quality depth in representing the original and considerately shades the atmosphere to be less vivid and culturally bound. Further, the richness and authenticity of the scene are reduced by avoiding main local architecture, traditional patterns, and other specific cultural motives. In addition, all the expressions on the cats and the postures of the birds are omitted, which reduces the depth and texture of the scene.

Although spirit-laden with the Pointillism treatment, the background lacks quality depth in representing the original. This shortcoming arises because AI systems like DALL-E rely heavily on pattern recognition from vast datasets, which can accurately reproduce visual features but struggle with capturing the nuanced emotional and cultural contexts that underpin a style. Pointillism, for instance, is not just about applying small dots of color; it's about creating a vibrant interplay of light and color that requires an understanding of both the scientific principles of color theory and the artist's emotional response to the subject. AI struggles to interpret these subtle connections because it lacks human experience and cannot emotionally engage with the artwork.

Moreover, AI often overlooks the cultural depth embedded in traditional art. For example, the specific symbolism associated with color choices in Pointillism may not be recognized by the model if these meanings are not explicitly present in the training data. AI's inability to understand cultural or historical context makes it less capable of replicating the deeper essence of a movement or the artist's original intent.

Impressionism

The term Impressionism defines a late 19th-century movement, most precisely dated from 1867 to 1886, that defines an art movement embracing those who shared related approaches and techniques. Modern life that was being lived and the fleeting effects of light and color were captured in the art. Viewed by today's standards, these may seem very ordinary, but they were truly revolutionary during the 19th century. During that period, the subjects that were the most prevalent were historical, biblical, and allegorical, where an extremely high finish in painting was expected. The Impressionists contributed much to changing the focus of art from the traditional subjects toward the expression of one's self and light and color.

The AI postcard tries to imitate the style of Impressionism. This is a painting characterized by loose strokes and a great deal of light and color used to make a vivid, joyful scene. On the card, there is a red post-box surrounded by white cats and flying doves with "Happy Postcrossing" underlined to underline joy and communication. Even though it didn't deviate too much from the general layout and main elements, all the cultural authenticity is replaced by the AI in avoiding specific Indian design features on the post-box, and culturally significant details in the flowers, which become more abstract and less detailed than those of the original. Compared to the source image, the background is impressionistic and lacks finesse in details and subtlety in depth. It misses altogether this kind of whimsical play that is a part of the cultural context for this original scene. The local architecture, traditional patterns, and cultural motifs are overlooked.

This lessens the richness and authenticity of this scene. Lacking cat expressions and postures for birds, or at best oversimplifying them, shrinks the depth and character of this image. It doesn't texturally align with its placement and styling, compared to the Impressionist theme in the original. Some of that feel of Impressionism was captured by this AI rendering in a visual sense but just didn't carry through on what brought life to the original postcard—that feel of culture and detailed texture. It should hence be more sensational and original, missing cultural and minute details if this is going to be a real contender in AI picture creation.

Impressionism captures transient moments of light and color, often depicting ordinary scenes. DALL-E's Impressionist postcards emulate this style but exclude the cultural features specific to Indian landscapes and social milieus. An Indian Impressionist scene might include bustling markets, richly dressed figures in traditional dress, or festivals like Holi with its explosion of colors. Adding textures of Indian foliage, banyan or neem trees, and culturally significant animals like peacocks or cows to the piece could make it culturally relevant. These elements are obviously missing in DALL-E's generic Impressionist interpretations.

The AI-generated postcard and Claude Monet's *Impression, Sunrise* both draw inspiration from Impressionist aesthetics but diverge significantly in execution and emotional depth. While Monet's work masterfully captures the transient interplay of light and atmosphere in a subdued harbor scene, the AI postcard takes a whimsical approach with vivid colors and playful imagery of cats, doves, and a red post box. However, the postcard lacks the cultural and contextual specificity that grounds Monet's painting, which reflects a moment in 19th-century France's industrial era. The AI piece, while visually engaging, simplifies textures, omits nuanced depth, and fails to evoke the fleeting, immersive quality characteristic of true Impressionism, instead presenting a more decorative and generic interpretation of the style.

Surrealism

Surrealism is a cultural and artistic movement that combines elements of the subconscious, dreams, and the irrational to build a world beside the one in which we live. That universe, full of magical and ludicrous features, can be described as something opposing and disturbingly disrupting the classic perception of real life. To the Surrealists, the subconscious mind was to be opened and explored into the psyche of humans, and this meant that every deep thought or aspiration had to be expressed regardless of whether it made sense or not. With its roots often traced back to the end of World War I - a time of huge disillusionment and trauma -, Surrealism was created out of the devastation brought by the war and new technologies and changes in society that created a demand for new art forms.

This AI Surrealist postcard deploys atypical Surrealist distorting forms and fantastic features—the general structure of a post box, red in color, with white cats, flying doves—but lacks cultural authenticity regarding Indian motifs and design features on the post-box that would impart real character to the image. These flowers in this picture are too abstract, lacking cultural importance and botanical and cultural detail that forms part of the original postcard. The surrealistic background, creative as it is, misses out on the depth and fine lines that characterize the original postcard, carrying a cultural essence. Although fun in its whimsical way, the AI barely measures up to display that light energy of the original. It misplaces these very essential cultural cues that give only the right texture to a scene: local architecture, traditional patterns, and culturally specific motifs that further complicate things and set a scene in its proper context.And it does so while also simplifying or entirely removing small but significant background details, like the cats' facial expressions or the postures of the birds—amongst many other typical background elements—that go a long way to adding richness and texture to a scene. In addition, the text on the AI postcard, "Happy Postcrossing", is not included in style, as in the original; it was not with this font and placement making it becoming quite out of place when combined with the surrealistic theme.

DALL-E's creations are dreamlike and irrational, like Surrealism, but they lack Indian cultural motifs that could make them more meaningful. For example, the Surrealist interpretation of Indian mythology, such as a multi-armed deity or floating mandalas, could merge the fantastical with the cultural. Traditional Indian art often blurs the line between reality and spirituality, as seen in miniature paintings or temple frescoes. Such elements as cosmic symbolism depicted in Madhubani art or surreal juxtapositions inspired by Kamasutra sculptures could be incorporated to give AI surreal works an undoubtedly Indian flavor.

The AI-generated postcard, with its whimsical surrealist composition of a red postbox surrounded by flying doves and white cats, contrasts René Magritte's *Philosopher's Lamp* in both cultural depth and execution. While both employ surrealist elements, Magritte's painting offers profound symbolic depth, blending objects like the pipe-nose and candle to provoke intellectual reflection, rooted in his signature style. The postcard, though imaginative, lacks the cultural authenticity and nuanced detail that might ground it in a specific context, such as Indian motifs or traditional patterns, which would elevate its significance. Furthermore, the AI's design simplifies textures and symbolic cues, resulting in a playful yet superficial image that misses the depth, fine details, and layered meaning seen in Magritte's work.

Expressionism

Expressionism is considered more of an international tendency, an art movement less coherent, particularly during the early years of the twentieth century. It stretched over all creative fields, from art and literature to music, theatre, and architecture. Expressionist artists attempt to express emotional experience and not the physical reality. Expressionism conventionally refers to the artistic tendency emerging in reaction to Impressionism in France or to the early twentieth-century movement that evolved in Germany and Austria. Expressionism expressed moral hypocrisy with society through themes of sexuality, death, and violence in intensive expressions of the environment and inner self.

In this Expressionist postcard created by AI, the lines are exaggerated, and the colors bright, and the overall expression is very emotive, with only the general layout and key objects maintained from the reference image. It misses any cultural authenticity completely while totally ignoring Indian design elements, motifs, or architectural details, due to which the replication becomes far less culturally relevant. While decoding the flowers in this AI version—it becomes conceptual and detailed less than the original, bereft of botanical detail, hence culturally symbolic. The background is dynamic, but it lost the subtlety and culture contained in the original. Very poorly embedded is the text "Happy Postcrossing." Somehow, it completely lost the harmony of style with the whole composition. It should, in general, contain elements of Indian-origin design and symbolic flowers and culturally relevant motifs. It should care about better text placement for improved aesthetics. An AI-created image would thus keep the vibrancy of Expressionism preserved, brushing in on the quirk of the postcard and its cultural context.

Expressionism is deeply emotional and raw, often emphasizing the artist's subjective experience. While DALL-E captures the emotive use of exaggerated lines and colors, it overlooks Indian cultural expressions of emotion. For instance, Indian Expressionism might draw from folk art like *Kalighat* paintings, which use bold lines and vivid colors to portray dramatic narratives. Themes of love, loss, and spirituality—ubiquitous in Indian art—could be depicted through exaggerated gestures, facial expressions, or culturally specific contexts like a religious procession or rural life during monsoons. DALL-E's generic approach to Expressionism fails to capture this depth of emotion tied to Indian traditions.

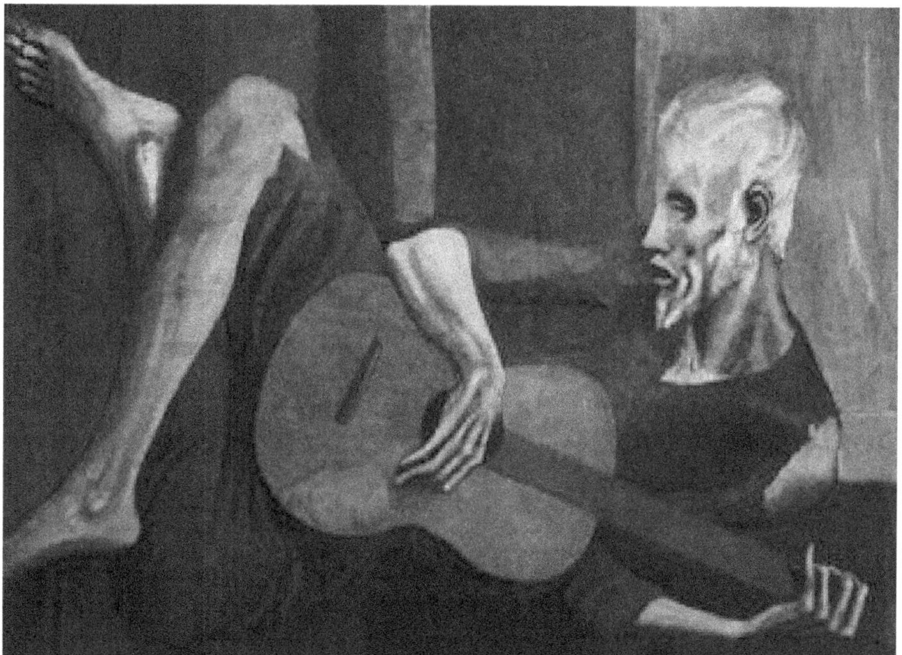

In contrast, Pablo Picasso's *The Old Guitarist* (1903–1904) embodies Expressionism through its muted blue tones and elongated, emaciated figure, evoking despair and melancholy. The guitar, as the central object, serves as both a literal instrument and a symbol of solace amidst suffering. Unlike the AI-generated image, which uses chaotic elements to communicate vibrancy, Picasso employs minimalism and stark contrasts to convey emotional depth. The posture and gaunt form of the guitarist amplify themes of poverty and human fragility, deeply tied to universal human experiences. While the AI image leans heavily on exaggerated whimsy, Picasso's work anchors its expression in human emotion and existential reflection, achieving a more profound and timeless resonance.

Findings

The varieties of art styles, from Fauvism to Surrealism, Pointillism, Impressionism, and Expressionism with AI-generated images, lacked nuanced cultural elements reflective of Indian origin and hence turned out generic and less real. There was a lack of richness in culture reflected in the artworks because traditional motifs, colours, and culturally significant details were missing. Equally, AI images lacked fine details, textures, emotional depth, or the capturing of subtle cultural cues, moods, and stylistic harmonies as seen in the original pieces. Although technically able to grasp these visual styles, it failed to convey the emotional essence and philosophical connotations that such art movements bore. In the future, improvement should head in a more culturally specific, detailed, and emotionally deep direction if AI-created art is to become more realistic and engaging.

To improve, the AI-generated photo needed far more unique Indian design and detailing intricate cultural flowers, with the backdrop being as decorative as the scene it wants to imitate. The architectural details, traditional patterns, and motifs representing the culture that the style does should be formulated in it to level up the scene's authenticity and relatability. It should wear the form of the text. The style and placement should both be done in a very meticulous way to balance the whole composition without cancelling out the illustrative view

Suggestions

In all styles, DALL-E's outputs demonstrate technical competence in replicating broad stylistic features but lack the cultural depth and specificity found in traditional Indian art. To enhance its outputs:

1. **Incorporate Indian Motifs:** Include *rangoli* patterns, architectural elements, tribal art motifs, and traditional floral and animal designs.
2. **Draw from Mythology and Festivals:** Indian art is rich in mythological themes and vibrant depictions of festivals like *Diwali* and *Holi*.
3. **Capture Local Landscapes and Daily Life:** Infuse local flora, fauna, and culturally rich scenes to create deeper resonance.
4. **Blend Style and Storytelling:** Indian art often serves as a narrative medium, which could be incorporated into AI outputs for authenticity.

By embedding these culturally specific elements into the stylistic frameworks, AI-generated art could better align with and respect the traditions of Indian artistry.

Conclusion

The infusion of AI into the world of art created a completely new dimension of imagination and innovation; it showed the potential of technology in changing the creative process forever. AI tools like DALL-E have already shown the capability to generate impressive visual artwork based on textual descriptions, offering artists and designers new ways to explore and experiment with a wide variety of styles and concepts efficiently. This technological innovation not only increases productivity but also enhances creativity by thinking of new perspectives and bringing forth new ideas. AI assists the artist in making the computer do all the repetitive work so that the artist's hands are free to indulge in higher order conceptualization and innovation. In this collaborative effort, some unique and newest forms of artistic expression can be created. AI generates images from textual descriptions in a jiffy, accelerating the whole process. This efficiency lets an artist try and re-try to make necessary changes before coming up with a more refined version of the work, thus enabling its realization more quickly. AI tools can imitate several artistic styles, thereby letting artists try many techniques and genres. This makes the domain of artistic research quite wide and possibly opens up new directions of creativity. The question of who should be considered an artist in AI-generated works remains the most difficult. To the contrary, the more powerful AI tools become in aid of creativity, the more difficult it becomes to tell how much of the art is created by a human and how much by AI. To address these limitations, future AI models could be trained with more culturally diverse and contextually rich datasets, ensuring that the model learns not just the visual aspects of art but also the cultural narratives and emotional expressions that are integral to various art movements. Additionally, integrating AI with collaborative human input, where artists guide the AI's output with cultural insights and emotional nuance, could improve the depth and authenticity of AI-generated artworks.This goes to the question of how AI art would handle respect for existing copyrights and not infringe on the intellectual property of human artists. There is a compelling need to set out clear lines in these areas of ownership and usage rights.

AI systems can reinforce biases in their training data. To ensure that AI-made art is diverse and inclusive, the algorithms behind these need continuous monitoring and adjustments to avoid harmful stereotyping. With AI reaching into all fields of creativity, AI can consequently affect jobs among human artists and designers. Modulating the gains from AI so that it also serves to nourish and continue human creativity is necessary to forestall undesirable economic and social consequences. The potential for misuse of AI-generated art in creating deep fakes or misleading representations underlines the need for ethical guidelines and responsible use of AI technologies in creative industries. Although AI means a giant jump in art through enhanced creativity, efficiency, and opportunities for exploration, it must address its process ethical issues so that technological progress would not be used against society. Provided that we can cultivate such collaboration, respecting human creativity and having regard for ethical concerns, we should be able to unfurl the complete potential of AI in art towards an innovative, inclusive future for the creative industries.

References

1. Baker, M., Gonzalez, A., Carter, J., & Turner, B. (2024). *AI-driven image generation and its transformative impact on art, design, and industry.*
2. Coeckelbergh, M. (2023). The work of art in the age of AI image generation: Aesthetics and human-technology relations as process and performance. *Journal of Human-Technology Relations, 1*(1), 1-13.
3. Chesher, C. (2022, November 29). *Autolography: The magical, multimodal invocation of images from text through AI* (Version 1.3). The University of Sydney.
4. The Editors of Encyclopaedia Britannica. (n.d.). Deconstruction. In *Encyclopaedia Britannica*
5. Kalive, P. (2021, July 22). Jacques Derrida's deconstruction theory – Explained. *Sociology Group.*
6. van Gerven Oei, V. W. J. (Ed.). (2017). *Going postcard: The letter(s) of Jacques Derrida.* punctum books.
7. Ben-Pazi, H. (2016). Subject, Other, and Human Dignity: Levinas' Reading of Kant. *Forum Philosophicum, 21*(1), 69-83.
8. Wolfreys, J. (1996). A note on a post card: Derrida, Deronda, Deguy. In J. Brannigan, R. Robbins, & J. Wolfreys (Eds.), *Applying: To Derrida* (pp. 71-95). Palgrave Macmillan.
9. Yang, L., Liu, W., Zhang, H., & Zhang, Y. (2023). From federated learning to federated decision-making: A survey. *IEEE Transactions on Neural Networks and Learning Systems.*
10. Liu, A. (2022). Taking text to image for spin via DALL-E.
11. Yang, Y., & Zhang, B. (2006). An evaluation of statistical approaches to text categorization. *Information Processing & Management, 42*(4), 473-487.
12. Snyman, G. F. (2006). Constructing and deconstructing identity in post-apartheid South Africa: A case for critical whiteness studies. *Patterns of Prejudice, 40*(1), 1-23.
13. Meron, Y. (2022). Graphic design and artificial intelligence: Interdisciplinary challenges for designers in the search for research

collaboration. In D. Lockton, S. Lenzi, P. Hekkert, A. Oak, J. Sádaba, & P. Lloyd (Eds.), *DRS2022: Bilbao, 25 June - 3 July, Bilbao, Spain.*

14. Engawi, D., Gere, C., & Richards, D. (2022). The impact of artificial intelligence on graphic design: Exploring the challenges and possibilities of AI-driven autonomous branding. In G. Bruyns & H. Wei (Eds.), *With Design: Reinventing Design Modes. IASDR 2021* (pp. 3567-3576). Springer.
15. Fatima, I. (2023). *Designing with AI: A user study to explore the future role of AI as a collaborative tool in graphics design* (Master's thesis, Södertörn University, School of Natural Sciences, Technology and Environmental Studies, Media Technology). DiVA.
16. Mustafa, B. (2024). *The Impact of Artificial Intelligence on the Graphic Design Industry.*
17. Al-Dulaimi, H. N. I. S. (2023). Applications of artificial intelligence in graphic design. *Al-Academy, Nineteenth Scientific Conference*, 109-124
18. Tomić, I., Jurič, I., Dedijer, S., & Adamović, S. (2024). Artificial Intelligence in Graphic Design. *ResearchGate.*
19. Liu, Y. (2023). Design of graphic design assistant system based on artificial intelligence. *International Journal of Information Technologies and Systems Approach (IJITSA)*, 16(3), 1-13.
20. Shi, Y. (2024). Research on the creation and innovation of graphic design driven by artificial intelligence. *Frontiers in Art Research*, 6(2), 12-18.
21. Lear, B. A. (2008). Wishing they were there: Old postcards and library history. *Libraries & the Cultural Record, 43*(1), 77-100. University of Texas Press.
22. Kearns, S. (1997). Picture postcards as a source for social historians. *Saothar, 22*, 128-133. Irish Labour History Society.

ChatGPT in Indian Newsrooms: Leveraging AI for Journalism, Ethical Insights, and Practical Applications

Mr Nithin Joseph Elanjimattom, Director of International Affairs, St Joseph College of Communication, Kerala. Email:inithin1011@gmail.com

Introduction

The development of artificial intelligence (AI) is reshaping every aspect of our lives and journalism is no exception (Elanjimattom, 2022). Among the many AI tools being integrated into newsrooms, ChatGPT, a generative AI model developed by OpenAI, stands out for its potential to change how news content is created, edited, and disseminated. News organisations around the world are exploring ways to leverage ChatGPT to streamline workflows, enhance content production, and assist journalists in their day-to-day tasks. However, the adoption of this technology also brings challenges, including concerns over ethical implications, accuracy, and the role of AI in a profession traditionally driven by human judgment and creativity. This study delves into the evolving role of generative AI, specifically ChatGPT, within the journalism industry, with a focus on its application in newsrooms. It seeks to provide an understanding of how this technology is being used by journalists in India, identifying both the opportunities and challenges it presents. Additionally, the chapter will explain how ChatGPT can be used effectively in newsrooms with the right prompting to assist the news personnel.

Generative AI and ChatGPT

Generative AI is an artificial intelligence system that is capable of creating new content, such as text, images, and music, by analysing and following patterns in existing data. Unlike traditional AI, which is focused on tasks like classification or prediction, generative AI produces original outputs based on what it has learned from existing data. Some of the best-known examples of generative AI are Dall-E for image creation, Sora AI for video creation, and ChatGPT for text generation. There are also other generative AI applications that can compose music, create graphics, write code, and more.

The origins of generative AI can be traced back to early developments in machine learning and neural networks in the mid-20th century. Key milestones include the formalisation of AI concepts in the 1950s by pioneers like Alan Turing (1950) and the research on Artificial Neural Networks (Haenlein & Kaplan, 2019). The 1990s saw the emergence of deep learning and its applications (Newborn & Newborn, 2023). A breakthrough came in 2014 with the introduction of Generative Adversarial Networks which significantly advanced the capabilities of AI in generating realistic synthetic data (Goodfellow et al., 2014).

Language models became a significant part of generative AI with the rise of the Transformer architecture, which revolutionised natural language processing (Cao, 2023). In 2018, OpenAI introduced GPT-1, a generative pre-trained transformer model that could generate coherent text after pre-training on large datasets (Radford et al., 2018). This was followed by GPT-2 in 2019, which, with its 1.5 billion parameters, sparked debates about the potential misuse of AI-generated text (Radford et al., 2019; Hern, 2019). GPT-3, released in 2020 with 175 billion parameters, took the technology further by enabling highly sophisticated text generation across various tasks, marking a significant advancement in AI's language capabilities.

ChatGPT, launched by OpenAI in November 2022, is a conversational AI tool built on the upgraded GPT-3.5 version and designed for real-time, interactive dialogue. Unlike earlier models, ChatGPT was optimised for conversation, allowing it to engage in detailed, context-aware exchanges (Open AI, 2022). In 2023, OpenAI introduced GPT-4, which enhanced ChatGPT's ability to handle complex prompts with better accuracy (Open AI 2023).

ChatGPT Applications in Journalism

In the newsroom environment, AI offers a range of applications that enhance journalistic productivity and engagement. From generating fresh story ideas to crafting compelling content, AI assists journalists in navigating the fast-paced demands of modern media (Simon, 2024). This section explores these key applications, highlighting how ChatGPT supports various aspects of journalism.

Idea Generation and Editorial Assistance

In the fast-paced environment of a newsroom, the ability to generate fresh story ideas and suggest alternative angles or perspectives is invaluable. ChatGPT can assist journalists by offering a wide range of potential story ideas based on current trends, social media activity, and other online sources. It can also analyse existing stories and suggest new angles or approaches, helping journalists to cover topics from multiple perspectives. Additionally, ChatGPT can help newsrooms stay ahead of the curve by identifying emerging trends and story leads, allowing them to respond quickly to new developments.

Content Creation and Social Media Management

ChatGPT can generate complete scripts for print, broadcasts or the internet, ensuring that content is not only informative but also well-structured and polished. ChatGPT's versatility extends to content creation, particularly in generating social media posts and drafting scripts for news broadcasts or podcasts. Journalists can leverage ChatGPT to create engaging tweets, Facebook posts, or Instagram captions that effectively promote their stories across various platforms. The AI can also suggest different headline variations, allowing journalists to choose the most impactful option for their audience. These features enable newsrooms to maintain a consistent and professional presence across multiple channels without overburdening their staff.

Content Summarisation and Data Extraction

One of the significant applications of ChatGPT in newsrooms is its ability to quickly summarise large amounts of text, such as reports, court judgments, public meetings, and other complex documents. Journalists often need to distill dense information into concise summaries that can be easily understood by the general public (Kunova, 2023). ChatGPT excels in this regard, offering quick summaries that save time and ensure key information is highlighted. Additionally, ChatGPT can extract relevant data from reports to create infographics, making it a powerful tool for transforming raw data into visually compelling narratives. This capability is especially beneficial for hyperlocal and independent news publishers, who often operate with limited resources and need to streamline their content production processes.

Personalisation and Audience Engagement

ChatGPT can enhance audience engagement by offering personalised recommendations for readers based on their interests and reading habits. For example, AI can generate customised newsletters tailored to individual preferences, making it easier for news organisations to deliver content that resonates with their audience. Furthermore, ChatGPT can analyse social media interactions and other online behaviours to suggest content that is likely to appeal to specific reader segments. By leveraging ChatGPT's capabilities, newsrooms can create more targeted, relevant, and engaging content, ultimately driving higher reader retention and loyalty. An example of generative AI in the news media is showcased by Nikkei, a leading Japanese publisher that employs AI to power its Minutes application. Minutes provide a concise, digestible news summary for the time-pressed readers (Beckett, 2024).

AI Policy of News Organisations

In recent years, many news organisations have begun developing and implementing policies regarding the use of generative AI technologies within their newsrooms. These policies generally focus on guiding the ethical and practical application of AI tools in journalism. Key considerations include transparency, accountability, and the maintenance of journalistic standards. For instance, some organisations mandate that AI-generated content must be clearly labelled to differentiate it from human-produced journalism, ensuring that audiences are aware of the nature of the content they are consuming. This approach aims to maintain trust and integrity in news reporting by providing clarity about the role of AI in content creation.

A study on the AI policies of 52 news organisations around the world reveals that a significant number of newsrooms, approximately 42%, allow journalists to use generative AI tools as aids in their work, such as drafting articles or summarising information while 4% disallow journalists from using AI tools while others do not mention anything about it (Becker et al, 2023). These policies typically outline permissible uses of AI while emphasising the need for human oversight to ensure the accuracy and reliability of the content. Here are two examples of AI policies of two major international news organisations.

> We are transparent about how and when we use AI. We use AI as a tool to support and accelerate our work in ways consistent with our news judgment and ethical standards. This means using AI to suggest related content, to translate between languages, or to sift through pages of documents or thousands of images. Whatever the task, we recognize this is a new and imperfect technology — meaning accuracy cannot be assumed and verification is critical (Washington Post, 2024).

The AI policy of The Guardian states so:

> We will seek to use genAI tools editorially only where it contributes to the creation and distribution of original journalism. We will guard against the dangers of bias embedded within generative tools and their underlying training sets. If we wish to include significant elements generated by AI in a piece of work, we will only do so with clear evidence of a specific benefit, human oversight, and the explicit permission of a senior editor. We will be open with our readers when we do this....
>
> When we use genAI, we will focus on situations where it can improve the quality of our work, for example by helping journalists interrogate large data sets, assisting colleagues through corrections or suggestions, creating ideas for marketing campaigns, or reducing the bureaucracy of time-consuming business processes (Guardian, 2023).

As AI technologies continue to advance, newsrooms must develop more detailed and universally applicable policies that address both the benefits and risks associated with AI (Merrefield, 2024). By doing so, they can better navigate the challenges of integrating AI into journalism while upholding the principles of transparency, accuracy, data protection and accountability. It is worth mentioning that the Indian newsrooms are yet to develop their AI policies or at least their AI policies are not in the public domain as of November 2024.

ChatGPT in Indian Newsrooms - Objectives and Methodology of the Study

As the role of AI in journalism continues to evolve, it is crucial to examine how these technologies are being adopted and understood by professionals in the field. Building on the discussion of generative AI's history, practical applications, and the AI policies of various news organisations, this section shifts focus to the specific objectives of this study. The research aims to investigate the extent to which Indian journalists are utilising ChatGPT, while also exploring the ethical implications of its use. Furthermore, it seeks to provide a practical guide for effectively integrating ChatGPT into journalistic workflows.

A questionnaire was developed to gather information on the usage of ChatGPT in the newsrooms, as well as to identify any benefits or challenges encountered in its use. This questionnaire was created using Google Forms, which allowed for easy distribution and collection of responses. The questionnaire was sent to journalists working in different English media across the country. The questionnaire was distributed via WhatsApp, a popular messaging app widely used by journalists in India.

One of the limitations of this study is that the sample size is limited to Indian journalists working in English (as ChatGPT is primarily an English language model). So this may not be a representation of the larger population of journalists or news organisations in India. The participants were assured that no personal information will be collected or stored.

Usage of ChatGPT in Indian Newsrooms

The questionnaire was sent to 217 journalists on WhatsApp as a personal message in February 2024, and 110 responses were received and analysed. Overall, the use of a questionnaire model allowed for the efficient collection of data from a large number of participants, and the use of Google Forms and WhatsApp made the distribution and collection of responses simple and straightforward. The data collected from the questionnaire allowed for the identification of trends and patterns in the responses. Out of the 110 participants who responded to the questionnaire, only eight reported having used ChatGPT as a tool in their journalism profession, while 102 reported that they do not use this tool in their profession.

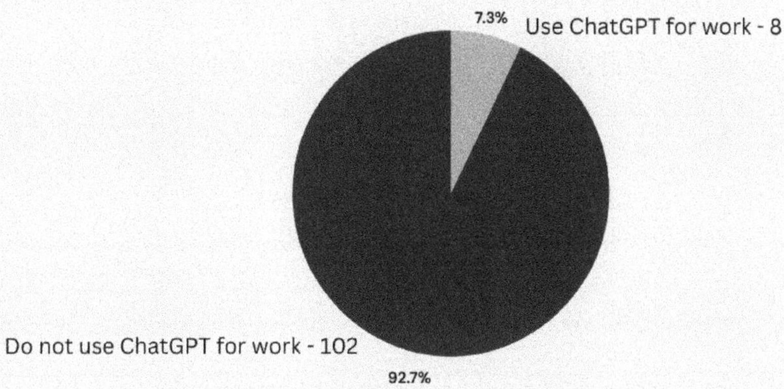

Use of ChatGPT by Indian journalists - 110 respondants

The participants were asked to mark the most important reason for not using ChatGPT in the newsroom. These were the options given them and the number of respondents to each reason was:

- Don't know how to use ChatGPT - nobody
- Not believing it would be useful at work - 12
- Company policy prohibiting the use of AI tools - 13
- Possibility of biased content - 17
- Possibility of plagiarism - 60

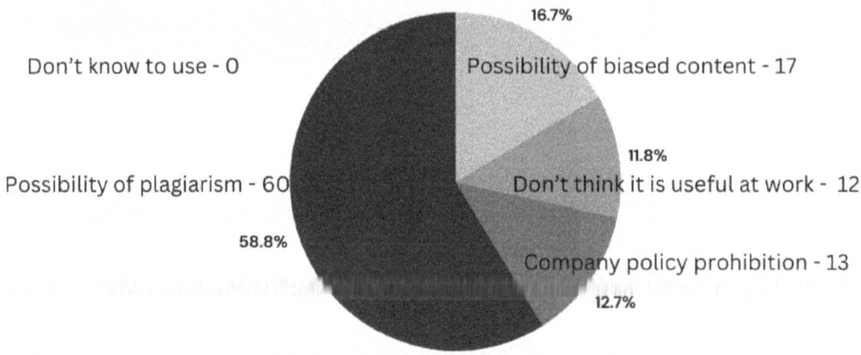

Indian journalists' reasons for not using ChatGPT

In addition to these reasons, a few participants also cited concerns about the non-reliable nature of ChatGPT, as well as personal satisfaction and ethical considerations.

Out of the eight respondents who had used ChatGPT, none of them reported using it regularly. Five respondents said they used it occasionally and three said they used it rarely. The ways in which ChatGPT had helped them included SEO writing, improving language, providing quick information, and generating story ideas. The respondents also reported challenges while using ChatGPT which included inaccurate information, irrelevant information, the limited scope of information, and difficulty in customising ChatGPT responses. They also reported certain ethical considerations including privacy concerns, bias in the information provided by ChatGPT, and the danger of the overdependence on technology.

Overall, the results suggest that ChatGPT is not widely used among Indian journalists working in English. These results suggest that there is potential for ChatGPT to be used more widely in the field of journalism. Additionally, efforts should be made to increase awareness and understanding of these tools among journalists and to promote their ethical and responsible use.

Systematic strategies for using ChatGPT in newsrooms

Leveraging ChatGPT for journalism requires a structured approach to maximise its capabilities in news writing and content creation. The key to effectively using ChatGPT lies in crafting well-designed prompts, providing clear context, and iterating on the responses until the desired outcome is achieved. This section will outline practical steps and use cases for journalists to integrate ChatGPT into their workflows, including examples and sample prompts.

Crafting Effective Prompts for News Writing

To harness the power of ChatGPT in journalism, creating well-crafted prompts is essential. A good prompt should be clear, and specific, and provide enough context to guide the AI's response. When using ChatGPT for news reporting, the prompt is the starting point for the AI's output, so it always includes relevant background information, constraints (such as word count or tone), and instructions on style (Amditis, 2023). For instance, when summarising a complex report, a journalist might provide specific instructions to focus on key findings and keep the summary concise.

Sample prompt generate summary: *Summarise the key findings from this government report on migration, highlighting the most significant points in no more than three paragraphs. Keep the language simple for a general audience.*

Sample prompt for news reporting: *Write a 300-word news article summarising the following press conference by the Finance Minister on the latest tax reforms. Focus on the key announcements and their potential impact on different classes of citizens. Use a formal tone and ensure the article is balanced and objective.* [Paste press release/notes]

Sample prompt for feature article: *Write a feature article based on the following interview transcript. The article should focus on the key themes discussed and provide a compelling narrative that highlights the interviewee's insights and experiences. Structure the article to include an engaging introduction, a detailed exploration of the main topics, and a reflective conclusion. The tone should be engaging and informative, suitable for a general audience. Include quotes from the interview to support the narrative.* [Paste transcript]

Adapting ChatGPT to Different Styles and Audiences

ChatGPT can be tailored to produce content in various writing styles, depending on the target audience. This is especially useful for journalists who write for different niches, such as financial news, entertainment, or political analysis. To achieve the desired tone, journalists can provide ChatGPT with examples of the required style, whether it's formal, casual, or technical.

Sample prompt for style adaptation: *Generate a 200-word review of the iPhone 16 from the following points in the style of a tech blog aimed at a Gen Z audience. The tone should be casual and engaging, with a focus on the most innovative ideas presented during the phone's launch event.* [Paste content]

Sample prompt for personal writing style: *Compose a feature article exploring the impact of Augmented Reality (AR) and Virtual Reality (VR) technology on journalism. The article should address both the positive effects and the ethical concerns associated with these technologies. Utilise the data provided here* [Paste the data for the article]. *Write in the style of my previous articles on this subject to ensure consistency in tone and approach.* [Paste writing sample]

Practical Applications: From Social Media to Script Writing

ChatGPT can assist journalists with a wide range of tasks beyond traditional news reporting. For instance, journalists can use ChatGPT to generate social media posts that promote news stories, ensuring consistency across platforms. The AI can also draft scripts for news broadcasts or podcasts, helping newsrooms streamline their production process. By providing ChatGPT with clear instructions, journalists can ensure the AI-generated content aligns with their editorial standards.

Sample prompt for social media posts: *Create three different X/ Twitter posts promoting this article about the Prime Minister's visit to Russia. The tone should be engaging, and each tweet should include a call to action to read the full article.* [Paste article]

Sample prompt for script writing: *Write a two-minute weather broadcast script summarising the current weather conditions in Kerala including temperature, humidity, and any significant weather phenomena such as rain. Include a brief outlook for the next 24 to 48 hours, highlighting any expected changes in weather patterns. The script should be formal in tone and crafted for smooth delivery on a teleprompter.* [Paste details]

Iterative Collaboration and Refinement

Journalists should view AI as a collaborative tool rather than a one-time command execution system. After receiving the initial output, they can refine the prompt to improve the response. This interactive approach allows for more accurate and tailored content that better meets editorial needs.

Sample Iterative Workflow

Initial prompt: *Draft a headline for this article about the latest developments in the solar panel industry.* [Paste article]

Follow-up prompt: *Suggest three alternative headlines that emphasise the environmental impact of these advancements.*

Final refinement: *Now rewrite the chosen headline to make it more SEO-friendly.*

By continually refining prompts and working with ChatGPT interactively, journalists can produce high-quality content that meets their specific requirements.

ChatGPT and Ethical Concerns

As AI tools like ChatGPT become increasingly integrated into journalism, they introduce a range of ethical challenges that must be carefully addressed. This section delves into the key concerns associated with the use of generative AI in newsrooms, including the risks of misinformation, inherent biases, and privacy vulnerabilities.

- **Misinformation and disinformation:** The potential for ChatGPT to produce or propagate misinformation is a significant ethical concern. Since the model generates content based on patterns from a broad dataset, it may spread false or misleading information (Moran, 2023). This risk is particularly concerning in journalism, where accuracy and reliability are paramount.
- **Bias and fairness:** ChatGPT's training data can contain biases present in the source material, which may lead to biased outputs. These biases can manifest in various ways, including gender, racial, or cultural biases. Such issues raise ethical concerns about fairness and representation in AI-generated content (AIJO, 2020).
- **Privacy and data security:** The use of ChatGPT involves processing large amounts of text data, which can include sensitive or personal information. There are concerns about how data is handled and whether it could be inadvertently exposed or misused (Gal, 2024).
- **Impact on employment:** The increasing use of AI tools like ChatGPT in journalism raises concerns about their impact on employment. As AI systems take on more tasks traditionally performed by human journalists, there is a risk of job displacement and a reduction in the diversity of voices and perspectives in news reporting.
- **Editorial independence:** Reliance on AI-generated content could potentially compromise editorial independence if journalists become overly dependent on automated tools.

Addressing the Limitations and Ethical Concerns

It is really important that the aforementioned concerns that AI raises have to be addressed. According to Yuval Noah Harari: "AI is an unprecedented threat to humanity because it is the first technology in history that can make decisions and create new ideas by itself. All previous human inventions have empowered humans, because no matter how powerful the new tool was, the decisions about its usage remained in our hands" (2024). In this context this section explores key measures for responsible AI usage in newsrooms, including the need for editorial vigilance and verification processes to ensure accuracy, the importance of robust policies to protect privacy, and the necessity of promoting transparency and accountability.

- **Implementing oversight and verification:** To address the limitations and ethical concerns associated with ChatGPT, it is crucial to implement strong oversight and verification processes. This includes ensuring that AI-generated content is rigorously fact-checked and reviewed by human editors to maintain accuracy and reliability.
- **Addressing privacy concerns with policy:** The recent European Union AI Act (2024) mandates organisations to establish and implement AI governance policies that address legal data processing obligations, conduct privacy impact assessments, and mitigate AI-related cybersecurity risks. Such effective policies ensure that AI tools comply with data protection regulations, safeguarding both the privacy of sources and the audience.
- **Promoting transparency and accountability:** Transparency about how ChatGPT is used and the limitations of its outputs is important for maintaining public trust. News organisations and content creators should openly communicate their use of AI tools and establish accountability mechanisms to address any issues that arise. The responsibility of the AI generated content still lies with the human journalists, who must review and refine AI-generated content to ensure it meets professional standards and avoids copyright violations.
- **Continuous training and improvement:** Regularly updating and fine-tuning the model to reduce biases and improve performance is essential. Engaging in ongoing research and development can help mitigate some of the inherent limitations of ChatGPT and enhance its usefulness while addressing ethical concerns.
- **Mitigating job loss through AI training:** To mitigate the growing concern over job displacement, news organisations

may focus on training journalists to leverage AI as a supportive tool rather than a replacement. By equipping journalists with the skills to maximise AI's potential, they can enhance their reporting capabilities and continue to produce high-quality journalism that AI alone cannot achieve.

By understanding and addressing these limitations and ethical concerns, journalists and content creators can better navigate the challenges of integrating ChatGPT into their workflows, ensuring that the technology is used responsibly and effectively.

Conclusion

The study revealed that 92% of Indian journalists are not utilising generative AI tools in newsrooms, despite the increasing automation of many tasks traditionally performed by humans. AI's potential to analyse data, summarise lengthy documents, and handle repetitive or routine tasks presents a significant opportunity for newsrooms to enhance productivity. By leveraging AI for such tasks, journalists can focus their creativity, experience, and skills on more meaningful and complex aspects of their work. In that context, this chapter has provided a simple practical guide on effectively incorporating ChatGPT into newsroom operations.

To make the most of ChatGPT's capabilities, tasks in journalism can be categorised into three levels: Correct Work, Good Enough Work, and Excellent Work (AI Exchange, 2023). Correct Work involves tasks with clear right or wrong answers, such as summarising key points in reports or organising content. ChatGPT excels at these tasks by automating routine activities, allowing journalists to focus on more significant responsibilities. Good Enough Work represents tasks that require a moderate level of quality, such as drafting articles or summarising meetings. ChatGPT can handle these efficiently, producing content that is coherent and reasonably polished, though human oversight remains essential for refinement. By delegating such work to AI, newsrooms can streamline processes and save valuable time for more critical tasks. Excellent Work demands creativity, deep understanding, and complex judgment, which are challenging for AI to achieve independently.

While ChatGPT can assist with idea generation, drafting, and initial research, these tasks ultimately require human expertise and insight. For these high-stakes tasks, ChatGPT should be seen as a supportive tool rather than a replacement, with human journalists providing the necessary oversight and final touches. In conclusion, ChatGPT offers a powerful toolset for newsrooms, but its application must be carefully managed. However, maintaining a "human-in-the-loop" approach (Chen et al., 2023) is crucial to ensuring the accuracy, ethics, and quality of the content produced. With the right balance, ChatGPT can enhance productivity in journalism while preserving the essential human touch that is central to the profession.

Reference

1. AI Exchange. (2023, September 5). AI task hierarchy. *The AI exchange.* https://news.theaiexchange.com/p/ai-task-hierarchy
2. AIJO. (2020, December 7). *Understanding newsroom biases. The AIJO Project.* https://www.aijoproject.com/post/understanding-bias-in-the-newsroom
3. Amditis, J. (n.d.). *Beginner's prompt handbook: ChatGPT for local news publishers.* Jamditis Notion. https://jamditis.notion.site/Beginner-s-prompt-handbook-ChatGPT-for-local-news-publishers-15d1f07d5b194265a41fdd42955679b4
4. Becker, K. B., et al. (2023, September 7). Policies in parallel? a comparative study of journalistic AI policies in 52 global news organisations. SocArXiv. Pre-print paper. https://doi.org/10.31235/osf.io/c4af9
5. Beckett, C. (2024, August 29). *Journalism and AI: balancing innovation and integrity*. LSE.https://blogs.lse.ac.uk/polis/2024/ 08/29/journalism-and-ai-balancing-innovation-and-integrity/
6. Cao, Y. et. al. (2023). A comprehensive survey of ai-generated content (aigc): a history of generative ai from gan to chatgpt. arXiv preprint arXiv:2303.04226.

7. Chen, X., et al. (2023). Constructing Ethical AI Based on the "Human-in-the-Loop" System. Systems, 11(11), 548.
8. Elanjimattom, N. J. (2022). Artificial intelligence as journalist and gatekeeper: ethics of automated journalism and algorithmic curation of news in the Indian context. Digital journalism in India. Media village publications. 10 - 33.
9. EU (2024). *AI act.* European union. Retrieved from https://digital-strategy.ec.europa.eu/en/policies/regulatory-framework-ai
10. Gal, U. (2024, June 5). *CHATGPT is a data privacy nightmare. if you've ever posted online, you ought to be concerned.* The Conversation. https://theconversation.com/chatgpt-is-a-data-privacy-nightmare-if-youve-ever-posted-online-you-ought-to-be-concerned-199283
11. Goodfellow, I. et al. (2014). Generative adversarial nets. *advances in neural information processing systems* (NeurIPS). Retrieved from https://papers.nips.cc/paper/5423-generative-adversarial-nets
12. Guardian. (2023, June 16). The Guardian's approach to Generative AI. *The Guardian.* https://www.theguardian.com/help/insideguardian/2023/jun/16/the-guardians-approach-to-generative-ai
13. Haenlein, M., & Kaplan, A. (2019). A brief history of artificial intelligence: on the past, present, and future of artificial intelligence. California management review, 61(4), 5-14.
14. Harari, Y. N. (2024, August 24). "never summon a power you can't control": Yuval Noah Harari on how AI could threaten democracy and divide the world. *The Guardian.* https://www.theguardian.com/technology/article/2024/aug/24/yuval-noah-harari-ai-book-extract-nexus#:~:text=AI%20is%20an%20unprecedented%20threat,usage%20remained %20in%20our%20hands.
15. Hern, A. (2019, February 14). New Ai fake text generator may be too dangerous to release, say creators. *The Guardian.* https://www.theguardian.com/technology/2019/feb/14/elon-musk-backed-ai-writes-convincing-news-fiction

16. Kunova, M. (2023, May 5). *Eight tasks CHATGPT can do for journalists*. journalism.co.uk.https://www.journalism.co.uk/news/how-can-journalists-use-chatgpt-/s2/a1005273/?s=08

17. Merrefield, C. (2024, June 11). Researchers compare AI policies and guidelines at 52 news organizations. *The Journalist's Resource.* https://journalistsresource.org/home/generative-ai-policies-newsrooms/#:~:text=Meanwhile%2C%2042%25%20allow%20journalists%20to,did%20not%20mention%20accountability%20mechanisms.

18. Moran, C. (2023, April 6). Chatgpt is making up fake guardian articles. here's how we're responding. *The Guardian.* https://www.theguardian.com/commentisfree/2023/apr/06/ai-chatgpt-guardian-technology-risks-fake-article

19. Newborn, M., & Newborn, M. (2003). Deep Blue: an artificial intelligence milestone. Springer Science & Business Media.

20. OpenAI. (2022). Introducing ChatGPT. *OpenAI blog*. Retrieved from https://openai.com/index/chatgpt/

21. OpenAI. (2023). GPT-4: Technical report. *OpenAI.* Retrieved from https://openai.com/index/gpt-4-research/

22. Radford, A., et al. (2018). Improving Language Understanding by Generative Pre-Training. *OpenAI.* Retrieved from https://cdn.openai.com/research-covers/language-unsupervised/language_understanding_paper.pdf

23. Radford, A., et al. (2019). Language models are unsupervised multitask learners. *OpenAI blog*, *1*(8), 9. Retrieved from https://d4mucfpksywv.cloudfront.net/better-language-models/language_models_are_unsupervised_multitask_learners.pdf

24. Simon, F. (2024). Artificial intelligence in the news: how AI retools, rationalizes, and reshapes journalism and the public arena. *Oxford internet institute.* Retrieved from https://ora.ox.ac.uk/objects/uuid:aeb25013-1d17-40b2-b471-5bdca309db87/files/s4t64gp800

25. Turing, A. (1950). Computing machinery and intelligence. *Mind.* LIX/236. 433-460.

26. Washington Post. (2024). Policies and standards - The Washington Post. *The Washington Post.* https://www.washingtonpost.com/policies-and-standards/

AI Literacy among Media Professionals in the Age of GPTs

Subhodeep Mukhopadhyay, PhD (Education) Student, Manipal GlobalNxt University. Email: subhodeepm.infinity@gmail.com

Introduction

Societies around the globe are witnessing major changes on account of the rapid advancement of artificial intelligence (AI) technologies. AI literacy is a critical competency required to effectively navigate the evolving technological landscape and to empower individuals to understand, interact with, and critically evaluate AI solutions (Ng et al., 2021). The rise of Generative Pre-Trained Transformers (GPTs), a specific type of AI technology, has further contributed to the widespread adoption of AI in various domains. From a communication perspective, AI may be seen as the latest entrant in a long line of disruptive technologies including printing press, radio, television and mobile phones, which have revolutionized the media and communication industry. Such disruptions not only create new markets and avenue for media consumption, but "can also upset the equilibrium of companies with good reputations and good products" (Christensen, 2002).

For media professionals grappling with the impact of automation, AI-generated content creation, and challenges like fake news and deepfakes, AI and especially GPTs present a reality that must be confronted and addressed intelligently. Depending on one's perspective, AI may be viewed either as an obstacle to ethical and human-centric mass communication or as an opportunity to make reporting and communication more authentic, responsible, ethical, and efficient. Those who become proficient in AI, and eventually go on to master it, will thrive and prosper in the coming age of mass AI integration in all aspects of the communication value chain. This paper assesses AI proficiency among mass media professionals using the four-aspect AI literacy framework proposed by Ng et al. (2021): know and understand, use and apply, evaluate and create, and ethical issues.

AI and GPTs

Artificial Intelligence (AI) encompasses the development of machines and systems capable of performing tasks that typically require human intelligence. These tasks include learning, reasoning, and decision-making. The High-Level Expert Group on Artificial Intelligence of the European Commission (EC) defines AI as computer systems that "display intelligent behaviour by analysing their environment and taking actions – with some degree of autonomy – to achieve specific goals" (AI HLEG, 2019). AI should not be seen as a revolutionary isolated technology but as part of a larger ecosystem of ever-evolving interconnected technologies. Like any computer system, how an AI system behaves is determined by its objectives and how it is used (Mukhopadhyay, 2023, p. 113). In an interview with Bloomberg in 2024, Satya Nadella, the CEO of Microsoft, observed the fact that AI was simply a "tool" and not a human-like entity with superior intelligence (Gairola, 2024).

Classic machine learning tasks in media studies typically involved analyzing articles to detect common patterns, themes and topics and subsequently categorizing new articles based on them. Generative artificial intelligence (GAI), a type of AI technology capable of creating new content across various media forms, including audio, code, images, text, and videos, enables AI systems to not only recognize but also generate brand new textual content on demand (McKinsey, 2024). Generative Pre-trained Transformers (GPT), a specific type of GAI have the ability to generate texts in various languages and can produce "human-sounding words, sentences, and paragraphs on almost any topic and writing style" (Jovanovic & Campbell, 2022, p. 107). ChatGPT is an example of a GPT chatbot that uses machine learning to generate human-like dialogue in real time (Figure 1). The release of ChatGPT in November 2022 is believed to have "triggered an exponential surge in the groundbreaking and widespread popularity of GAI to the general public" (Bengesi et al., 2024).

Figure 1: Types of AI

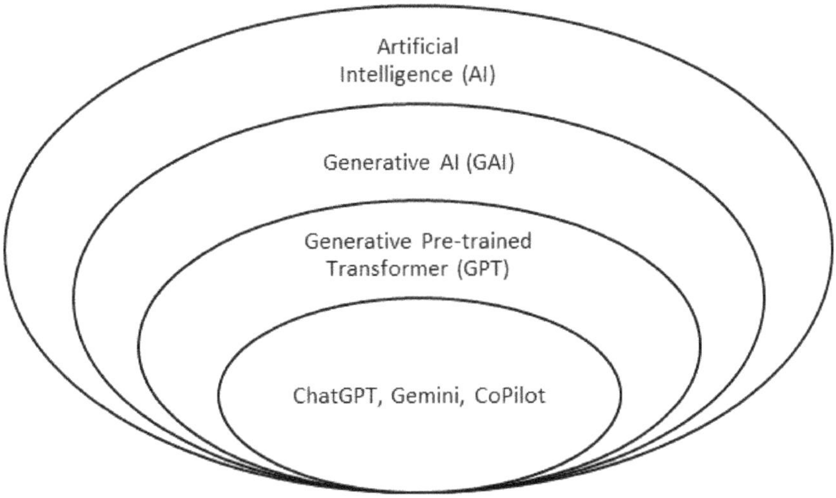

AI in Mass Media

AI integration has the potential to impact the entire value chain of media production including audience engagement, augmented audience experience, message optimization, content management, content creation, audience insights, and operational automation (Chan-Olmsted, 2019). In the areas of audience engagement and content personalization, AI plays a major role in understanding audience sentiment and preferences, and matching the right content to the right consumers. There are several other avenues for integrating AI in journalism, including automated news writing, fact-checking, personalized news, and content recommendation (Dhiman, 2023). AI is also being used in the transcription of interviews, translation of regional news stories, and data-driven journalism. Two factors are seen driving the productivity gains in mass media industry on account of AI integration: enhancement of journalists' capabilities and streamlining of new-making processes (Noain-Sánchez, 2022).

Despite these positive perceptions, there are concerns about the propensity of Large Language Models (LLMs) like ChatGPT to "hallucinate" data, a "phenomenon where AI generates a convincing but completely made-up answer" (Athaluri et al., 2023). AI hallucination can have adverse effects on decision-making and pose ethical and legal dilemmas as well (Zhang et al., 2023). It undermines the credibility and reliability of mass media and journalism by generating false or misleading information. Another significant issue pertains to biases within AI systems. If the training datasets exhibit biases or inaccuracies, the AI will inevitably learn and perpetuate these biases in its predictions and content generation (Schwartz et al., 2022; Rosário, 2024). Even if unintended, this can severely undermine public trust in AI. This issue is particularly critical for journalists and media professionals who must maintain the highest ethical standards despite the challenges of AI-generated content, fake news, and deepfake videos.

AI Literacy

AI literacy can be defined as the knowledge and skills necessary to understand, interact with, and critically evaluate artificial intelligence technologies and their impacts, and encompasses ethical, social, and practical dimensions as well. Ng et al. (2021) outline four key aspects of fostering AI literacy:

- **Know and Understand AI:** This involves educating learners about fundamental AI concepts, skills, knowledge, and attitudes without requiring prior expertise. The focus is on how learners acquire foundational AI knowledge.
- **Use and Apply AI:** This highlights the importance of educating learners to apply AI concepts in various contexts and everyday applications.
- **Evaluate and Create AI:** This aspect engages learners in higher-order thinking activities, encouraging them to critically evaluate AI technologies and effectively communicate and collaborate with AI.
- **AI Ethics:** This deals with human-centered considerations such as fairness, accountability, transparency, ethics, and safety.

AI literacy enables individuals and professionals to engage with AI systems in an informed manner, critically assess their outputs, and implement these technologies to enhance productivity and innovation. Understanding

AI's ethical and social implications is crucial for mitigating issues related to bias, quality control, and equitable access (Su & Zhong, 2022). However, the fast-paced development of AI can outstrip the growth of corresponding literacy, creating a significant knowledge gap. As Christensen (2002, p. 278) notes, the "trajectory of technological progress almost invariably outstrips the ability of customers to utilize those improvements; companies can almost always innovate faster than people's lives can change to fully utilize those innovations." AI literacy is, therefore, a critical competency for media professionals and an essential requirement for examining AI's transformative impact on the media and communication industry.

India's National AI Programme

Over the past several years, the Government of India has taken concrete steps to encourage the responsible adoption of AI and build public trust in its use in order to harness its potential for social development and inclusive growth. The Ministry of Electronics and Information Technology (MeitY) has undertaken various initiatives to promote the 'AI for All' initiative. The policy position is that the advancement of AI technology will generate a large number of jobs in India across various industries, including media and entertainment (MeitY, 2023, p. 78). With this objective in mind, the government has set-up a number of working groups focusing on different aspects of AI integration (MeitY, 2023, p. 5). One such focus area is AI-based skilling solutions to promote continuous AI learning and the government has come up with guidelines for model curricula involving K-12 interventions, graduate/postgraduate-level interventions, AI-based research, and competency/design considerations (MeitY, 2023, p. 78).

The chapter is driven by two goals: to identify the most challenging AI literacy issues among mass-media professionals in the context of rapid GPT integration in various parts of the communication value chain, and to examine how media professionals perceive the advent of GPTs in terms of their work. This study applies qualitative methods to gather the required information, as this enables us to acquire a deep understanding of the phenomenon and facilitates our investigation into 'how' and 'why' research questions (Yin, 2003). Qualitative methods allow us to explore new dimensions of a phenomenon and are critical in helping us uncover unique, useful, and meaningful insights from complex data, providing for both relevance and rigor (Eisenhardt & Graebner, 2007; Kiger & Varpio, 2020).

Primary data included semi-structured interviews with media, communication, and research professionals across various domains of mass media and communication (Table 1). Purposive sampling was used for data collection and sixteen media professionals in different parts of India were chosen for in-depth interviews. The respondents were primarily from middle to senior management roles, including multimedia director, managing editor, digital marketing head, assistant vice-president, senior research fellow, and general manager rank. Two senior freelance media professionals were also part of the interview participants. The domains included content creation and editing, multimedia and video content production, transcription, translation, podcasts, blogs, and social media management. This added to the diversity of occupational backgrounds.

Table 1: Participants Profile

Domain	No of Participants
Content creation and editing	5
Secondary Research	2
Multimedia/ video content production	2
Transcription and Translation	2
Online news portals/ Blogs	2
Social media	2
Podcasting	1
Total	**16**

In terms of geographic location, the participants came from different cities, as below:

- Kolkata – 5
- Delhi – 4
- Bengaluru – 4

- Pune – 3

Prior consent was taken from each of the participants and interviews were scheduled accordingly. All the interviews were conducted in online mode using Zoom platform. Most of the interviews were of 1 hour duration with a few interviews taking up to 2 hours. Each interview was recorded using Zoom's recording feature and transcribed manually by the author. The data analysis process involved a number of steps: obtaining raw transcript with timestamps, converting the transcript to raw conversation, editing the file to generate full interview conversation and classifying the data into the different dimensions as applicable.

Data saturation was achieved with 15 interviews. Typically, a qualitative study requires 6-12 interview participants to ensure data saturation (Johnson & Christensen, 2004; Baumgartner et al., 2006). For the purpose of our analysis, we establish a mapping between the four aspects of Ng et al.'s (2021) AI literacy framework and twelve specific guidelines from the national AI curriculum framework (Table 2). This methodological approach enables an in-depth exploration of AI literacy among media professionals in India, contextualized within the country's unique socio economic landscape.

Table 2: Mapping AI literacy to national policy guidelines

AI Literacy: Ng et al. (2021)	**AI-based curriculum guidelines: MeitY (2023)**
Know and Understand AI	○ What is AI? ○ Basics of AI ○ AI based tools and applications ○ Comfort with AI interface (MeitY, 2023, p. 89)
Use and apply AI	○ Problem Identification ○ Process to identify AI based solutions ○ Industry use cases (MeitY, 2023, p. 89)

Evaluate and create AI	○ Evaluation ROI of AI projects ○ Generate Innovative solutions (MeitY, 2023, p. 89)
Ethical Issues	○ Privacy concerns ○ Potential for AI systems to be used for malicious purposes ○ Potential for AI systems to be biased or discriminatory (MeitY, 2023, p. 82)

Consistent with Pettigrew's (1990) qualitative research guidelines, the research questions were based on established theoretical constructs from AI literacy literature. However, a conscious effort was made to avoid imposing these constructs universally to the entire dataset, and to use evidence from the field guide to corroborate and build upon existing theories. Relevant codes were created by condensing the meaning into compact categories through extraction and abstraction of relevant information and ideas (Lee, 1999).

The length of the coded text in this study ranged from one sentence to several sentences. The resulting codes were analyzed, combined and re-organized to extract relevant categories and themes from the data. The first level coding was focused on uncovering common themes and concepts. The data analysis involved an iterative process of theory and data analysis leading to the emergence and refinement of additional codes (Eisenhardt, 1989). This was followed by a second round of coding where similar codes were collapsed into second-order code categories, and themes were extracted from the same. In the next section, the analysis and interpretation of the data is presented.

Results

Factor 1: Know and Understand AI

This factor is used to evaluate the fundamental AI concepts, skills, knowledge, and attitudes of our respondents, with a focus on foundational AI knowledge.

Dimension 1.1: Understanding AI

All participants emphasized two major aspects of AI-based systems: the ability to perform thinking tasks that replicate human intelligence and the distinction between traditional computing and AI-based computing, wherein AI can learn, improve, and requires data for these processes, unlike older systems. Around 20% of respondents also discussed other technical aspects of AI like machine learning algorithms based on error minimization.

Around 70% of the interviewees felt that AI-generated content and output, as relevant to media professionals, was as good as humans. One interviewee, for example, said that there was "no way of telling if any human input is there in what you see or if it is entirely generated by a bot," and that she found this "scary." However, the remaining 30% believed that the actual output of AI systems fell short of expectations, especially considering the exaggerated claims and media depiction of AI as a game-changing technology. One of the interviewees says:

> "We are basically into research and writing reports and other material for online consumption. This is basically what we do, and I have used AI for some research work. My personal opinion about that experience is that it is not very helpful... I mean, as of now, it is not satisfactory and it's not only the fact that the data is not current, that is part of the thing, but it's also very verbose and less analytical."

Dimension 1.2: Basics of AI

Seventy percent of the interviewees correctly identified machine learning on large datasets as a major concept underpinning artificial intelligence. The remaining 30%, while aware that AI-based systems could learn and improve their performance, did not immediately associate the learning aspect of AI with machine learning as a concept. Only one interviewee discussed additional aspects and foundational elements of AI, including mathematical optimization and artificial neural networks modeled on the human brain. He also touched upon the interdisciplinary nature of AI spanning computer science, linguistics, psychology, neuroscience, and philosophy:

> "Artificial intelligence is powerful because all these different experts in different technological areas are coming together and trying to imitate a human brain. This is what I feel. Of course, I'm not

a computer scientist, so I don't have too much idea about what technologies are involved."

A small number of participants demonstrated a basic awareness of the role of Natural Language Processing (NLP) in AI, highlighting its function in facilitating more natural and conversational interactions with humans. Another interviewee emphasized the importance of data quality in AI systems and the applicability of the principle of "garbage in, garbage out": poor-quality data can result in unreliable and biased AI outputs

Dimension 1.3: AI-Based Tools and Applications

Over 87% of the interviewees reported using at least one AI-based tool or application for their job-related tasks on multiple occasions. The remaining interviewees had seen demonstrations and tested a few AI-based applications but had not utilized them for work or personal purposes. The tools explored and utilized by participants included:

- OpenAI ChatGPT
- Google Gemini (earlier Bard)
- Microsoft Copilot
- Adobe AI Assistant
- Midjourney
- AI-based transcription and translation tools

Dimension 1.4: Usability of AI Tools

Among those who used at least one or more AI tools periodically, constituting 75% of the interviewee sample, all reported finding the various tools easy to use, interactive, and requiring minimal learning curve. One interviewee suggested that even if some users found it initially challenging, a few days training and use were sufficient to become proficient. Another significant observation by a participant was that it was important to ask the right questions to ChatGPT to obtain relevant and useful answers. While ease of use is crucial, it does not necessarily translate to useful results—the human component remains essential. She says:

"ChatGPT is very easy to use. An average person just needs to ask a question. But the actual value in the answer you get from that depends on your skill in asking the right question. That again is very important. Eventually, the human component is not going anywhere. If you can communicate exactly what you want, then it helps you."

Factor 2: Use and Apply

We use this factor to assess the ability of media professionals to apply AI concepts in various contexts and everyday applications.

Dimension 2.1: Problem Identification for AI use

The key applications of AI tools by the participants included content generation, data summarization, content editing, image generation, transcription, and translation (Table 3).

Table 3: Major Application of AI Tools & Software

Generative	Search and Retrieval	Others
Content generation	Multiple keyword searches	Transcription
Image generation	Topic and concept searches	Translation
Content editing	Summarization	

Dimension 2.2: Factors to Identify AI-Based Solutions

Two major factors were identified by the interviewees as determinants in their choice of a specific AI solution or software for a work task:

- Neutrality and Lack of Bias: The neutrality of the output was crucial, with a preference for results that were fair, context-specific, and free from civilization or societal biases.
- Type of Task: AI was preferred for objective and repetitive tasks rather than for subjective or complex problem-solving.

Additional factors influencing the choice of an AI-based solution included:

- ease of use
- cost or affordability
- speed and efficiency
- accuracy of the output

Moreover, 20% of the interviewees felt that there was a need to conduct a trial run or proof of concept test to assess the quality of the AI generated output before considering other factors.

Dimension 2.3: Industry Use-cases

Beyond the applications of AI-based solutions discussed in Dimension 2.1, the interviewees expressed interest in a wide spectrum of industry use cases where AI could be beneficial. These use cases include:

Use Case 1: Advanced Integrated Search

Approximately two-thirds of interviewees expressed interest in AI applications for advanced, end-to-end integrated searches across multiple sources and media types. They anticipate AI aiding in narrowing down searches within vast collections of books, reports, secondary sources, videos, audio files, and podcasts. Ideally, they would like AI systems to create a relevant shortlist based on specific research criteria, providing easy access to specific information and generating content such as images or summaries from the search results.

Use Case 2: Journalism

Around one-third of the interviewees felt that AI could greatly improve efficiency in journalism by automating tasks such as page-making. This would allow journalists to focus on core activities such as news selection, editing, and writing. A senior editor from a major English daily observed:

> "...if we have an evolving intelligence helping us, then at least the page-making can easily be shifted onto it. I think if they can make the page, we can focus our, not we, journalists can focus their energies on actual journalism, selecting their news, doing their

> editing, writing the captions… I personally feel that would be a good thing."

Factor 3: Evaluate and Create

We use this factor to understand how media professionals evaluate AI technologies and whether they use AI to assist in higher-order thinking activities and for fostering innovation in the workplace.

Dimension 3.1: Evaluation of ROI of AI Projects

Around two-thirds of respondents reported increased efficiency and time savings after using AI-based applications. The amount of time saved, however, was different for different types of activities. For those involved in secondary and archival research, AI summarization has resulted in substantial gains, enabling tasks that would typically take several days to be completed in minutes. This resulted in several days or even weeks saved over the course of a project. For content generation and editing tasks, a minimum of 30% efficiency gains were noted for most tasks. One respondent, a regular user of AI tools observed:

> "It is very efficient. And I told you the study that we did, it varies. Like for some articles, more personal work is required. Those would be like 30 to 40% benefit, but for other articles, it goes up to 60 to 70% time-saving."

However, one-third of the participants noted that the results of AI systems were at best mixed. While I did speed up their work, when the quality of output was poor or not as expected, the initial time savings were negated by manual rework. Additionally, during brainstorming and idea generation sessions, AI tools often generated random or irrelevant ideas that consumed time leading to decreased productivity. One interviewee notes:

> "It improves, but it decreases in a way. Like, it keeps on giving me many random ideas which I haven't asked for, and to go through all those things, I lose my time. So, in that sense, sometimes my productivity is decreased. But otherwise, I also find many benefits while using the tools provided by AI… So, it's a mixed experience with AI. Not fully 100% happy, not very depressed as well."

Dimension 3.2: Higher Order Thinking and Innovation

The participants discussed a number of higher-level uses of AI tools, which they have either used or see using in the near future:

- Research
- Idea generation
- Language enhancement
- Narrative building
- Messaging Platform
- Storytelling
- Increasing content engagement

One interviewee said that she used AI to automate repetitive technical tasks, freeing up his team to focus on more creative and strategic tasks. With regards to using AI for idea generation, an interviewee explained how ChatGPT and Gemini helped her generate new ideas:

> "I use these softwares, and these softwares help me a lot in my work. In a way, like sometimes when I'm stuck with some idea, there are many suggestions from which I can go and refer and read, and then my work gets enhanced and I can do better when I'm using these AI softwares... I get loads of help from this AI-based tool, ChatGPT. How to make it interesting, how to get more ideas, how to get more suggestions."

None of the interviewees found conclusive evidence of AI tools fostering innovation, although they acknowledged that it was possible. One interviewee noted that the effectiveness of AI in generating innovative solutions in media and communication largely depends on the skill of the user. Skilled users can leverage AI to achieve significantly higher output and innovative results. The interviewee noted that AI's potential to drive innovation is closely linked to the user's ability to effectively interact with the AI tool in question and apply it creatively to solve complex problems:

> "If I want to do something innovative, the amount of effort that I, as a creator, will have to put in is much, much more. Finally, it depends on the quality of the human being in charge of using

> that tool. That is my personal opinion. You have a smart human being who knows how to use the tool, but the basic intelligence is required, the basic thought process. All that is inescapable."

Factor 4: Ethical Issues

We use this factor to evaluate the respondents' awareness of issues such as fairness, accountability, transparency, ethics, and safety in the context of AI.

Dimension 4.1: Privacy Concerns

All respondents expressed significant concerns about privacy and the implications of AI-enabled surveillance using terms like "alarming," "eerie," "frightening," invasion of privacy," and "sense of threat" to convey the gravity of the issue. They discussed the constant monitoring by AI systems such as Alexa and Siri, noting that these devices listen to conversations and that social media tools use AI algorithms to track user behavior. Some respondents highlighted the risks associated with the storage of conversation data by AI chatbots like ChatGPT, which they felt could be used for user profiling.

A few participants pointed out the potential repercussions of AI-based analysis of behavioral data. They warned that it could have a potentially disastrous effect on societies, leading to major shifts in behavior, customs, spending habits and social trends. One respondent cautioned that in an Indian context, this could further exacerbate societal divisions by politicizing caste or regional spending patterns, or behaviors:

> "I would say that a lot of multinationals, if not outright having goals such as thought control, definitely do want to be able to control your spending habits. It could be as simple as you are providing data. For you, it may be that you have just given a peek into the kind of television you're buying, but when companies collect this data at the level of society and mine it, they can use it in ways that are kind of scary. For Indians, it could be like, which caste is spending on what? This is not something you want to further divide society on, but I see risks in this."

Dimension 4.2: Malicious Use of AI

All participants expressed significant concerns regarding the potential misuse of AI-based systems. Their concerns can be broadly categorized as follows:

Fake News and Deepfakes: The significant risks posed by AI-generated fake news and deep fakes was highlighted by all the interviewees. Misleading or false information AI-generated content can lead to identity theft by making it appear as though individuals are saying or doing things they have not. AI-generated images of people and incidents can harm reputations and cause severe emotional distress. One respondent notes:

> "We have heard of... Why, this election that got over, there was so much of a biased narrative that was being consumed very freely and trustingly by so many people. That itself shows how problematic such things can be. We heard about a deep fake video going viral, saying that reservations will be pulled out and things like that, and people falling for all that, not even knowing that they are being manipulated."

Propaganda: All interviewees noted a significant danger of AI-generated content amplifying the spread of incorrect and often harmful information. In situations where misinformation already exists, false but credible sounding AI-generated content can cause significant polarization of views and societal rifts. One participant discusses the dangers of AI-generated content with ideological slant.

> "That brings us to the dangerous part. If things, especially ideological content, can be generated, then how reliable is it? A big danger is that AI trains itself on what is already available out there. Right now, if the media has a lot of ideological content that is very strongly biased in one direction, the danger is that effect could only snowball."

Impact on Children and Teenagers: Some participants were particularly concerned about the negative impact on children through harmful AI-generated content. Children's thoughts and behaviors can be influenced in harmful ways, often without parental awareness. Biased or malicious messaging in social media or promoted by AI-bots can potentially turn children against their own identity, culture, and family. One respondent, who runs a Podcast dedicated to parenting challenges and issues, notes:

> "Considering that I work with parents and children, I'm naturally inclined to see this as the biggest risk: the fact that children can be manipulated, and parents would still not be able to understand the bigger forces operating, and we will then push the children into ways that are inimical to their well-being. For example, if you notice these days, AI has a lot of articles, bots on social media generating content that children especially are very influenced by."

Dimension 4.3: Bias in AI Systems

Every participant expressed concerns about biases in AI systems. They noted that the outputs from ChatGPT, image generation AI tools, and even summarization and paraphrasing tools seemed to propagate specific views. The output often exhibited ideological bias, with a tendency to align more closely with Western viewpoints.

> "As I said, just try to know anything related to Indian civilization. Most of the answers are what the Western academicians understand India to be... Maybe it's intentional also, or it could be bias, but definitely due to lack of understanding or due to ill intention, they give you answers which, at least for me, don't satisfy me. If they are really interested, they are really very serious, very keen to provide the correct answer, then they should take people who are experts in these areas from India on board."

Discussion and Analysis

This study aimed to qualitatively understand AI literacy among media professionals in India. The objective was not only to explore the technical and work-related aspects of AI usage but also to delve into what AI meant to these individuals at a personal level. On certain issues, such as the ethical implications there were similar views and concerns. However, participants had diverse perspectives on AI itself. Some viewed AI as a tool to improve efficiency and augment human performance. Others remained indifferent, perceiving it as a normal part of the evolution of computing technology. One respondent cautioned against becoming too dependent on AI:

> "There are pros and cons. If you get too much involved, too much dependent on AI, then, you know, of course, as a human being, as a researcher, your potential will degrade with time. So you have to use it very intelligently."

For a subset of participants, AI was associated with job loss and other negative impacts. One interviewee, a veteran freelance content creator, transcriptionist, and translator who has had many major media clients, bluntly stated that she was a victim of AI.

> "Actually, my work got affected because of AI only. I used to write a lot of website content; article writing was my main job work. But around one and a half years ago, my clients took their hands off because they said artificial intelligence can do the work you can do, and it's faster and easier... So my work got affected. And gradually, right now, I don't get any article writing work from my clients. So artificial intelligence—I am one of the first batch of victims that got affected by artificial intelligence. So I have a little bad experience."

One of the other issues raised by participants was the quality of output produced by AI-systems. Apart from irrelevance and verbosity, in some cases, the answers to specific questions asked to ChatGPT or Gemini were said to have been wrong. While bias in data sets as well as data hallucination can partially explain wrong answers, another factor as pointed out by participants is the correct use of AI systems to get the desired output.

> "If you want a 2+2=4, that is something that a person without too much training or putting in a lot of thought can probably get... it depends on the quality of the human being in charge of using that tool. That is my personal opinion. You have a smart human being who knows how to use the tool, but the basic intelligence is required, the basic thought process. All that is inescapable."

Conclusion

AI is an integral part of our present reality. It is no longer a futuristic idea or a distant prospect. AI literacy is therefore an essential requirement for navigating the future of the media industry, and systematic studies are needed to thoroughly understand AI literacy among media professionals. This will enable a more equitable and effective integration of AI in journalism and communication processes, and to develop targeted educational interventions. This study is a small step in that direction. The current study has a number of limitations, including a sample size of 16 participants and geographic focus on media professionals in India. Mass media is a vast field, from which a few activities like content generation and editing, multimedia content production, blogging and podcasts, transcription and translation, were chosen. Moreover, all the participants came from an urban background and work in metro cities. There was no representation of the views of rural India in this study. Future research should aim to examine larger samples, catering to different demographic segments, including rural, semi-urban as well as urban areas. A variety of methods such as surveys on large population samples, focus groups and other interviews should be employed to gather more comprehensive insights. Such research could triangulate the data, thereby strengthening and validating the insights gained.By developing an understanding of AI technologies, media professionals can maximize their advantages while minimizing potential drawbacks.

References

1. Athaluri, S. A., Manthena, S. V., Kesapragada, V. K. M., Yarlagadda, V., Dave, T., & Duddumpudi, R. T. S. (2023). Exploring the boundaries of reality: investigating the phenomenon of artificial intelligence hallucination in scientific writing through ChatGPT references. *Cureus, 15*(4). https://doi.org/10.7759/cureus.37432

2. Baumgartner, T.A., Strong, C.H. and Hensley, L.D. (2006). *Conducting and Reading Research in Health and Human Performance*. McGraw-Hill, New York.

3. Bengesi, S., El-Sayed, H., Sarker, M. K., Houkpati, Y., Irungu, J., & Oladunni, T. (2024). Advancements in Generative AI: A Comprehensive Review of GANs, GPT, Autoencoders, Diffusion Model, and Transformers. *IEEE Access, 12*, 69812-69837. http://dx.doi.org/10.1109/ACCESS.2024.3397775

4. Broussard, M., Diakopoulos, N., Guzman, A. L., Abebe, R., Dupagne, M., & Chuan, C. H. (2019). Artificial intelligence and journalism. *Journalism & mass communication quarterly, 96*(3), 673-695. https://doi.org/10.1177/1077699019859901

5. Chan-Olmsted, S. M. (2019). A review of artificial intelligence adoptions in the media industry. *International journal on media management, 21*(3-4), 193-215. https://doi.org/10.1080/14241277.2019.1695619

6. Christensen, C. M. (2002). The opportunity and threat of disruptive technologies. *MRS Bulletin, 27*(4), 278-282.

7. Dhiman, D. B. (2023). Does Artificial Intelligence help Journalists: A Boon or Bane?. *Available at SSRN 4401194.* http://dx.doi.org/10.2139/ssrn.4401194

8. Eisenhardt, K. M. (1989). Building theories from case study research. *Academy of management review, 14*(4), 532-550. https://doi.org/10.2307/258557

9. Eisenhardt, K. M., & Graebner, M. E. (2007). Theory building from cases: Opportunities and challenges. *Academy of management journal, 50*(1), 25-32. https://doi.org/10.5465/amj.2007.24160888

10. Gairola, A. (2024). Microsoft CEO Satya Nadella Says Stop Treating AI Like Humans: 'I Sort Of Believe It's A Tool.' MSN. https://www.msn.com/en-us/money/news/microsoft-ceo-satya-nadella-says-stop-treating-ai-like-humans-i-sort-of-believe-its-a-tool/ar-BB1mORVQ

11. AI HLEG. (2019). *A definition of AI: Main capabilities and disciplines.* High-Level Expert Group on Artificial Intelligence: European Commission. https://digital-strategy.ec.europa.eu/en/library/definition-artificial-intelligence-main-capabilities-and-scientific-disciplines

12. Johnson, R. B., & Christensen, L. (2004). Quantitative, qualitative, and mixed research. *Educational Researcher, 33*(7), 14-26.

13. Jovanovic, M., & Campbell, M. (2022). Generative artificial intelligence: Trends and prospects. *Computer, 55*(10), 107-112. https://doi.org/10.1109/MC.2022.3192720

14. Kiger, M. E., & Varpio, L. (2020). Thematic analysis of qualitative data: AMEE Guide No. 131. *Medical teacher, 42*(8), 846-854. https://doi.org/10.1080/0142159x.2020.1755030

15. Lee, T. W. (1999). *Using qualitative methods in organizational research.* Sage.

16. Lewis, J. E. (2023). Imagining Indigenous AI. In S. Cave & K. Dihal (Eds.), *Imagining AI: How the world sees intelligent machines* (pp. 210-217). Oxford University Press.

17. McKinsey. (2024). What is generative AI? https://www.mckinsey.com/featured-insights/mckinsey-explainers/what-is-generative-ai

18. MeitY. (2023). *IndiaAI 2023: Expert Group Report – First Edition.* Ministry of Electronics and Information Technology. https://www.meity.gov.in/writereaddata/files/IndiaAI-Expert-Group-Report-First-Edition.pdf

19. Mukhopadhyay, S. (2023). Chat GPT adoption in cultural domains in India: A diffusion of innovation analysis. *Asian Journal of Management and Commerce, 4*(2), 112-117. https://doi.org/10.22271/27084515.2023.v4.i2b.200

20. Ng, D. T. K., Leung, J. K. L., Chu, S. K. W., & Qiao, M. S. (2021). Conceptualizing AI literacy: An exploratory review. *Computers and Education: Artificial Intelligence, 2*, 100041. https://doi.org/10.1016/j.caeai.2021.100041

21. Noain-Sánchez, A. (2022). Addressing the Impact of Artificial Intelligence on Journalism: The perception of experts, journalists and academics. *Communication and Society, 35* (3), 105–121. https://doi.org/10.15581/003.35.3.105-121

22. Pettigrew, A. M. (1990). Longitudinal field research on change: Theory and practice. *Organization science, 1*(3), 267-292.

23. Rosário, A. T. (2024). Generative ai and generative pre-trained transformer applications: Challenges and opportunities. *Making Art With Generative AI Tools*, 45-71. http://dx.doi.org/10.4018/979-8-3693-1950-5.ch003

24. Schwartz, R., Vassilev, A., Greene, K., Perine, L., Burt, A., & Hall, P. (2022). *Towards a standard for identifying and managing bias in artificial*

intelligence. US Department of Commerce, National Institute of Standards and Technology. https://doi.org/10.6028/NIST.SP.1270

25. Su, J., & Zhong, Y. (2022). Artificial Intelligence (AI) in early childhood education: Curriculum design and future directions. *Computers and Education: Artificial Intelligence*, *3*, 100072. https://doi.org/10.1016/j.caeai.2022.100072

26. Yin, R. K. (2003). Designing case studies. *Qualitative research methods*, *5*(14), 359-386.

27. Wresch, W. (1996). *Disconnected: Haves and have-nots in the information age*. Rutgers University Press.

28. Zhang, Y., Li, Y., Cui, L., Cai, D., Liu, L., Fu, T., ... & Shi, S. (2023). Siren's song in the AI ocean: a survey on hallucination in large language models. *arXiv preprint arXiv:2309.01219*. https://doi.org/10.48550/arXiv.2309.01219

Artificial Intelligence in Media and its Impact on Socio-Cultural-Economic Constructs

Dr. Ramya K. Prasad, Associate Professor, Department of Visual Communication, Amrita Vishwa Vidyapeetham, Mysuru Campus. Email: kp_ramya@my.amrita.edu/ drramyakprasad@gmail.com

Introduction

In the media and entertainment industry, the infusion of Artificial Intelligence has set the stage for a remarkable change. AI has emerged as a formidable force in the realms of game development, movie production, and advertising, innovating creative processes across industries. Artificial intelligence (AI) provides ample opportunities for enabling effective knowledge sharing among organizations seeking to foster open innovation. AI has the potential to revolutionize less structured application fields, such as innovation management (Füller et al., 2022, Haefner et al., 2021).

Business studies have extended general definitions of AI to conceptualize the tasks or functions that AI applications can perform. For instance, Huang and Rust (2021) propose that AI can perform *mechanical* tasks such as documentation, *thinking* tasks including analysis and estimation, and *feeling* tasks like communication. Others, such as Rai et al. (2019), focus on human cognitive functions such as perceiving, reasoning, problem-solving, decision-making, and creativity. (Thijs Broekhuizen, Henri Dekker, 2023).

AI has become a catalyst in the media and entertainment sector, sparking strategic investments and anchoring a determined pursuit to satisfy ever-growing viewer demands.

In this era of innovation, robots and augmented intelligence have become the architects of unforgettable, next-generation consumer experiences. Giants in both the media and entertainment and technology spheres, including Blizzard Entertainment, Walt Disney World, Google, Microsoft, and Intel, have converged their expertise to craft, launch, and refine a plethora of AI-driven innovations, propelling the industry into uncharted territories of imagination and spectacle. As per Grand View Research, the global AI in the media & entertainment market reached a significant valuation of USD 10.87 billion in 2021. This thriving sector is poised for remarkable expansion, with a projected CAGR of 26.9% anticipated from 2022 through 2030. (Akash Takyar, CEO LeewayHertz, https://www.leewayhertz.com/ai-in-media-and-entertainment/)

Films like "Ex Machina," "Blade Runner 2049," and "Her" have captured the essence of AI's influence on our imagination and the profound questions it raises about the future. These cinematic creations have entertained and served as thought-provoking windows into artificial intelligence's potential and ethical complexities.

AI in the Media Industry

The media and entertainment industries are early adopters of contemporary technology, embracing the digital revolution and exploiting the ever-changing technology to create better content, improve user experience, and establish a robust brand presence.

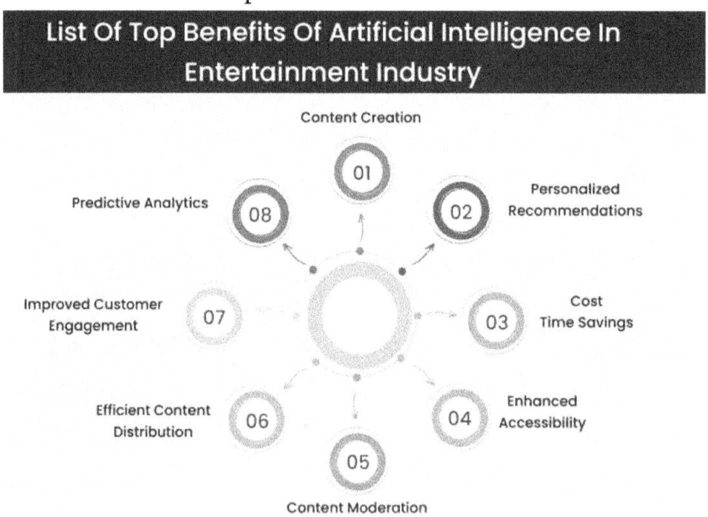

Pic 1 - Source:

https://www.bigscal.com/blogs/entertainment-industry/top-benefits-implementing-ai-entertainment-industry/ Top Benefits of Implementing AI in the Entertainment Industry - Deep Vador

One of the ways the media and entertainment industries have embraced the digital revolution is by using data-driven insights to better understand current consumer centric marketplaces and adapting operational processes to improve user experiences. As a result of artificial intelligence AI in media and entertainment, predictive analytics, recommendation engines, customer journey mapping, and audience segmentation are now widely used. AI's impact extends across film, television, over-the-top (OTT), music, and gaming, improving content creation, music composition, and gameplay for a more engaging and collaborative future. AI also contributes to the growing desire for curated and tailored experiences, making it easier for people to find the material they enjoy. The market size for AI in media and entertainment As we approach 2024, the $2.3 trillion media and entertainment sector faces a critical crossroads. The digital revolution has not just arrived; it is reshaping the landscape. The media and entertainment sector is thriving in today's globe. Whether it's social media networking, news websites, or OTT platforms, the business has much to offer the general population. Statistics estimate that the M&E business will be worth $2.9 trillion by 2026.

The AI market is expected to reach $312.4 billion USD by 2027, according to ReportLinker. Any businesses must stay current on the newest developments in order to decide where they can utilise this technology to not only boost productivity but also remain competitive. AI has been a major changer, quickly permeating practically every aspect of our lives and increasing company efficiency. The expanding number of linked devices and the Internet of Things (IoT) are the primary drivers of market growth. The PwC's Entertainment & Media Outlook points iut that with more people staying home and switching on their streaming services, COVID 19 has catalyzed the adoption. AI is being used in media and entertainment in many ways.**The impact of AI in media and entertainment**

The impact of AI in media and entertainment industry has been significant, with many companies utilizing AI to improve their operations, enhance the consumer experience, and create more personalized content.

One of the major areas in which AI impacts media and entertainment is content creation. AI algorithms can now analyze vast amounts of data to create content tailored to specific audiences. For example, Netflix uses machine learning algorithms to analyze viewing data and recommend content to users, while companies such as Jukin Media and Storyful use AI to analyze user-generated content and identify potential viral hits. AI is also being used to create new forms of content, such as virtual influencers and computer-generated actors.

AI is also being used to enhance the consumer experience in entertainment. For example, chatbots are increasingly being used by entertainment companies to provide customer service and answer frequently asked questions, while voice recognition technology is being used to allow consumers to control their entertainment experience hands-free. AI-powered personal assistants such as Amazon's Alexa and Google Assistant are also being integrated into entertainment systems, allowing consumers to control their entertainment experience with voice commands.

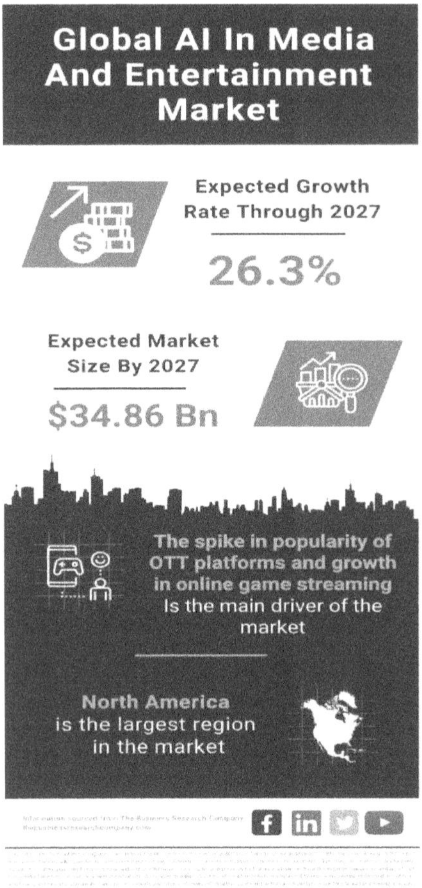

Pic 2 Source:

https://www.thebusinessresearchcompany.com/infographics/ai-in-project-management-global-market-report.
The Business Research Company

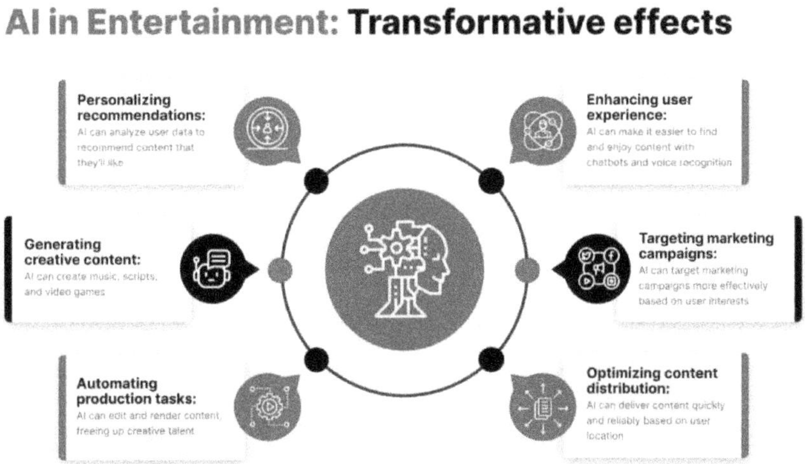

Pic 4 Source: How AI Revolutionizes Personalization: A Deep Dive- Emily Winslet

Personalization is a key facet of AI's influence in media and entertainment. Music and content recommendation systems use AI algorithms to deliver tailored suggestions,enhancing user satisfaction by demonstrating content aligned with individual preferences. Personalized experiences keep players engaged in gaming by dynamically adjusting difficulty levels to match their skills and preferences.

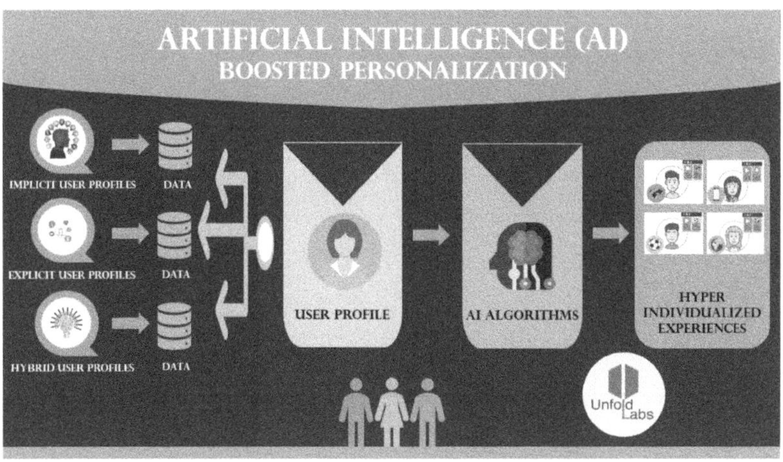

Pic 3 Source: https://blog.robosoftin.com/ai-impact-in-shaping-the-entertainment-industry/ How AI is Shaping the Digital Age - By Akhila Bharanya

The media and entertainment industry has also benefited from the efficiency AI brings. Automated tools like AI-driven animation and character modeling improve the realism of 3D models in films and video games. AI-powered music composition tools make it easier for composers to produce original soundtracks. Additionally, AI streamlines the content creation process by automating tasks like video editing, proofreading, and even generating ad copy, leading to cost savings and increased productivity.

Pic 6 Source: Transforming the Entertainment Landscape: How AI is Shaping the Digital Age – Akhila Bharanya

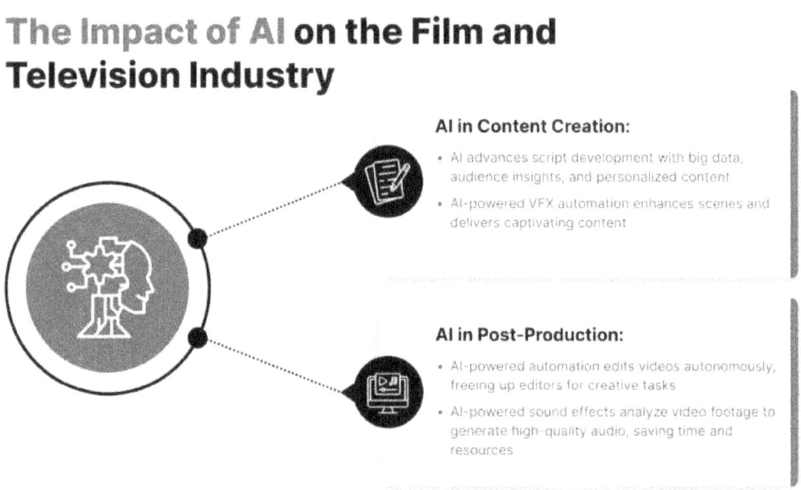

Pic 5 Source: https://618media.com/en/blog/the-future-of-ai-in-video-from-sora/#exploring-ethical-considerations-and-societal-impact

Lastly, AI plays a pivotal role in marketing and audience engagement. It allows for precise targeting of advertisements, ensuring that content reaches the right audience. Social media analysis helps businesses refine their strategies by identifying trends and measuring their online impact more accurately. AI's impact on the media and entertainment industry is transformative, enhancing creativity, personalization, and efficiency while optimizing marketing efforts for better results.

Pic 7 Source: CTV Advertising for SMEs in 2023: A Complete Guide – Vaishali Tripathi

AI is also being used to improve marketing and advertising in the media and entertainment industry. By analyzing data on consumer behavior and preferences, AI algorithms can help companies create more targeted and personalized marketing campaigns. For example, companies like Amazon and Netflix use AI to recommend content to users based on their viewing and purchasing history.

Use Cases of AI in Media and Entertainment

AI is seamlessly weaving its magic across the vibrant landscape of the media and entertainment industry, notably revitalizing diverse domains such as music, film and TV, gaming, advertising, book publishing, and content creation. These use cases, each unique, illustrate a panorama where technological innovation harmoniously meets creative expression, augmenting the evolution of media production, distribution, and consumption in a digital age.

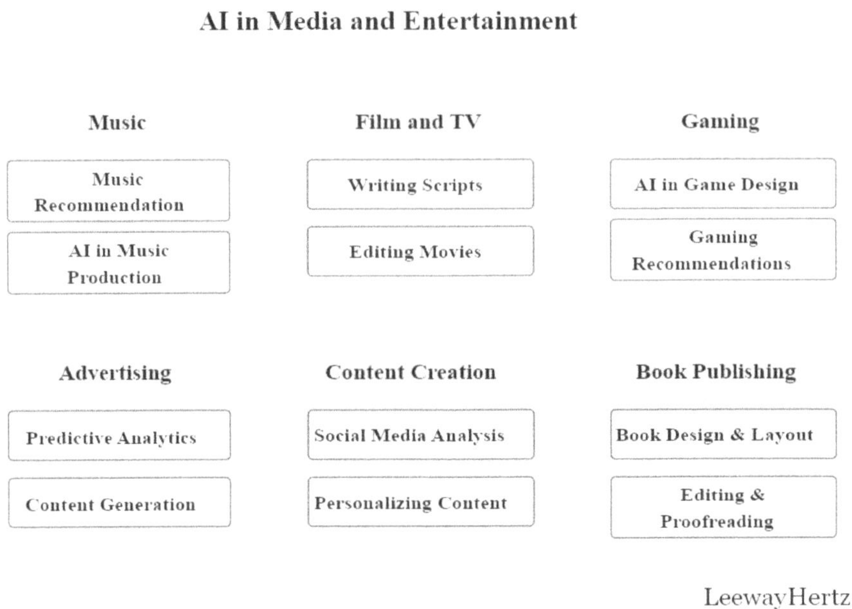

Pic 8 Source: AI in the Entertainment Industry: A Glimpse into the Future of Film and TV - Vasukam

Benefits of AI in Media and Entertainment Industry

AI has impacted various industries, and media and entertainment are no exception. Here are some of the advantages of AI in media and entertainment:

Personalization: AI algorithms can analyze user data to offer personalized recommendations for movies, TV shows, and music. This helps entertainment companies to retain customers and improve their engagement with their content.

Production efficiency: AI can help improve the efficiency of production processes in the entertainment industry. For example, AI can automate video editing, voiceover, and post-production tasks, reducing the time and resources required.

Audience analysis: AI can analyze audience behavior and feedback to provide insights on improving content and increasing engagement. This information can be used to create better content that resonates with audiences and improves the overall user experience.

Marketing and promotion: AI can analyze user data and social media trends to develop targeted marketing and promotion strategies. This helps entertainment companies to reach the right audiences and improve their overall marketing ROI.

Better decision-making: AI enhances business decision-making by analyzing extensive data for valuable insights. Predictive analytics anticipates customer behavior, aiding in product development and marketing decisions. AI-driven sentiment analysis offers valuable brand perception insights, allowing businesses to refine branding and marketing strategies for improved outcomes.

Reduced costs: AI aids businesses in media and entertainment by cutting costs through task automation. This diminishes labor expenses by reducing the reliance on human work, while AI-driven optimization concurrently curtails energy consumption, thereby lowering utility costs. For instance, AI-driven content creation in media slashes the demand for writers and editors, reducing labor expenses. AI optimization minimizes energy consumption in data centers, resulting in decreased energy expenditures.

AI in Media and Entertainment Industry: Real-World Examples

AI in media and entertainment industry is exemplified through various real-world examples, including the following:"

- **Scriptbook:** Scriptbook is an AI-powered script analysis tool used by film studios to predict the commercial success of a screenplay. The tool analyzes the script's characters, themes, and plot points and then compares this data to the performance of similar films in the past to predict box office success.

Pic 9 Source: https://news.futuretools.io/tag/ai-code/ - Devin Wikks

AIVA: AIVA (Artificial Intelligence Virtual Artist) is an AI-powered music composition tool that can create original music tracks based on user preferences. The tool analyzes data points such as genre, tempo, and mood to create unique compositions that can be used in films, TV shows, and video games.

- **DeepMotion:** DeepMotion is an AI-powered animation tool that can create realistic 3D animations for video games and films. The tool uses machine learning algorithms to simulate human movement and behavior, allowing for more realistic and natural-looking animations.

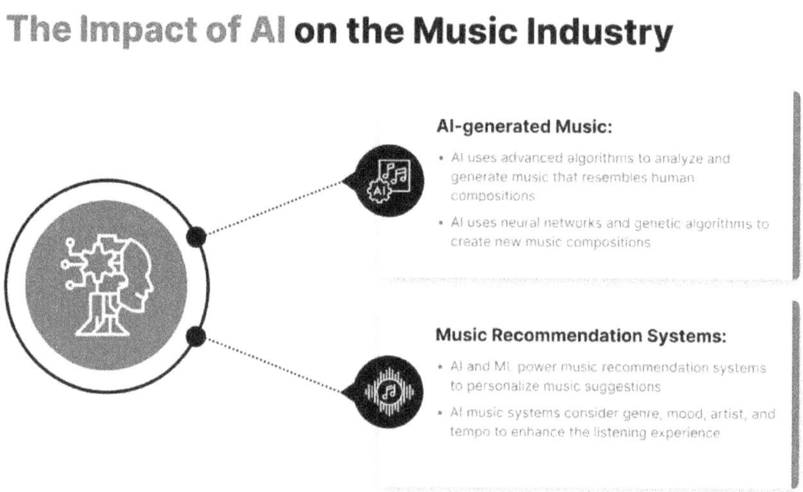

Pic 10 Source: The Amazing Ways Artificial Intelligence Is Transforming The Music Industry – Bernard Marr

Ziva Dynamics: Ziva Dynamics is an AI-powered software tool for creating realistic 3D character models for films and video games. The tool uses machine learning algorithms to simulate the movement of muscles and skin, allowing for more realistic and detailed character models.

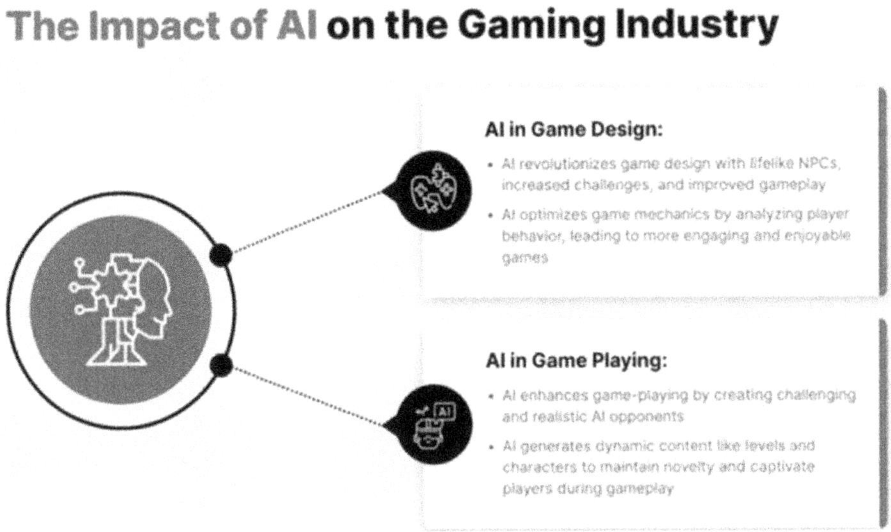

Pic 11 Source: How to Build a gamification Platform: A blueprint for Success – Ms. Madhu Kadiyala

LyricFind: LyricFind is an AI-powered lyrics search engine that allows users to search for song lyrics using natural language queries. The tool uses natural language processing algorithms to understand user queries and provide accurate and relevant results.

Future Trends in Media and Entertainment Industry

The entertainment industry constantly evolves and adapts to new technologies and consumer demands. One of the biggest future trends expected to shape the industry is using virtual and augmented reality (VR and AR) to provide audiences with more immersive and interactive experiences. As the technology for VR and AR continues to improve, we can expect to see it increasingly integrated into various entertainment areas, from gaming and live events to film and television. For example, VR concerts and events have become increasingly popular, allowing audiences to experience the event as if they were there. In film and television, VR and AR could create more immersive and interactive experiences for viewers, allowing them to explore the story's world in more detail or even participate in the narrative.

Another trend expected to continue is the growing emphasis on personalization. With the help of AI and machine learning, entertainment companies can analyze vast amounts of data to create personalized content recommendations, targeted advertising, and more. This trend has already been seen in streaming services such as Netflix and Amazon Prime, which use algorithms to suggest content to viewers based on their viewing history and preferences. As this technology continues to improve, we expect more companies to adopt personalized strategies to engage consumers and increase revenue.

AI-generated avatars or virtual news anchors will become commonplace, presenting news in a lifelike and engaging manner, catering to different demographics and languages, and offering a more immersive news experience.

Furthermore, AI-powered content moderation tools will become vital for media platforms in the digital age. They can act as gatekeepers, swiftly detecting and filtering inappropriate or harmful content. This ensures a safe online environment and upholds the responsible use of digital media.

In live broadcasting, AI automation will take center stage. It effortlessly handles real-time tasks such as closed captioning and provides dynamic graphics and informative overlays for sports events, news programs, and live shows. This can enhance the quality and accessibility of live content.

AI's utility doesn't stop there; it can extend to media archive management. Advanced categorization and tagging can simplify the search and retrieval of historical content, ensuring that valuable media assets remain easily accessible.

Finally, as deepfake technology continues to advance, AI is indispensable for developing sophisticated detection tools. These tools play a pivotal role in identifying manipulated or fabricated media content and preserving the authenticity and trustworthiness of the media landscape.

In a time where technology is tightly intertwined with our daily activities, AI has subtly but powerfully reshaped our media and entertainment experiences. This vibrant industry, shaped by fast technological changes and changing consumer wants, has experienced a notable transformation. From changing the way we consume content with new streaming platforms to putting a necessary focus on diversity and representation, the future is bright with endless possibilities.

As we move forward, both creators and audiences must recognize the media's strong influence in shaping our views, values, and culture. It not only carries a heavy responsibility regarding ethical discussions and inclusiveness but also opens up a platform for sharing varied narratives, enabling a rich exchange of cross-cultural stories and insights. Let's navigate this colorful landscape, aware of its influences, responsibilities, and the diverse stories it can tell across our worldwide community.

Socio-Economic Impacts of AI

AI is a real revolution because it allows the creation of advanced technologies in a variety of fields. We can consider that the concept of AI was born in 1950, with the Turing test, which is a test designed by mathematician and cryptologist Alan Turing, aimed at measuring the ability of an AI to imitate a human conversation.

AI was then defined by Marvin Lee Minsky in 1956, as "the construction of computer programs that engage in tasks performed unsatisfactorily by human beings". This definition is used in most reports on AI and in particular in the "Villani report" (Villani, 2018).

AI covers an artificial rationality that optimizes the resolution of more or less complex problems, in a logical-deductive mode and in specific fields. It is part of cognitive science and the internet ecosystem, which also includes Internet of Things (IoT), big data, cloud computing and block chain. The dissemination of AI cannot be as inclusive and systematic as that of computers or the Internet, because AI covers a set of models and methods whose fields and modes of application are heterogeneous. 3D image recognition is, for example, used to make medical diagnoses and to steer self-driving cars.

Recently, Yong, Zeshui, XinXin, and Marinko (2023) show that the proliferation of AI in the economy has been unprecedented. In particular, the advent of the post-pandemic era has intensified the reliance on and desire for AI for economic development.

AI today is segmented into two main streams. The first current is "symbolic AI" where the computer is programmed so that it can manipulate knowledge. The second consists of "machine learning" which covers advanced statistical models and in which we find in particular neural networks (Le Cun, 1987). The processing of big data is becoming one of the major techniques of AI because of the computing power of current computers.

A third wave is emerging which combines symbolic AI, machine learning and natural language, capable of merging knowledge of various origins and above all for which explanation and transparency are the main properties (Pearl & Mackenzie, 2018).

But while AI can solve complex problems, it cannot replace all forms of human intelligence, including intuition and emotion (Houdé, 2019). While AI has tangible effects on the real economy and the financial economy, it alone cannot alter the paradigms.

When it came to understanding what AI can do, review of literature shows that most respondents believe that AI could "replace human jobs" but few thought that it could "feel emotion." Most respondents were optimistic about the future and impact of AI, though about one third were not sure. Most respondents also did not think they could develop an emotional bond with or be comfortable being provided care by an AI. Regarding the influence of entertainment media on perceptions of AI, it was found that there was a significant relationship ($p < 0.5$) between people's beliefs about AI in entertainment media and their beliefs about AI in reality. Those who believe AI is realistically depicted in entertainment media were more likely to see AIs as potential emotional partners or apocalyptic robots than to imagine AIs taking over jobs or operating as surveillance tools.

In particular, by canvassing the relationship between the portrayal of AI in entertainment media and the general public's attitudes toward AI, we lay a foundation for assessing how these media shape public beliefs and attitudes. Such an assessment should in turn help public interest technologists who seek to design and deploy AI to better craft their outreach to the general public on behalf of which AI is presumably being developed. (Kirby 2010; Menadue and Jacups 2018; Parikka 2019; Jordan et al. 2016.)

Many surveys have been conducted to understand the public's concerns about possible developments in AI, including fears related to what people believe AI can do. That people harbor such fears is not to say that the public does not simultaneously believe that AI will lead to improvements in our everyday lives: in one survey, "respondents thought Al would start having a positive effect on humankind in four years (4.32) and a negative effect in five years (4.74)" (Holder et al. 2018). Again, such results show that the public does not believe that AI is widely used and deployed today but thinks it will be in the future. Some respondents bring up concerns that are not inherent to AI but result from social inequalities. For example, in one survey, most respondents report believing that AI will benefit the wealthy and harm the poor (Edelman AI Center of Expertise 2019).

In another survey, a majority of respondents indicated that AI is used in virtual assistants, smart speakers and driverless cars, but did not believe that Facebook photo tagging, Google Search, Netflix or Amazon recommendations use AI (Dafoe and Zhang 2019), showing that people are less likely to detect AI algorithms when they work in the background.

Economic Impact

AI Impact on Economic Growth

Dr. Mark Cotteleer, research director of Deloitte's Center for Integrated Research, explains that if "we want to use technology growth as a means to drive economic growth, we need to think about what the people on the ground being asked to use these technologies are going to think about it" (Robinson 2019).

AI economy is essentially about data (Agrawal, Gans, & Goldfarb, 2016). The results of economics studies on AI are heterogeneous. The research methodologies applied to the AI ecosystem bear on either top-down (based on value creation hypotheses) or bottom-up (by consulting users and experts) type approaches.

Most relevant studies emphasize that AI has the potential to significantly impact economic growth in various ways. However, it is worth noting that the impact of AI on economic growth is not uniform across all sectors and regions. Some industries may experience more significant changes and growth, while others may face challenges or disruptions. Additionally, the successful adoption and integration of AI technologies need adequate infrastructure, data availability and supportive policies, which can vary across different economies.

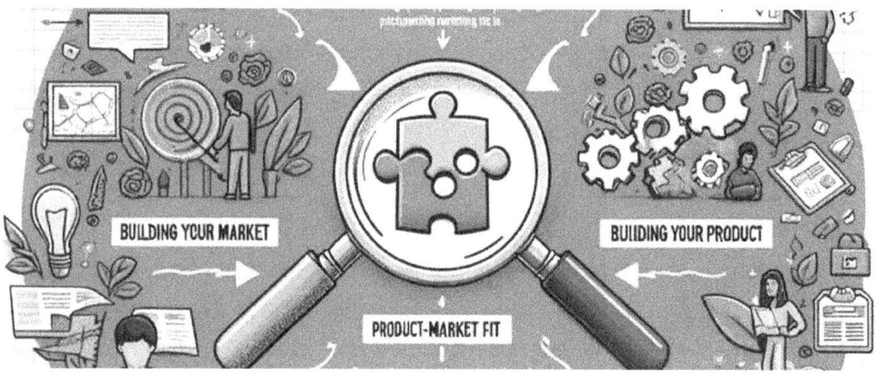

Pic 12 Source: Understanding Product Market Fit (PMF) Through a Real-World Example -Hitheshwar Upparapalli

In its 2017 study, the British consulting company Pricewaterhouse Coopers (PwC) estimates the specific contribution of AI to global GDP at $15,700bn between 2018 and 2030, an increase of 14%. Value creation should be higher in Asia Pacific (26%) and North America (14.5%) than in Europe (9.9% to 11.5%) and developing countries. It would mainly lead to productivity gains (55%) and a recovery of consumption (45%) until 2030, but this ratio should be reversed beyond these benchmarks, because of an optimal productivity threshold.

According to the Stanford University report, “2023 AI index report”, the countries that invested the most in AI during the 2013–2022 period are the United States of America, with an amount of 248.9bn dollars, followed by China, with $95.1bn. The data for the main countries is represented in the following Table 1. In 2022, the largest investments in AI were made in medicine and healthcare ($6.1bn), according to the same report.

On the other hand, and according to the latest study by the International Federation of Robotics, the number of operational robots in the Chinese manufacturing industry reached a ratio of 322 units per 10,000 employees in 2021, followed by the American industry with 274 units per 10,000 employees. China now ranks fifth in the world, behind South Korea (1,000 per 10,000 employees), Singapore (670), Japan (399) and Germany (397). Note that the global average is 141 units per 10,000 employees.

The consulting company Accenture (2017) argues that AI could double the growth rates of twelve major Western countries by 2035. They explain this by the fact that automation, using AI, improves productivity.

According to the Accenture company, the impact of AI-based technologies is expected to improve work efficiency by up to 40% in some countries. The company then calculated the impact of AI on the productivity of companies in each country. For France, the study estimates that companies will increase productivity by 20% because of AI and increase annual GDP growth from 1.7% to 2.9%. According to the economist Philippe Aghion (2023), AI should however also have negative effects on economic growth, due to the brakes (or hidden costs) weighing on the development of AI.

These Obstacles are Mainly of the Following Nature

Technological: some technologies have reached an insufficient stage of maturity to assess their economic benefits, such as the autonomous vehicle which is at an experimental stage or the quantum computer which is at an exploratory stage;

Legal: protection of personal data, cybersecurity and the competitive environment of the AI ecosystem remain insufficiently regulated;

Socio-professional: the effects of skills deficits and resistance to organizational change are difficult to measure;

Organizational: AI models in current business and government management systems are still insufficiently integrated;

Institutional: public action on training (initial and continuous) in AI, in order to reduce the digital divide and promote the retraining of professions, is not equally promoted. It depends on the country and region.

The potential brakes can also be of a competitive nature. AI markets are controlled by "fringed oligopolies", with a few leaders in a situation of quasi-monopoly on their market segments (GAFAs – Google, Amazon, Facebook and Apple) and a galaxy of small players (start-ups). In order to conquer pioneering competitive advantages, the big players absorb or control the most innovative start-ups, thus strengthening their dominant positions and control of their markets. In fact, GAFA thus controlled more than two thirds of global internet traffic in 2018.

Scope for Economic Growth for Media Organisations with AI Applications

Music Industry

AI-Generated Music

Merging technology with melody, AI-generated music leverages sophisticated algorithms to construct musical compositions. These machine learning models scrutinize ample data from existing compositions, identifying and learning patterns across varied styles and genres. Consequently, the algorithms generate new, distinct musical pieces. It's worth noting that the emotional depth and nuance of AI-created music might spark diverse opinions among audiences, fluctuating significantly across different genres and uses. Hence, the exploration of artificial intelligence within the musical landscape reveals an intriguing confluence of technological and creative expression.

Music Recommendation Systems

Music recommendation systems analyze user data, such as the user's listening history, music preferences, and behavior. The system will then use this data to create a unique profile for each user, which it will use to make recommendations. The recommendations can be based on genre, mood, artist, and tempo. For example, Spotify uses AI algorithms to analyze user data and create personalized playlists.

Mastering the Art of Music

The incorporation of AI into the domain of audio mastering presents an intriguing development in music production. Historically, audio mastering necessitated specialized studios and expertise, focusing primarily on ensuring optimal sound quality and identifying imperfections. In contemporary practices, AI technologies have begun to find a place in mastering, aiming to increase efficiency and minimize errors, specifically in providing accessible mastering options. Platforms like LANDR leverage AI to offer artists, especially those who are emerging or working independently, a straightforward and cost-effective mastering solution. While the technology facilitates a quicker and more affordable process, it's also worth acknowledging that discussions continue among professionals regarding the comparative quality and nuance of AI-assisted mastering versus traditional methods.

AI in Music Production

AI is making significant strides in music production, capable of analyzing aspects like melodies and rhythms and even generating creative inputs for compositions. Additionally, AI technologies can process and potentially enhance sound quality through automated mastering services. LANDR, an AI-driven music mastering platform, analyzes frequencies, dynamics, and tonality to improve tracks and offers valuable suggestions for overall enhancement. AI tools further streamline production by automating mixing and mastering processes, significantly expediting high-quality music creation.

Film Production

Writing Scripts

Leveraging AI to craft impactful and revenue-generating film scripts is a strategic move for filmmakers. Once ingested with extensive script data, machine learning algorithms swiftly generate fresh and unique scripts, saving filmmakers valuable time and resources. Additionally, AI aids in the analysis of scripts destined for the screen, dissecting storylines to identify questions, uncertainties, and recommendations, simplifying and expediting the script evaluation process.

Assisting with Pre-production

AI is paving the way for enhanced efficiency in film pre-production by automating and refining various tasks. It assists in creating optimized schedules by analyzing and predicting task durations, suggests potential filming locations through virtual exploration, and aids in preparing for shoots by breaking down scripts and organizing logistical elements. While AI offers valuable support, the crucial decisions and creative insights of production teams remain irreplaceable in crafting meaningful cinematic experiences.

Predicting the Success of a Film

AI plays a pivotal role in predicting a film's potential revenue by analyzing its script. While algorithmic forecasts may not always be spot-on, they are gaining traction among major film studios. Notably, Warner Bros. utilizes the Cinelytic AI platform for box office predictions. 20th Century Fox employs the Merlin system, which uses AI and machine learning to match films with target audiences and provide comprehensive demographic insights. Sony Pictures relies on ScriptBook, another AI-based system, to assess 62 of its movies for revenue forecasting.

Editing Movies

Artificial Intelligence offers valuable support in crafting compelling trailers and editing full-length films. AI systems excel at identifying action-packed and emotionally charged scenes, aiding editors in the creation of enticing trailers. IBM Watson is used in producing a trailer for the sci-fi movie "Morgan" and serves as a real-world illustration of AI in movie editing. Furthermore, AI proves invaluable in editing entire films, utilizing facial recognition to identify central characters and key plot-related scenes, streamlining the editing process for full-length features.

Producing Movies

Last but certainly not least, Artificial Intelligence ventures into film creation itself. In partnership with Ross Goodwin, Benjamin AI crafted the science fiction movie "Zone Out" in a mere 48 hours. While it may not be an award-winner, this endeavor marks a remarkable stride in automating video production through intelligent AI technology. Across various aspects of moviemaking, AI offers a wealth of advantages, enhancing the filmmaking process, economizing time and resources, and boosting revenue generation.

Gaming Industry

AI in Game Design and Playing

AI enriches game design by enhancing non-player characters (NPCs) and refining game mechanics through its capability to create realistic and challenging behaviors, subsequently elevating the player's experience. Furthermore, in gameplay, AI not only develops formidable opponents, providing a heightened and immersive experience, but also ingeniously generates procedural content, such as new levels and characters, ensuring a continually fresh and engaging gaming journey for players.

Personalized Gaming Recommendations

AI algorithms excel at delivering personalized game suggestions, considering players' preferences, gameplay styles, genre inclinations, in-game choices, and past feedback to recommend game titles aligned with their interests. Moreover, AI can dynamically tailor in-game content, like missions and challenges, according to individual player behavior and decisions. This predictive personalization elevates user engagement, crafting immersive, one-of-a-kind gaming experiences that resonate uniquely with each player.

Adaptive Difficulty

Adaptive difficulty, a gaming system, employs real-time player behavior analysis to customize game challenges. It evaluates factors like skill, response time, strategy, and progress speed to create personalized difficulty levels. For instance, if a player excels, the AI ramps up the challenge for engagement, while it eases difficulty if a player struggles, reducing frustration. Dynamic difficulty adjustment (DDA) through AI ensures game balances between challenge and accessibility, tailoring the experience to individual player capabilities and preferences.

Advertising Industry

Audience Targeting and Segmentation

AI enhances audience targeting by analyzing vast data, predicting behavior, and enabling real-time personalization. It segments users based on behavior, facilitates A/B testing, and optimizes campaigns for better results. AI-driven automation streamlines marketing efforts, making them more cost-efficient and customer-centric.

Predictive Analytics

Predictive analytics powered by AI leverages historical data to forecast consumer behavior and buying trends. This empowers advertisers to fine-tune their ad placements and timing, maximizing the effectiveness of their campaigns for better results.

Personalized Content

AI-powered systems create tailored content and recommendations based on individual preferences, boosting engagement and conversion rates. This personalization enhances the user experience, making marketing efforts more effective and relevant.

Content Generation

AI-generated content, such as ad copy and articles, offers significant time and cost savings in content production. Its automated generation capabilities streamline the creative process and enhance efficiency.

Social Media Analysis

AI-driven social media analysis involves trend identification, brand mention monitoring, and assessing the effectiveness of advertising campaigns. It leverages data analytics to gain valuable insights, enabling businesses to refine their social media strategies and measure their online impact more accurately.

Cross-Channel Marketing

AI seamlessly integrates data from multiple advertising channels, offering a holistic approach to the customer journey. This unified perspective empowers advertisers to coordinate campaigns more effectively and optimize strategies for maximum impact and engagement.

Book Publishing

Manuscript Submission and Evaluation

Authors send their work to publishers or literary agents in the manuscript submission and evaluation process. Editors and agents meticulously assess manuscripts, considering factors like quality, market potential, and alignment with the publisher's existing catalog. Artificial Intelligence plays a pivotal role in the manuscript submission and evaluation process. It aids in automating initial manuscript screening, categorizing submissions based on predefined criteria, and expediting the sorting process.

Predictive modelling utilizes AI to analyze market trends and reader preferences, helping in forecasting a manuscript's market potential and guiding informed publishing decisions. AI also assists in efficient manuscript tracking, organized feedback management, and streamlining decision-making processes, ultimately enhancing the overall efficiency and effectiveness of the evaluation and publication process.

Editing and Proofreading

In the critical editing and proofreading phase of manuscript preparation, Artificial Intelligence proves to be a valuable tool. AI-driven grammar and spell-checking tools swiftly identify and rectify typographical and grammatical errors, ensuring an error-free manuscript. Moreover, AI ensures adherence to style guidelines and consistency in writing style and formatting, ensuring a coherent and professional final output. AI can also assess text for clarity and readability, offering suggestions for enhancing sentence structure and overall coherence. Additionally, it plays a pivotal role in version control, facilitating the management of different manuscript versions ensuring that the editing and proofreading process is streamlined and efficient, ultimately enhancing the overall quality of the manuscript before publication.

Book design and Layout

Graphic designers play a crucial role in book publishing by crafting book covers, interior layouts, fonts, chapter headings, and text formatting. Collaboration between designers and approval processes ensures visual elements align with the book's theme and message. AI aids in this by providing design software with advanced features, like automated font suggestions based on genre, layout templates, and even predictive analytics to optimize design choices. Additionally, AI-driven tools can streamline collaboration by offering real-time feedback and version control, enhancing the efficiency and quality of the design process.

Printing and Distribution

After finalization, books undergo two primary distribution paths: physical printing for retail shipment and eBook distribution setup. These processes encompass logistics, inventory management, and channel coordination. AI aids by optimizing supply chain logistics through predictive analytics, automating inventory tracking to reduce overstock or shortages and using data-driven insights to target specific eBook distribution platforms for maximum reach. Additionally, AI-powered chatbots and customer service solutions enhance customer support in efficiently managing orders and resolving distribution-related inquiries.

Marketing and Promotion

Publishers and authors utilize marketing strategies to connect with their book's intended readers. This encompasses crafting promotional content, orchestrating book launch events, and harnessing social media and advertising channels. AI assists in this process by streamlining campaign management, precisely targeting the desired audience through data analysis, optimizing ad placements, and providing real-time analytics to gauge the effectiveness of marketing efforts. AI-powered tools can help refine strategies, identify trends, and adapt marketing tactics for improved book visibility and sales.

Storytelling

AI aids in storytelling by enhancing various aspects of content creation and delivery. It analyzes vast datasets to provide insights for character development and plot structures, helping authors craft more engaging narratives. Emotion detection and sentiment analysis tools help writers fine-tune their stories to evoke specific emotional responses, ensuring a deeper connection with the audience.

Content creation

Personalizing Content & Recommendations

From music streaming apps to OTT platforms, AI leverages machine learning to personalize both audio and visual content based on user preferences and past interactions. These advanced algorithms analyze user behavior and demographics to recommend movies, music, and videos tailored to individual tastes. This level of personalization enhances user engagement and enables media and entertainment companies to outperform competitors by expanding their user base and delivering superior service.

Online Advertising with Targeted Audiences

Online advertising is pivotal for branding and business promotion in the media industry. AI, exemplified by platforms like Google AdSense and AdWords, leverages user browsing history and preferences to target ads precisely. This intelligent targeting ensures advertisers reach the most relevant audience, ultimately maximizing their campaigns' effectiveness and conversion rates.

Regulating the Transmission of Online Content

The media and entertainment sector hosts a wide range of content, including offensive ones. Regulatory authorities necessitate control over such content, and AI plays an important role in detecting and filtering objectionable content. AI can ascertain a user's age and gender, ensuring appropriate content delivery, or it can employ automated content moderation to ensure that objectionable content is not broadcasted without appropriate audience categorization, such as for children or adults only.

Content Classification and Categorization

Online streaming platforms rely on AI to enhance content discovery. AI analyzes scenes, objects, and metadata to categorize movies and shows, enabling more accurate genre classification and recommendations. This automated process streamlines content categorization, making it easier for users to find relevant content based on genre, cast,

AI solutions development for media and entertainment typically involves creating systems that enhance decision-making, automate routine tasks, and personalize audience experiences. These solutions integrate key components such as data aggregation technologies, which compile and analyze media-related information from diverse sources. This comprehensive data foundation supports predictive analytics capabilities, allowing for the forecasting of content trends that inform strategic decisions.

Additionally, machine learning algorithms are employed to tailor content recommendations to individual audience profiles, ensuring that each viewer's unique preferences and viewing habits are considered. These solutions often cover areas like content creation, audience engagement, rights management, and advertising optimization.

Overall, AI solutions in media and entertainment aim to optimize content delivery, improve operational efficiency, and elevate the audience experience.

AI Agent/Copilot Development for Media and Entertainment

Leeway Hertz built custom AI agents and copilots that enhance various media and entertainment operations, enabling companies to save time and resources while facilitating faster decision-making. Here is how they help:

Content Analysis:

- Performing media data analysis and generating content reports.
- Identifying potential content opportunities based on predefined criteria or rules.
- Identifying and analyzing audience trends by processing historical and real-time data, helping to predict future content preferences.

Audience Engagement:

- Analyzing audience data and past interactions to provide personalized recommendations and content.
- Automating routine communication tasks like show reminders and updates.
- Offering 24/7 virtual assistance to answer audience queries and provide basic information.

Compliance and Rights Management:

- Automating regulatory document analysis, ensuring compliance with ever-evolving regulations.
- Monitoring content portfolios for compliance with predefined rules and policies.
- Automating documentation and reporting processes.
- Flagging any potential compliance violations or discrepancies.

Process Automation:

- Automating repetitive tasks such as data entry and report generation.
- Automating data validation and verification tasks.
- Automating content onboarding and metadata management processes.

Content Planning:

- Gathering and analyzing data from diverse sources, providing content planners with a holistic view of audience preferences.

- Recommending content scheduling and prioritization based on audience insights and historical performance.
- Providing real-time insights into market conditions and content performance, supporting timely and informed decision-making.

Content Distribution and Optimization:

- Recommending content distribution strategies based on predefined models or rules.
- Identifying imbalances in content libraries and suggesting rebalancing actions within defined thresholds.
- Optimizing content delivery across various platforms based on audience engagement data.

Fraud Detection:

- Monitoring media transactions for predefined patterns or rules associated with potential fraud.
- Flagging suspicious activities based on predefined criteria or models.

Marketing and Content Generation:

- Generating personalized marketing communications or promotional materials based on templates or structured data inputs.
- Assisting with content creation for websites, social media, and marketing campaigns within defined parameters.

Customer Segmentation and Targeting:

- Analyzing audience data to segment viewers based on predefined criteria (e.g., demographics, viewing preferences, engagement levels).
- Identifying potential cross-promotion or upselling opportunities based on audience segments.

AI agents/copilots don't just increase the efficiency of operational processes but also significantly enhance the quality of customer service and strategic decision-making. By integrating these advanced AI solutions into their existing infrastructure, media and entertainment companies can achieve a significant competitive advantage, navigating the complex media landscape with innovative, efficient, and reliable AI-driven tools and strategies.

For example: Generative AI platform, ZBrain, plays a transformative role in transforming content creation processes within the media and entertainment industry. As a comprehensive, enterprise-ready platform, ZBrain empowers media and entertainment businesses to design and implement applications tailored to their specific operational requirements. The platform leverages clients' data, encompassing text, images, or documents, to train advanced LLMs such as GPT-4, Vicuna, Llama 2, or GPT-NeoX for developing contextually aware applications capable of performing diverse tasks.

In the dynamic landscape of content creation within the media and entertainment sector, enterprises often face challenges such as maintaining consistency, generating innovative ideas, ensuring originality, and meeting tight deadlines. ZBrain effectively addresses these challenges through its distinctive feature called "Flow," providing an intuitive interface that enables users to create intricate business logic for their apps without the need for coding. Flow's easy-to-use drag-and-drop interface seamlessly integrates large language models, prompt templates, and media models into the app's logic, facilitating easy conceptualization, creation, or modification.

To comprehensively understand how ZBrain Flow works, explore this resource that outlines a range of industry-specific Flow processes. This compilation highlights ZBrain's adaptability and resilience, showcasing how the platform effectively meets the diverse needs of various industries, ensuring enterprises stay ahead in today's rapidly evolving business landscape

ZBrain apps within the media and entertainment industry enable organizations to streamline content workflows, foster creativity, refine content ideation, and facilitate diverse content generation. All of this is achieved while upholding stringent data privacy standards, amplifying creative output, reducing errors, boosting productivity, increasing customer engagement, and ensuring the delivery of high-quality content across music, gaming, TV, and other media domains.

Social Impact of AI

In the academic literature, concerns have been voiced about the business drivers for monetizing AI (see Baldini et al. 2018; Bauer and Dubljević 2019), especially since the most successful strategies for AI development (bottom-up approaches and, to a certain extent, hybrid approaches) and monetization create a lack of transparency. Additionally, the media has a large impact on the way issues are framed to the public in every field (Racine et al. 2005; Royal Society 2018; Chuan et al. 2019), so public opinion and acceptance of AI will likely be impacted by the media they consume about it. Because the members of the general public, as both consumers in the market economy and constituents of a liberal democracy, are key stakeholders for technology adoption—and, to a certain extent, for public policy and regulatory oversight—public opinion could affect what kind of AI is developed in the future and how AI is regulated by the government. For these reasons, it is important to analyze how issues of AI and ethics are portrayed in the media. In certain instances where a topic is highly stigmatized, there is a marked disconnect between media representation and public opinion (see Ding 2009), but there are no initial reasons to suspect that would be the case with AI ethics. Going forward, it is important to gather more data and ascertain if a mismatch in public expectations is actually occurring.

AI has a significant impact on skills transformation, both in terms of the skills needed to work with AI technologies and the broader skills required in a world where AI is increasingly prevailing.

Studies on the mutation of skills caused by AI pointed to uncertain results. McKinsey Global Institute estimates that 90% of jobs will be transformed by AI. Only 1% of them could be fully automated, but 60% could be for at least a third of the tasks. The Institute drew up a list of the 25 key skills of an economy and projected their evolution by 2030. It believes that repetitive tasks in interaction with customers, standard manipulation, some administrative support functions, accounting, etc... are threatened, while manager, expert and technician activities (especially digital) should prosper.

The Boston Consulting Group estimates that 32% of companies in China have already adopted AI in their daily process, compared to 22% in the United States and 20% in France and Germany.

The OCED (2019) considers that the impact of AI on jobs and skills in developed countries should be profoundly different from one sector to another. The OCED (2019) rejects the hypothesis of "mass technological unemployment" and underlines the urgency of a partial and gradual retraining of agents exercising low-skilled robotic jobs towards "phygitalisable" jobs with higher skills. The jobs most affected would be those in large manufacturing, logistics, trade, banking and insurance. The OCED (2019) argues in favor of reducing the digital divide within populations, due to a better integration of AI into educational programs under educational technology "edtech".

Overall, AI drives a shift in the skill sets required for the workforce. While technical skills remain important, there is an increasing emphasis on complementary skills such as data literacy, critical thinking, collaboration, adaptability and ethical understanding.

AI is seen by many as an engine of productivity and economic growth. It can increase the efficiency with which things are done and vastly improve the decision-making process by analyzing large amounts of data. It can also spawn the creation of new products and services, markets and industries, thereby boosting consumer demand and generating new revenue streams. However, AI may also have a highly disruptive effect on the economy and society. Some warn that it could lead to the creation of super firms that could have detrimental effects on the wider economy. It may also widen the gap between developed and developing countries. On the other hand, there have been many debates about the dangers associated with the development and application of AI, especially ChatGPT.

The added value of AI mainly bears on effects on consumption, productivity gains and better risk management. These value creation levers vary according to the business (more or less automatable), but also time (duration of the technological cycles) and space (geographical areas).

It is important to note that the impact of AI on economic growth is not uniform across all sectors and regions. Access to AI technologies, digital infrastructure and AI skills can influence the extent to which countries and industries benefit from AI. Addressing ethical considerations, data privacy and ensuring inclusive access to AI benefits are also crucial for maximizing the positive impact of AI on economic growth. In this regard, Nguyen and

Doytch (2022) found a positive and significant effect of total patents on economic growth for advanced economies, but the magnitude of the effect of the technology variable weakens for emerging economies.

On the other hand, absence of human reasoning in automated procedures can generate or amplify inequity, discrimination and racism.

Socio-Cultural Impact

The impact of AI on Cultural Expression and Diversity

AI has the potential to impact cultural expression and diversity in a variety of ways. On the one hand, AI can provide new opportunities for cultural expression by enabling the creation of new types of content and experiences. For example, AI-powered tools can be used to create art, music, and literature that may not have been possible before. This can lead to greater diversity and creativity in cultural expression, as well as increased accessibility to cultural experiences for people around the world.

At the same time, there is concern that AI may also have a negative impact on cultural diversity. If AI systems are not designed to be culturally sensitive and inclusive, they can perpetuate existing biases and stereotypes that limit the representation of diverse cultures and perspectives. This can be particularly challenging when it comes to the curation and distribution of content, as AI algorithms can easily amplify the popularity of content that is already popular, leading to a lack of diversity in the content that is promoted and distributed.

Another challenge is the potential for AI to reinforce cultural barriers and limit cross-cultural communication. If AI-powered translation tools are not able to accurately translate the nuances and cultural references of different languages, this can limit communication and understanding between cultures. Additionally, if AI systems are not designed to be inclusive of diverse perspectives, this can lead to the exclusion of certain cultural groups from the development and distribution of content.

Ultimately, the impact of AI on cultural expression and diversity will depend on how it is used and developed. If AI systems are designed with cultural sensitivity and inclusivity in mind, they have the potential to enable greater diversity and creativity in cultural expression. However, if AI is developed without considering cultural diversity, it may perpetuate existing biases and stereotypes that limit the representation of diverse cultures and perspectives. By working to develop AI that is respectful and inclusive of all cultures and perspectives, we can ensure that it has a positive impact on cultural expression and diversity.

Limitations of AI when it Comes to Cultural Representation

AI is a powerful tool, but it is not without limitations when it comes to cultural representation. One of the biggest challenge with AI is ensuring that it is trained on diverse data sets that represent a range of cultures and perspectives. If the data used to train AI systems is biased or incomplete, the resulting algorithms can perpetuate existing stereotypes and biases, which can lead to inaccurate or offensive cultural representations.

For example, AI-powered language translation tools can struggle to accurately translate idioms or cultural references that are specific to certain cultures. This can lead to confusion or misunderstanding, and can also perpetuate stereotypes or misrepresentations of a culture.

Another limitation of AI when it comes to cultural representation is its inability to understand the nuances and complexities of human culture. AI can recognize patterns and make predictions based on data, but it cannot fully grasp the subjective experiences and cultural practices that shape our worldviews. This can lead to oversimplification or misrepresentation of cultures, and can also reinforce existing biases and stereotypes.

Furthermore, AI systems are only as unbiased as the data they are trained on. If the data is biased or incomplete, the AI system will also be biased or incomplete. This is a significant challenge when it comes to cultural representation, as many data sets used to train AI are not diverse enough to represent the full range of cultural perspectives and experiences.

While there are certainly limitations to using AI when it comes to cultural representation, there are steps that can be taken to address these challenges. One important step is to ensure that AI systems are trained on diverse data sets that represent a range of cultural perspectives and experiences. Additionally, human oversight and ethical guidelines can help ensure that AI systems are not perpetuating stereotypes or harmful cultural representations.

Ultimately, it's important to recognize that AI is not a silver bullet for cultural representation, and that human creativity and expertise are still essential in creating culturally sensitive and accurate content. By working together, humans and AI can create content that is respectful and inclusive of all cultures and perspectives.

The Need for Cultural Sensitivity in the Development of AI Technology

As AI technology becomes more integrated into our daily lives, it is becoming increasingly important to consider the cultural implications of its development. The need for cultural sensitivity in the development of AI technology is driven by the recognition that AI has the potential to impact cultural representation, reinforce biases, and perpetuate discrimination if it is not designed with inclusivity and diversity in mind.

AI translations often miss the mark when it comes to cultural nuances. For instance, idiomatic expressions and metaphors can be tricky. An AI might translate "kick the bucket" literally, which can confuse or offend. Similarly, names with cultural significance might be translated inaccurately, leading to misunderstandings.

Strategies for Incorporating Cultural Sensitivity into AI Training Datasets

One important consideration in the development of AI technology is ensuring that the data used to train AI systems is diverse and representative of a range of cultural perspectives and experiences. If the data is biased or incomplete, this can lead to the perpetuation of stereotypes and biases, which can have negative consequences for cultural representation and inclusivity.

Another important consideration is the need to ensure that AI systems are designed to be culturally sensitive and inclusive. This means considering factors such as language, cultural references, and social norms in the development of AI systems, as well as taking into account the diverse perspectives and experiences of different cultural groups.

There is also a need to ensure that AI systems are not reinforcing existing cultural biases or perpetuating discrimination. This can be achieved through ongoing monitoring and evaluation of AI systems to ensure that they are not perpetuating stereotypes or biases that limit the representation and inclusion of different cultural groups.

In order to achieve these goals, it is essential that AI developers work closely with cultural experts and community representatives to ensure that AI systems are designed with cultural sensitivity and inclusivity in mind. By taking these steps, we can ensure that AI technology is developed in a way that promotes cultural diversity, inclusivity, and respect for all cultures and perspectives.

Examples of AI-Generated Content and their Impact on Cultural Sensitivity

As AI technology continues to advance, we are seeing more examples of AI-generated content in various forms, including art, music, and literature. While these examples of AI-generated content can be impressive and innovative, they also raise important questions about their impact on cultural sensitivity and inclusivity.

One example of AI-generated content is the creation of art. Some AI-powered tools can analyze patterns and styles from different artists and create new pieces that mimic these patterns. While this may lead to the creation of new forms of art, it also raises questions about the authenticity and cultural significance of the resulting art. If the AI system is not trained to recognize and incorporate diverse cultural styles, it may create art that perpetuates existing biases and stereotypes.

Similarly, in the music industry, AI has been used to generate new songs based on popular music styles. While this may lead to the creation of new forms of music, it can also perpetuate the dominance of certain music styles and genres, limiting the representation of diverse cultural perspectives and experiences.

Another example of AI-generated content is the creation of literature. Some AI-powered tools can generate new text based on existing works of literature. While this may lead to the creation of new and innovative stories, it also raises questions about the cultural sensitivity of the resulting works. If the AI system is not designed to be culturally sensitive and inclusive, it may create literature that perpetuates existing biases and stereotypes, limiting the representation of diverse cultural perspectives and experiences.

In order to ensure that AI-generated content is culturally sensitive and inclusive, it is important to ensure that the data used to train AI systems is diverse and representative of a range of cultural perspectives and experiences. Additionally, it is essential to ensure that AI systems are designed with cultural sensitivity in mind and to incorporate diverse perspectives and experiences in the development process.

Overall, while AI-generated content has the potential to lead to new forms of creative expression, it is important to consider its impact on cultural sensitivity and inclusivity. By working to develop AI systems that are respectful and inclusive of diverse cultures and perspectives, we can ensure that AI-generated content has a positive impact on cultural representation and diversity.

Ethical Dilemmas for Considerations on AI and Cultural Sensitivity

As AI technology continues to advance, it is important to consider the ethical considerations that come with its impact on cultural sensitivity. While AI has the potential to create innovative and exciting forms of content, it is important to ensure that these creations are ethically sound and culturally sensitive.

One ethical consideration for AI and cultural sensitivity is the need to ensure that AI systems do not perpetuate biases or stereotypes. This means that AI systems should be designed to recognize and incorporate diverse cultural perspectives and experiences. It is essential to ensure that the data used to train AI systems is diverse and representative of a range of cultural perspectives and experiences. Additionally, it is important to ensure that AI systems are designed with cultural sensitivity in mind and incorporate diverse perspectives and experiences in the development process.

Another ethical consideration for AI and cultural sensitivity is the need to ensure that AI systems are transparent and accountable. This means that it should be clear how AI systems are making decisions and creating content. Transparency is important because it helps ensure that AI-generated content is culturally sensitive and ethical. Additionally, it is important to have systems in place to monitor and correct any unintended consequences or negative impacts of AI-generated content.

Finally, it is important to ensure that AI systems are being used ethically and in a way that benefits society as a whole. This means that AI-generated content should not be used to perpetuate harmful stereotypes or to create content that is offensive or inappropriate. Instead, it should be used to create innovative and exciting forms of content that promote cultural sensitivity and inclusivity.

In conclusion, ethical considerations are crucial when it comes to AI and cultural sensitivity. By ensuring that AI systems are designed with cultural sensitivity in mind, transparent, and accountable, and used in an ethical and responsible manner, we can unlock the full potential of AI-generated content while minimizing the risk of unintended consequences or negative impacts.

The Future of AI and its Impact on Cultural Diversity in Content Creation

As AI technology continues to advance, it is clear that it will have a significant impact on cultural diversity in content creation. AI has the potential to create innovative and exciting forms of content that incorporate diverse perspectives and experiences, while also minimizing the risk of unintended biases or negative impacts. However, the future of AI and its impact on cultural diversity in content creation will depend on a number of factors.

One key factor is the continued development of AI technology. As AI systems become more advanced, they will be able to incorporate more diverse perspectives and experiences into content creation. Additionally, as the use of AI in content creation becomes more widespread, it is likely that AI-generated content will become more culturally sensitive and inclusive.

Another factor that will impact the future of AI and its impact on cultural diversity in content creation is the role of human oversight. As mentioned previously, human oversight is crucial to ensuring that AI-generated content is culturally sensitive and appropriate. As AI systems become more advanced, the role of human oversight will likely become even more important, as it will be necessary to ensure that AI systems are creating content that meets the needs and expectations of diverse audiences.

Finally, the future of AI and its impact on cultural diversity in content creation will depend on how AI systems are used in practice. If AI-generated content is used to perpetuate harmful stereotypes or to create content that is offensive or inappropriate, it could have a negative impact on cultural diversity in content creation. However, if AI-generated content is used to create innovative and exciting forms of content that promote cultural sensitivity and inclusivity, it could have a positive impact on cultural diversity in content creation.

Conclusion

In conclusion, the future of AI and its impact on cultural diversity in content creation is complex and multifaceted. While there is certainly potential for AI to promote cultural diversity in content creation, this will depend on a number of factors, including the continued development of AI technology, the role of human oversight, and the ethical and responsible use of AI-generated content. As AI technology continues to advance, it will be important to consider these factors and work towards creating a future where AI-generated content is culturally sensitive and inclusive.

The media and entertainment industry has entered a transformational era by integrating Artificial Intelligence (AI), which has revolutionized many content development, delivery, and audience interaction elements. The cooperation of major players in the market, including Blizzard

Entertainment, Walt Disney World, Google, Microsoft, and Intel, highlights the shared dedication to utilizing AI's potential for previously unheard-of levels of innovation and spectacle. The AI in the media and entertainment sector is well-positioned for future developments that will influence the production and consumption of content as AI drives efficiency, creativity, and innovation. Artificial intelligence is changing the media and entertainment industries. It is undoubtedly having a significant impact on raising the effectiveness of the procedures used in the entertainment industry. Businesses in the entertainment and media sectors should collaborate with AI consulting firms to guarantee data compliance and maximize the use of cutting-edge technology to increase income. Proper use of AI in media and entertainment will result in favorable improvements for the worldwide industry.

AI also has a significant impact on content diversity and cultural sensitivity. AI has the potential to create innovative and exciting forms of content that incorporate diverse perspectives and experiences, while also minimizing the risk of unintended biases or negative impacts. However, there are limitations to the ability of AI to represent diverse cultural perspectives, and ethical considerations are important when developing and using AI-generated content. Human oversight is also crucial to ensure that AI-generated content is culturally sensitive and appropriate.

To ensure that AI promotes cultural diversity and sensitivity, there is a need for continued development of AI technology, responsible use of AI-generated content, and consideration of the role of human oversight. Overall, the impact of AI on content diversity and cultural sensitivity is complex and multifaceted, and it will be important to consider these factors as AI technology continues to advance.

References

1. Brewer, P.R., Cuddy, L., Dawson, W. *et al.* Artists or art thieves? media use, media messages, and public opinion about artificial intelligence image generators. *AI & Soc* (2024). https://doi.org/10.1007/s00146-023-01854-3

2. Li-juan zhao.(2023). Looking at the transformation of the advertising industry from the new era of digital intelligence: take the introduction of artificial intelligence as the cutting-edge technology as an example [J]. News, (12), 145, 146.

3. Hai-yan wang.(2023). AI technology enables advertising: a deep understanding and matching of customer behavior and demands [J]. Business era, (36), 197, 198.

4. Brewer PR, Bingaman J, Paintsil A, Wilson DC, Dawson W (2022) Media use, interpersonal communication, and attitudes toward artificial intelligence. Sci Commun 44(5):559–592. https://doi.org/10.1177/10755470221130307

5. Nader K, Toprac P, Scott S, Baker S (2022) Public understanding of artificial intelligence through entertainment media. AI Soc. https://doi.org/10.1007/s00146-022-01427-w

6. Stonehouse, G. H., & Konina, N. Y. (2020). Management challenges in the age of digital disruption. 1st International Conference on Emerging Trends and Challenges in the Management Theory and Practice (ETCMTP 2019), 1-6. https://www.atlantis-press.com/proceedings/etcmtp19/125934002

7. Ouchchy, L., Coin, A. & Dubljević, V. AI in the headlines: the portrayal of the ethical issues of artificial intelligence in the media. *AI & Soc* **35**, 927–936 (2020). https://doi.org/10.1007/s00146-020-00965-5

8. Hall S (2018) Encoding/decoding. In: Culture, media, language. Routledge

9. Oren TE, Petro P (2004) Global currents: media and technology now. Rutgers University Press, New York, p 273

10. https://www.sas.com/en_us/insights/analytics/what-is-artificial-intelligence. html #:~:text=Artificial%20intelligence%20 %28AI%29%20makes%20it,learning% 20and%20natural%20 language%20processing.

11. https://verbit.ai/ai-in-media-industry-latest-technology/ y/#:~:text=AI%20in%20 the%20media%20industry,creators%20 to%20work%20more%20efficiently.

12. https://www.globallogic.com/insights/blogs/ai-is-the-future-of-media/.https://www.adriel.com/blog/the-future-of-advertising-is-ai.

13. Budge, K. and Burness, A. (2017). Museum objects and Instagram: agency and communication in digital engagement. Continuum, 32(2), pp.137-150. doi:https://doi.org/10.1080/10304312.2017.1337079.

14. Drew, R. (2016). Technological Determinism. A Companion to Popular Culture, pp.165-183. doi:https://doi.org/10.1002/9781118883341.ch10.

15. Smith, A. (2017). Social Innovation, Democracy and Makerspaces. SSRN Electronic Journal. doi:https://doi.org/10.2139/ssrn.2986245

16. Breyer, C., Heinonen, S. and Ruotsalainen, J. (2017). New consciousness: A societal and energetic vision for rebalancing humankind within the limits of planet Earth. Technological Forecasting and Social Change, [online] 114, pp.7 doi: https://doi.org/10.1016/j.techfore.2016.06.029.

17. Dafoe, A. (2015). On Technological Determinism: A Typology, Scope Conditions, and a Mechanism. Science, Technology, & Human Values, 40(6), pp.1047-1076. doi: https://doi.org/10.1177/0162243915579283.

18. Ruotsalainen, J. and Heinonen, S. (2015). Media ecology and the future ecosystemic society. European Journal of Futures Research, 3(1). doi:https://doi.org/10.1007/s40309-015-0068-7.

19. https://www.linkedin.com/pulse/ai-media-entertainment-use-cases-examples-parangattechnologies2uixf#:~:text=Many%20companies%20use%20AI%20to,content%20intended%20for%20specific%20audiences.

20. https://www.linkedin.com/pulse/applications-ai-media-entertainment-industry-yamini-m

21. https://www.neilsahota.com/the-transformative-impact-of-ai-on-media-and-entertainment-sectors/

22. Matt, C., Hess, T., & Benlian, A. (2015). Digital transformation strategies. Business & Information Systems Engineering, 57, 339-343.

23. Guszcza, J., Evans-Greenwood, P., & Lewis, H. (2017). Cognitive collaboration Why humans and computers. Deloitte Review, 20(January), 8-29.

24. Jarrahi, M. H. (2018). Artificial intelligence and the future of work: Human-AI symbiosis in organizational decision making. Business Horizons, 61(4), 577-586. https://doi.org/10.1016/j.bushor.2018.03.007.

25. Thijs Broekhuizen, Henri Dekker, Pedro de Faria, Sebastian Firk, Dinh Khoi Nguyen, Wolfgang Sofka (2023). AI for managing open innovation: Opportunities, challenges, and a research agenda, Journal of Business Research, 2023. Volume 167, 2023. https://doi.org/10.1016/j.jbusres.2023.114196.

Artificial Intelligence and Knowledge Development

A Critical Analysis of Using ChatGPT in Kolkata

Nazrul Ahmed Zamader, Ph.D Scholar; Department of Adult, Continuing Education and Extension, Jadavpur University. Email:nazrulahmedzamader1978@gmail.com

Prof. (Dr) Santwan Chattopadhyay, Professor, Department of Adult, Continuing Education and Extension, Coordinator, Mass Communication, Jadavpur University. Email:santwanchattopadhyay@yahoo.com

Introduction

"Our intelligence is what makes us human, and Artificial Intelligence is an extension of that quality."

The above single-line quotation of Yann LeCun, Professor of New York University, carries explicitly the main essence of Artificial Intelligence. AI has revolutionized all spheres of human life including information and knowledge. The right to information and knowledge is now a kind of fundamental right in most of the democratic countries including India. Citizens want to enjoy this right not only through queries to government information officers; but they want to utilize this right in all spheres of life. At present, internet-driven social media and AI tool ChatGPT have become the popular platform to acquire information and gather knowledge. Present day information-sphere has now been controlled and dominated by five big corporations- Google, Apple, Facebook, Amazon and Microsoft (GAFAM). Capital, market and profit – are their darling playing fields. They have been controlling the information flow of the world through capital and market with sole intention of gaining profit. To gain more profit, these five corporations have also been engaged in competition with each other. "Information" is being used as an instrument in this competition. It perhaps needless to say that there exist huge differences between information and knowledge. However, big corporations pose to consider and define information as knowledge. They easily earn profit by selling information; therefore, the information-centric economy has been termed as knowledge economy. The monetary value of GAFAM is near about 600 lakh crores (Bhattacharya, 2023, 17 and 20). Technological intervention like launching of many artificial intelligence tools like ChatGPT has a distinct economic vision and outcome. Here, all functions have been done by a data-controlled machine, where the role of human beings is in gradual decline. As an outcome, it bears a direct threat of unemployment along with spread of fake news, propaganda, hate speech, and destruction of the environment for ensuring more profit.

Focusing on Knowledge and information is an intrinsic part of human culture. Human beings have been collecting knowledge and information for thousands of years to understand and perceive society. But now knowledge and information have become valuable parts of big corporate organizations. Capitalistic intervention has made knowledge a commodity to earn profit. The most recent instance of that is Artificial Intelligence (AI) tools. These tools are being used to collect information and make that easily available. In this situation, ChatGPT, a powerful AI tool, has reached the doorstep of the common people. Educated and tech-savvy people now can readily use ChatGPT to access unfathomable information and generate knowledge from that. This study examines how knowledge and information are generated through ChatGPT. Whether knowledge development is possible through ChatGPT is being critically analyzed. This study also explores the embedded existence of technology i.e. ChatGPT and capitalism in the context of knowledge development. The impact of ChatGPT on the contemporary generation has also been studied in this chapter.

Despite these shades of concern, the common people have been using ChatGPT primarily because of its apparent democratic and easy features in terms of knowledge and information gathering. This has created a space where information is available at the fingertips of the internet users. In that context, AI-controlled technology has given the common people a chance to widen their understanding (Bhattacharya, 2023, 91). It helps further in using and sharing the pieces of information. It, indeed, is an added feature in network-friendly social media. The use of this aid is on the rise with clear warning of curtailing individual effort for obtaining the information and a kind of possibility of similar angle while disseminating that information.

Artificial Intelligence

It is really hard to describe Artificial Intelligence in a straight jacket definition. The understanding of AI evolves with technological advancement, and the idea of intelligence itself is very complex and therefore cannot be clearly defined (Garrel and Mayer, 2023). AI is a multi-disciplinary and interdisciplinary field and can therefore be studied from different outlooks (Lu, 2019). AI is a sub-field of computer science that focuses on creating intelligent machines that can perform human-like tasks. It may require learning new information, solving problems, making decisions and speech recognition (Ge and Lai, 2023). AI is an umbrella term that encompasses a wide variety of technologies, including machine learning, deep learning and natural language processing (Coursera, 2024).

ChatGPT (Chat Generative Pre-trained Transformer) is one popular tool of AI. ChatGPT is a language model developed by the US-based company OpenAI (Ferguson, 2023). OpenAI was launched in 2015 by a group of tech innovators and it has received considerable funding from tech giants such as Microsoft, Amazon and Alphabet (Dempere, Modugu, Hesham and Ramasamy, 2023). ChatGPT is a search-scan-and-paraphrase program. It is powered by the natural language processing program GPT-3. It has a conversational feature (Jose. P, 2023). It communicates in natural language. The system was constructed to imitate human conversation and help users with various tasks (Marbun, 2023). It represents a significant breakthrough in natural language processing (NLP), a subfield of computer science that deals with the interaction between commuters and human language (Ferguson, 2023). ChatGPT can also produce chatbots, virtual assistants, language translators, and many other applications that can comprehend and create human-like language with greater accuracy and speed than ever before (Ferguson, 2023). A Chabot is a computer program through which human and technology communicate with each other. The GPT in ChatGPT is mostly two interconnected algorithms: GPT 3.5 Turbo and GPT 4. The GPT 4 is only for ChatGPT Plus subscribers (Guinness, 2023). ChatGPT can learn and produce text responses like humans since it is based on a deep-learning neutral network architecture built after the human brain. Here, the model is trained using vast volumes of text data from books, journals, the internet and other written sources (Ferguson, 2023 & Guinness, 2023). During the training phase, the model can forecast the next word in a sentence related to the context of the previous words (Ferguson, 2023). The model's training becomes better with additional data (Jose P, 2023).

The idea of a machine that might mimic human intelligence tasks was initially originated by Alan Turing, who is regarded as the father of computing science and a pioneer in AI. He introduced this idea in 1947 when he said, "What we want is a machine that can learn from experience" (Khare, 2023 & Sundaresan, 2023). Turing said a computer might be deemed artificially intelligent if it could replicate human responses under particular conditions (Sundaresan, 2023). Turing's work opened the door for making artificially intelligent machines. In 1948, William Grey Walter made two autonomous robots named "Elmer" and "Elsie". "Eliza", the world's first Chatbot, was developed in 1964. The first AI-controlled robot in the world, named "Shakey" was created in 1970 (Sundaresan, 2023). A computer program named "Deep Blue" set a record in 1997 when it defeated world chess champion Gary Kasparov (Bhattacharya, 2023, 14). The strategic board game "Go" is very popular in countries like South Korea, Japan and China. At the time, Lee Sedol, a South Korean, was the world's best player in this game. Lee Sedol lost against "AlphaGo", a google-built artificial intelligence system, in 2016. AlphaGo is a "Deep Learning" computer application. It mimics the neural network of the human brain through different complex algorithms (Bhattacharya, 2023, 14). The year 2018 marked a turning point in the field of natural language processing. Microsoft and Ali Baba separately developed two AI programs. In 2018, these two programs defeated humans in a reading comprehension test (Sundaresan, 2023). Through numerous advancements in computing and technologies in the 21st century, ChatGPT was launched in November 2022.

In 2018, American entrepreneur and businessman Mark Cuban said in 2018 that AI would create the first trillionaires in history (Bhattacharya, 2023, 20). This prediction proved to be accurate. Human relations, demand, and all emotions have been transferred to commodification. Then it is expensively sold to the advertiser. Corporate entities became trillionaires in this way (Bhattacharya, 2023, 20). The launch of ChatGPT is a significant occasion in human history. However, if the main aim is to establish an economy that works for all people, then AI should not be considered a reliable tool (Sundaresan, 2023).

Experts have also questioned the morality of using ChatGPT and other AI tools. Generative AI or ChatGPT can create 'deepfakes' where audios or videos generate an entirely new, untrue perception of reality. In the media, film and advertising industries, generative AI is creating a synthetic world where actors and anchors are being replaced by actors-like bots (Kodali, 2023). In his book 'Simulacra and Simulation', post-modernist French thinker Jean Baudrillard introduced the idea of simulations and hyper-reality while also posing the question of what constitutes reality. According to the concept of Baudrillard, 'hyper-reality' is the creation by models of a real without a genesis' (Baudrillard, 1994). Though at the time of Baudrillard, there was no such generative AI, ChatGPT can also be explained through his work.

It is easy to become confused between information and knowledge. Without realizing it, people frequently use the two words synonymously. However, there is a distinction between knowledge and information. These are two key ideas in knowledge management systems. Information means processed data about someone or something while knowledge refers to useful information gained through learning and experience (Surbhi, 2018). Knowledge development is an ongoing repetitive process performed at strategic, operational and tactical levels to give the decision-maker a thorough understanding of complex environments, including behavior, relationship and interactions between systems and interactors. The knowledge development process is assisted by the knowledge management process which assists the information, intelligence and knowledge development requirements. Thus, the knowledge development process utilizes knowledge management for the development of knowledge. Knowledge, therefore, is the nucleus of both AI and knowledge management. AI provides the mechanism to enable machines to learn. AI enables machines to gather, process and apply knowledge to carry out tasks. It also unlocks knowledge that can be transferred to humans to enhance the decision-making process (Rhem, 2017). As an AI tool ChatGPT has a connection to Knowledge management systems.

Research Methodology and Data Collection

This chapter has followed a research work which is qualitative by nature. Under qualitative research methodology, intensive interviews, focus group interviews, discourse analysis and content analysis methods have been explored. Senior Consultant of an American MNC and Software Analyst Shankhadeep Bhattacharya and Senior Deputy Editor of Frontline magazine Suhrid Sankar Chattopadhyay have been interviewed. Two focus group interviews have been conducted. The first focus group consisted of seven B.Tech. (Mechanical) pass out students and one post-graduation (English) student at Jadavpur University, while the second group consisted of five M.Tech. (Nano Science) students at Jadavpur University. Various magazines and online sources have also been introspected. Some points have also been noted from the answer given by ChatGPT itself. Other than that, a qualitative interview of fifty people of Kolkata has been conducted to understand the general attitude of the people towards the topic.

Findings

The Worldwide Trend of ChatGPT Usage

Despite numerous ethical concerns, the popularity of ChatGPT is unquestionable. ChatGPT has over 180 million users. ChatGPT surpassed 10 lakh users in just five days after its inception (Duarte, 2024). Every day,

25 million people visit the ChatGPT website. Its total number of traffic so far is 619 million. After releasing ChatGPT, OpenAI was ranked 44th in January 2023 based on global traffic rankings (Sundaresan, 2023).

Table 1. Source: Statista, Reuters, Similarweb

Platform	Launch Year	*Time taken to reach 1 million users*
ChatGPT	2022	5 days
Instagram	2010	2.5 months
Facebook	2004	10 months
Netflix	1999	3.5 years
Spotify	2008	5 months
Twitter	2006	2 years

Table 2. Source: Frontline March 24, 2023

Platform	*Time taken to reach 100 million users*
ChatGPT	2 months
Tik Tok	9 months
Instagram	2.5 years

ChatGPT's users are located around the world, with the largest proportion (an estimated 15.3%) being from the USA. The second-largest proportion of users is thought to be from India, with around 7.06% of users living here. Kolkata is not an exception to this trend. Among fifty interviewed people, forty-eight people use ChatGPT. All ChatGPT users are educated, as well as tech-savvy. Most of them use ChatGPT for getting specific and relevant information in real time. According to some respondents, they use ChatGPT for educational purpose. The common view is that ChatGPT is very helpful for building a basic and primary concept on different subjects within a very short span of time.

Table 3. Source: SimilarWeb

Country	Percentage of ChatGPT users
USA	15.3%
India	7.06%
Philippines	3.68%
Colombia	3.66%
Peru	2.92%
Others	67.37%

According to OpenAI, ChatGPT is currently supported in 163 countries. It is available in all countries except China, Russia, Ukraine, Belarus, Venezuela, Afghanistan and Iran (Robert and Cai, 2024). 65.68% of ChatGPT users are male, while 34.32% are female. The majority of ChatGPT users are young - 62.52% are between 18 and 34 years old. The lack of proper internet facilities and language barriers significantly limit the accessibility of ChatGPT. According to a report of the World Economic Forum, there are many countries in the world where internet access is still an issue. Only 35% of people in the developing countries have internet facilities compared to over 80% in the developed world (Broom, 2023). The language barrier has also been considered as a concern for access, but now ChatGPT can translate messages of many different languages instantly. More than 50 languages are currently supported by ChatGPT including Spanish, Arabic, English and French.

ChatGPT and its Democratic Features of Information and Knowledge

The acquisition and dissemination of knowledge and information among a larger segment of the population is known as the 'democratization of knowledge and information'. Democracy creates a pluralistic environment where all people are supposed to enjoy space to think freely and critically. True knowledge development is possible through a democratic environment. ChatGPT has provided a democratic space to common people in terms of accessing the platform. ChatGPT offers numerous features, one of which is epistemological plurality. It means that knowledge acquisition is a right of all people and is not just the domain of experts and scholars. ChatGPT has allowed all people to access information and knowledge. Millions of people, globally, use the free version of ChatGPT. But one of the major challenges for accessing ChatGPT is the digital divide. The digital divide is the gap between people who have access to digital technology and the internet, and those who do not. It can be caused by a number of factors including socio-economic status, geographical proximity etc. The digital divide can lead to disparities in information and knowledge. According to a joint survey report of the Internet and Mobile Association of India (IAMAI) and Kantar, 45% of the Indian population, or about 665 million citizens, do not access the internet as of 2023. According to the second focus group, marginal and underprivileged people are deprived of accessing ChatGPT because they do not have any opportunities for getting access to the internet. Digital illiteracy can also be considered as a point to consider. Though mainly people acquainted with English language can use ChatGPT, now people can also communicate with ChatGPT in many other languages, even in Bengali. According to the opinion of the first focus group, ChatGPT is a capitalist product, and it was developed for profit making. Not only that, a new ChatGPT Plus version (the subscription-based version) has already been launched. It is faster, more efficient, and more capable than the free version. But it is a paid version. So the issue of free accessibility has already been reduced after launching the new version. ChatGPT disapproves of mental labour which is required to gain a basic understanding of an intricate political or scientific topic. Even one highly skilled and talented individual cannot discuss any complex subject correctly or simply through a search on the internet in 5 seconds. But ChatGPT is capable of that. Nonetheless, ChatGPT gives access to this larger universe of knowledge and information (Bhattacharya, 2023, 91). Inquiry-based learning can be aided by using ChatGPT for information-seeking purposes. Inquiry-based learning is the process of gaining knowledge and skills by seeking information (Lee, 2014). Inquiry-based learning is used in higher education. It is an effective teaching technique. The updated version of ChatGPT, based on GPT-4 technology, guarantees that disabled students can access information in a format appropriate for them (Adarkwah, Ying, Mustafa and Huang, 2023). One of the major features of inquiry-based learning is asking questions. Questions increase curiosity and motivates one to ask further questions. In this way critical thinking can be developed. ChatGPT is a tool through which students can get primary answers to their questions. The answers given by ChatGPT can further be analyzed and evaluated once again through ChatGPT.

Though ChatGPT has a democratic feature, it cannot be termed a democratic tool unconditionally. In this context, Shankhadeep Bhattacharya said, 'Democracy' is a political term. ChatGPT cannot have any specific political inclination, as it is an AI tool. Suhrid Sankar Chattopadhyay also expressed his doubt in this respect. According to his opinion, I am not sure if there is any specific relationship between ChatGPT and the democratic freedom to gather information. ChatGPT is just like any other tool. It cannot be said that ChatGPT supports the democratization of knowledge. The internet itself is the biggest source of free knowledge. When we search through Google, we are presented with a wide range of possible results and their sources. Forty people said they use ChatGPT for seeking information. They felt the presence of a democratic space through ChatGPT. ChatGPT has also been questioned in this context. Is there any democratic feature of ChatGPT in terms of knowledge-seeking? ChatGPT answered that ChatGPT embodies several democratic features in terms of knowledge-seeking. Is ChatGPT a democratic tool? The answer ChatGPT produced was many democratic features in its design and functionality, promoting equitable access to information and user participation. However, the extent to which it can be considered a fully democratic tool is influenced by factors such as accessibility, content moderation, and the inherent biases in its training data. After being questioned again is ChatGPT a democratic tool? Clearly say yes or no. ChatGPT replied, no, ChatGPT is not inherently a democratic tool!

ChatGPT and Knowledge Development

Like Wikipedia and many social media platforms, ChatGPT is being used as a knowledge- gathering tool. However, how long knowledge development is possible through ChatGPT is a subject of serious doubt. Having analyzed the first focus group interview it can be said that ChatGPT only gives the information, not true knowledge. According to the group opinion, they use ChatGPT for information and basic concepts. Knowledge gain depends on how that information or source of the information is used. Knowledge cannot be acquired through mere copy and paste of the information after retrieving it from ChatGPT. There is a possibility of plagiarism if it is done in such fashion. If the information is used according to the user's own filtered judgement, then it is correct, but if it is used directly then the user falls under plagiarism. It, surely, is not suitable for knowledge development. The gist of the second focus group interview is that serious knowledge development is not possible through ChatGPT. They said the information of ChatGPT is not reliable because ChatGPT does not give any reference. In the future, if ChatGPT is developed and gives information with reference, then it will be treated as a reliable knowledge tool. But now it can hardly be termed a knowledge tool. Different opinions have been reflected in the qualitative interview in this context. Ten people clearly said they achieve knowledge through ChatGPT. According to twenty-five users, true knowledge development is not possible through ChatGPT because it gives only some short-cut answers and true knowledge gain is not possible through a short-cut answer.

In this respect Shankhadeep Bhattacharya said ChatGPT does not give knowledge, it gives informative-knowledge. According to his opinion, there is a huge difference between information and knowledge, the two terms are not the same at all. If one says the term 'The Communist Manifesto', it is data; it is not information. Then if it is mentioned that 'The Communist Manifesto' was first published in 1848 and written by Karl Marx and Frederick Engles – then also it is not knowledge, but information. But one must thoroughly read the book and draw upon personal experience what has been discussed in Communist Manifesto and then knowledge is generated. So primarily, one has to put data in; information is formed from that data, and then it is transformed into knowledge.

ChatGPT acknowledges its limitations in the context of knowledge development. While answering whether ChatGPT is a tool for knowledge development ChatGPT answered, yes, ChatGPT can be considered a tool for knowledge development. It helps users access, understand, and generate information across various topics. Then after being asked, ChatGPT gives only information, not knowledge. Do you believe it? ChatGPT replied, I understand the distinction you are making between information and knowledge. While ChatGPT primarily provides information, it can also help users develop knowledge by contextualizing information, encouraging critical thinking and interactive learning. When further being asked, if ChatGPT gives the information without any reference, then how can one believe it is true? ChatGPT answered: If you have specific information that needs verification or references, let me know, and I can help you find reliable sources. Finally, being asked - can ChatGPT develop that knowledge achieved by reading different books, journals and individual experiences, ChatGPT expressed its limitation and replied, while ChatGPT can significantly support the acquisition and development of knowledge, it is most effective when used in conjunction with traditional methods like reading books, academic journals, and gaining personal experiences. It serves as a powerful supplement that can enhance and accelerate the learning process but cannot fully replace the depth and richness of knowledge gained through comprehensive and experiential learning.

Capitalism, ChatGPT and Features of Knowledge

According to the opinion of Shankhadeep Bhattacharya, ChatGPT has been intended to resolve a contradiction in capitalism. One can find numerous research articles on various sites but cannot access those without payment. ChatGPT is empowered to access information globally, but cannot access those paid articles. In this pretext, Knowledge is not accessible for all the users and it becomes a kind of commodity. This, to a major extent, denies that knowledge is primarily a social resource. Mr. Bhattacharya explained why knowledge is social in character. He elaborated, if any researcher initiates writing a research article, he/she must have some background knowledge acquired by reading books. The books' authors also must have gone through some books as well. That is why knowledge has a social nature. But restricting access or privatizing knowledge in the form of a commodity, is contrary to this spirit.

But what is the exact contradiction arising out of this scenario? The interview of OpenAI CEO Sam Altman published during July 2023 in Forbes magazine can focus on this. In that interview, he expressed that he is a capitalist but AGI (artificial general intelligence) - could possibly disrupt the current economic system. He said, "I think capitalism is awesome. I love capitalism. Of all of the bad systems the world has, it is the best one or the least bad one we found so far. I hope we find a way better one. And I think that if the artificial general intelligence ChatGPT really truly fully happens, I can imagine all these ways that it breaks capitalism" (Konrad and Cai, 2023). In this context, some questions were asked to ChatGPT itself. These questions and answers are highlighted below-

Question: Capitalism created ChatGPT to solve its contradiction. Please say something about this statement.

ChatGPT: Capitalism leverages ChatGPT to address contradictions related to labor, knowledge commodification, innovation, and market expansion. While it resolves some tensions like reducing costs and democratizing access, it also introduces new challenges, such as labor displacement and data privacy concerns. This dual role highlights the complex relationship between capitalism, technology, and societal progress. ChatGPT is also automating customer support jobs, and this is a direct example of how AI technologies like ChatGPT are addressing certain contradictions within capitalism, particularly the tension between labor costs and profit maximization.

Question: Does Sam Altman really want to break capitalism?

ChatGPT: Sam Altman has expressed views that suggest he is interested in transforming or reforming aspects of capitalism rather than outright breaking it.

Question: So can I say ChatGPT was created to advance capitalism?

ChatGPT: You can say that ChatGPT, like many technological innovations, was created within the framework of capitalism and serves to advance it in several ways.

Question: Do you believe the nature of knowledge is always social? Clearly say yes or no.

ChatGPT: Yes

Question: If the nature of knowledge is social, then why does capitalism want to privatize knowledge?

ChatGPT: Capitalism seeks to privatize knowledge primarily due to the profit motive and competitive advantage, despite the inherent social nature of knowledge.

Question: Does OpenAI want to privatize knowledge?

ChatGPT: OpenAI's approach to knowledge and technology distribution is not about fully privatizing knowledge but rather balancing openness with responsible access and financial sustainability.

Ethical Concern

ChatGPT has given common people the opportunity to get favorable and likeable information at any time and any moment. Common people are happily grabbing this opportunity. But the introduction of the subscription model of ChatGPT has raised ethical questions about fairness. Economic affordability, hence, becoming a precondition of accessing the paid platform. It, therefore, shows an element of inequality.

ChatGPT and Misinformation

There exist many shades of doubt about the authenticity and credibility of ChatGPT. At present, ChatGPT is a strong AI tool for information and knowledge dissemination, but it may generate and spread misinformation. Suhrid Sankar Chattopadhyay expressed his concern about the reliability of the information and knowledge provided by ChatGPT. He said that, like anything else, ChatGPT can be utilized as a tool for collecting information and achieving knowledge. But at the same time, the accuracy of that information is also something that should be double-checked, since the information that is produced by ChatGPT is from numerous web sources. All information available on the internet is not necessarily accurate. It has many gaps and loopholes, but in the future, it may be a powerful tool, for that it may need some more time. In this context Shankhadeep Bhattacharya said, ChatGPT gathers all information and knowledge from the internet. ChatGPT does it through its algorithm which uses natural language processing (NLP). So the ChatGPT response depends on the information that is available on the internet. Lakhs of people put information on the internet and without cross checking it is not possible to accept it as authentic. So, whether the information provided by ChatGPT is true or false is dependent upon the ideas and thoughts of the people. It is a subjective matter. Professor of Computer Science at Princeton University, AI expert and author Arvind Narayanan also raised questions about the transparency of ChatGPT. In an interview with Frontline magazine, he termed the plausible text that ChatGPT generates as "bullshit". According to his opinion, ChatGPT has been trained to produce plausible text, and it is extraordinarily good at it. That means the bot can be very convincing. But it has no way to distinguish truth from falsehood (Jose P, 2023). Many people interviewed in Kolkata also expressed their doubt about the information given by ChatGPT.

ChatGPT and its Impact on Intelligence Development

Some ethical and harmful concerns about ChatGPT are also being discussed in the public sphere of Kolkata along with the issue of authenticity and credibility. The main concern is that ChatGPT may be harmful to the development of child intelligence. According to the two focus group interviews, ChatGPT has no positive impact on the intelligence development of human beings. Rather, it may be harmful to the intelligence development of the child. One student of the first focus group said that the excessive use of ChatGPT may badly impact the child's thinking ability. The other two students in this group supported it. One student in the second focus group clearly expressed his concern and said that ChatGPT may restrict the broad thinking process. One student in the first focus group explained that if ChatGPT is harmful for us, it depends on how we use it. It may help with documentation and primary planning but it does not increase creativity. ChatGPT will never be equivalent to human creativity. Use of ChatGPT should be done considering its limitations. ChatGPT relies on existing internet data to generate its responses. It can never replace the human brain and creative faculty.

Conclusion

The study says that ChatGPT is a very popular instrument among the middle-class people of Kolkata. The students of the educated middle-class families are rampantly using this AI tool. After analyzing the data collected from different sources, it can be said that information and knowledge seeking are the main focus for using ChatGPT. Different AI tools like ChatGPT are also being used in higher education, especially for inquiry-based learning. However, after analyzing the answers given by experts and users it cannot be considered that ChatGPT is a knowledge generating tool in the true sense. Knowledge development is a continuous process. In-depth knowledge is not possible only through searching some information in ChatGPT. It gives something that can be called informative knowledge. ChatGPT gives a gist or summary of a particular subject. True knowledge development is not possible with a summary of a subject.

Through ChatGPT, people can easily access any desirable and likeable information. People can freely interact with ChatGPT. So, users perceive ChatGPT as a democratic space. But it is not a democratic tool in the true sense. According to findings, democracy is a political term. ChatGPT cannot have any political inclination but it depends on who is using the tool with what intention. It is a capitalist product. It is controlled by capitalist organizations with its eternal zeal of profit earning. So the capitalist tendency of ChatGPT has impacted its democratic features and some social ethics. ChatGPT gives an answer that is censored, filtered and sometimes biased. Not only that, experts and users have raised questions in terms of the transparency, credibility and authenticity of the information and knowledge generated by ChatGPT. However, according to the interpretation of some findings, it cannot be surely said that the answer given by ChatGPT is true or false. ChatGPT is trained by some data available on the internet. So the answers given by ChatGPT have to be double-checked. Renowned US thinker and linguist Noam Chomsky criticized the use of ChatGPT in education. In an interview with YouTube channel EduKitchen, he said, ChatGPT is 'basically a high-tech plagiarism' and a 'way to avoid learning' (EduKitchen, 2023). Long before the creation of ChatGPT, world famous scientist Stephen Hawking predicted the harmful effect of artificial intelligence. In an interview with BBC, he said "The development of full artificial intelligence could spell the end of the human race" (Jones, 2014). However, according to experts and users, AI tools like ChatGPT may be detrimental human civilization depending on how it is being used.

References

1. Adarkwah, Ying, Mustafa & Huang. (2023). Prediction of learner information-seeking behavior and classroom engagement in the advent of ChatGPT. ResearchGate. https://www.researchgate.net/publication/373853048_Prediction_of_Learner_Information-Seeking_Behavior_and_Classroom_Engagement_in_the_Advent_of_ChatGPT.
2. Baudrillard, J. (1994). Simulacra and Simulation (Sheila Faria Glaser, Trans). The University of Michigan Press.
3. Bhattacharya, S. (2023). Ajantriker Karcha: Krittim buddhir britte manuser ajj o agami. Kolkata: Saros.
4. Broom, D. (2023). https://www.weforum.org/stories/2023/09/broadband-no-luxury-basic-necessity/
5. CIMIC Handbook, (2012). Knowledge Development. https://www.handbook.cimic-coe.org/4.knowledge-development/4.1aim/#:~:text=The%20knowlwdge%20development%20process%20overview,that%20it%20can%20be%20shared. Retrieved June 23, 2024.
6. Christodoulou, E and Iordanou, K. (2021). Democracy under attack: Challenges of addressing ethical issues of AI and big data for more democratic digital media and societies. *Frontiers in Political Science.* 3:682945. doi: 10.3389/fpos.2021.682945.
7. Coursera. (2024, April 4). What is Artificial Intelligence? Definition, uses, and types. Coursera. https://www.coursera.org/articles/what-is-artificial-intelligence. Retrieved June 20, 2024

8. Dempere, J, Modugu, K, Hesham, A & Ramasamy, L. K. (2023). The impact of ChatGPT on higher education. Fontiers. Education. 8:1206936. doi: 10.3389/feduc.2023.1206936.

9. Duarte, F. (2024). Number of ChatGPT Users (Jul 2024). Exploding Topics. https://explodingtopics.com/blog/chatgpt-users. Retrieved June 19, 2024

10. EduKitchen. (2023, January 21). *Chomsky on ChatGPT, Education, Russia and the unvaccinated* [video]. YouTube. https://youtu.be/IgxzcOugvEI?si=o9IK6JWgrPZeb-hW.

11. Ferguson, G. B. (2023). ChatGPT for Dummies: The most complete and easy-to-use guide for writers, programmers, businesses and content creators: Henry C. Billings.

12. Garrel, Jorg von & Mayer Jana. (2023). Artificial Intelligence in studies-use of ChatGPT and AI-based tools among students in Germany. Humanities & Social Science Communications, https://doi.org/10.1057/s41599-023-02304-7.

13. Ge, J & Lai, J. C. (2023). Artificial Intelligence-Based text generators in Hepatology: ChatGPT is just the beginning. Hepatology Communications, 7(4). https://journals.lww.com/10.1097/HC9.0000000000000097

14. Guinness, H. (2023). How does ChatGPT work? Zapier. Retrieved October 20, 2023 https://zapier.com/blog/how-does-chatgpt-work/

15. Jones, R. C. (2014). Stephen Hawking warns artificial intelligence could end mankind. BBC. https://www.bbc.com/news/technology-30290540. Retrieved July 5, 2024.

16. Jose P, J. (2023). ChatGPT for dummies: A comprehensive explainer that addresses all the doubts and apprehensions about the newest AI kid on the block. Frontline, Published on March 24, 2023. Page 20.

17. Khare, Y. (2023). From Turing test to ChatGPT: The remarkable journey of AI. Analytics Vidhya. Retrieved October 20, 2023. https://www.analyticsvidhya.com/blog/2023/04/from-turing-test-to-chatgpt-the-history-and-evolution-of-ai/

18. Kodali, S. (2023). Unreal, and unsetting. Frontline. Published on March 24, 2023. Page 17-19.

19. Konrad, A & Cai, K. (2023). Exclusive Interview: OpenAI's Sam Altman Talks ChatGPT and How Artificial General Intelligence Can 'Break Capitalism'. Forbes. https://www.forbes.com/sites/alexkonrad/2023/02/03/exclusive-openai-sam-altman-chatgpt-agi-google-search/. Retrieved June 29, 2024.

20. Lee, H. Y. (2014). Inquiry-based teaching in second and foreign language pedagogy. *Journal of language teaching and research, 5(6)*, pp 1236-1244. https://doi.org/10.4304/jltr.5.6.1236-1244.

21. Lu, Yang. (2019). Artificial intelligence: a survey on evolution, model, applications and future trends. Journal of Management, 6(1), 1-29. https://doi.org/10.1080/23270012.2019.1570365.

22. Marbun, T. O. (2023). The Implementation of Artificial Intelligence, ChatGPT, and Critical Thinking Method for Academic Endeavors at Theological Higher Education. Journal Didaskalia, 6(2), 84-100. https://doi.org/10.33856/didaskalia.v6i2.309.

23. Novabear. (2023). https://medium.com/@NOVABEAR/breaking-the-language-barrier-how-chatgpt-can-help-you-translate-messages-in-real-time-1a5883519a4a

24. Rhem, A. J. (2017). The Connection between Artificial Intelligence and Knowledge Management. KMI. https://www.kminstitute.org/blog/connection-between-artificial-intelligence-and-knowledge-management#:~:text=KM%20and%20AI%20at%20its,improve%20the%20decision%2Dmaking%20process. Retrieved June 23, 2024.

25. Robert & Cai. (2024). ChatGPT Statistics 2024-All the latest statistics about OpenAI's chatbot. Tooltester. https://www.tooltester.com/en/blog/chatgpt-statistics/. Retrieved June 19, 2024.

26. Sundaresan, E. (2023). Disruption or fantasy? Frontline. Published on March 24, 2023. Page 6-16.

27. Surbhi, S. (2018). Difference between Information and Knowledge. Key Differences. https://keydiffrence.com/diffrence-between-information-and-knowledge.html. Retrieved June 23, 2024.

28. Vempati, S. S. (2016). India and the Artificial Intelligence revolution. Washington DC: Carnegie Endowment for International Peace.
29. Whittaker, J. (2019). Tech Giants, Artificial Intelligence, and the Future of Journalism. New York and London: Routledge.

Algorithmic Governance and Democratic Integrity: Assessing the Impact of Computational Intelligence on Media, Human Rights, and the Rule of Law

Dr. Archan Mitra, Assistant Professor, SOMS, Presidency University, Bangalore India. Email: archan6644@gmail.com

Prof. Rajesh Sisodia, Director, UIMS, Chandigarh University, Chandigarh India. Email: director.uims@cumail.in

Introduction

The rapid advancement of computational intelligence has transformed various sectors, including media governance and the judicial system. This paper, "Algorithmic Governance and Democratic Integrity: Assessing the Impact of Computational Intelligence on Media, Human Rights, and the Rule of Law," systematically investigates the intersection of algorithmic governance and democratic integrity. It explores how these technologies influence media practices, human rights, and the rule of law. Algorithmic governance, characterized by the use of algorithms and machine learning in decision-making, poses significant implications for democratic processes. This study encompasses theoretical foundations, research questions, methodologies, data collection techniques, and analytical strategies to provide a comprehensive understanding of these implications. The background and rationale section discusses the dual nature of algorithmic governance: enhancing efficiency, transparency, and accountability, while raising critical questions about media representation, human rights protection, and adherence to the rule of law.

Media theory highlights the transformative impact of algorithms on content curation, distribution, and consumption, often prioritizing sensational content and impacting public opinion and democratic discourse. The human rights framework examines privacy, freedom of expression, and protection against discrimination, emphasizing the need for robust legal frameworks. Rule of Law Theory explores the alignment of algorithmic processes with established legal principles and accountability mechanisms. The primary objective of this research is to explore the impact of algorithmic governance on democratic integrity. The study investigates how algorithms influence media content and its consumption, the implications of algorithmic processes on human rights, and the impact on the rule of law. A mixed-methods approach, combining quantitative and qualitative methodologies, ensures a robust analysis. Quantitative methods include content analysis, surveys, and statistical analysis, while qualitative methods involve interviews, case studies, and ethnographic observations. Findings reveal significant biases in algorithmically curated content, impacting media narratives and public opinion. A majority of respondents perceive algorithmic content as biased or lacking in diversity.

Interviews highlight the "filter bubble" effect, where algorithms reinforce existing beliefs and limit exposure to diverse perspectives. Human rights concerns include privacy violations, with a significant relationship between algorithmic data collection and privacy concerns. Interviews reveal dual effects on freedom of expression, amplifying marginalized voices while potentially suppressing dissent. Case studies of algorithmic moderation during political protests illustrate these effects. Discriminatory outcomes, such as higher error rates for minority groups in facial recognition algorithms, underscore the importance of fair and transparent algorithms.

The chapter also examines the implications of algorithmic governance for the rule of law, revealing tensions between efficiency and fairness. Lack of transparency in algorithmic processes can undermine public trust in legal decisions. Comparative analysis indicates that robust regulatory frameworks mitigate risks associated with algorithmic governance. The study emphasizes the need for transparency, accountability, and tailored regulatory approaches to uphold the rule of law. The research contributes to the academic discourse on algorithmic governance and informs policy and practice. It offers evidence-based recommendations for policymakers, media practitioners, and civil society organizations to navigate the complexities of algorithmic governance. By addressing these critical issues, the study aims to support democratic integrity in an increasingly digital world.

Computational Intelligence

The rapid advancement of computational intelligence has revolutionized various sectors, including media, governance, and the legal system. Algorithmic governance, characterized by the use of algorithms and machine learning techniques in decision-making processes, poses significant implications for democratic integrity. This paper seeks to systematically investigate the intersection of algorithmic governance and democratic integrity, focusing on how these technologies influence media practices, human rights, and the rule of law. The framework developed for this study encompasses theoretical foundations, research questions, methodologies, data collection techniques, and analytical strategies. Algorithmic governance, a central concept in this research, refers to the use of algorithms—sets of rules or instructions executed by computers—to automate decision-making processes in governance and public administration. For instance, algorithms used in social media platforms curate news feeds by analyzing user behavior to prioritize content likely to engage them. While this can enhance efficiency and personalization, it also raises concerns about transparency, bias, and accountability.

Computational intelligence is developing at a rapid pace, revolutionizing a number of industries, including media governance and the judicial system. The application of algorithms and machine learning techniques in decision-making processes is known as algorithmic governance, and it has a big impact on the integrity of democracy. In order to better understand how algorithmic governance and democratic integrity interact, this article will examine how these technologies affect media practices, human rights, and the rule of law. This study's framework includes theoretical underpinnings, research topics, methodology, tactics for gathering data, and analytical approaches.

A significant amount of scholarly research has been conducted recently to better comprehend the varied effects of artificial intelligence on different disciplines. As an illustration of the multifaceted nature of these technologies, Das and Mitra (2024) provide a thorough examination of lightweight digital trust structures in the Internet of Medical Things. In their discussion of biomimicry's useful applications in bio-inspired optimization, Jain and Mitra (2024) considered the nexus between natural laws and scientific discoveries.

Das and Mitra (2024) made another important addition to the field of ethical marketing in the era of big data by looking at data governance guidelines and the function of useful technology. Additionally, Jain and Mitra (2024) conducted a critical analysis of the ethical ramifications of media discourse, environmental sustainability, and AI-driven consumer behavior. These studies highlight the complex nature of algorithmic governance and its wider societal effects, as do others by Mitra and colleagues on topics like sustainable gastronomy tourism, energy harvesting system design, the effects of IoT on the environment, and the role of digital celebrities (Das & Mitra, 2024; Jain & Mitra, 2024; Mitra & Das, 2024).

These contributions offer a rich context for the analysis that is presented in the current work. This research attempts to provide a detailed understanding of the consequences of algorithmic governance for democratic integrity by utilizing a wide range of views and approaches. The analytical framework is further enhanced by the incorporation of theoretical ideas from human rights frameworks, media theory, and rule of law concepts, which guarantee a thorough examination of the opportunities and difficulties associated with algorithmic governance.

Background and Rationale

Algorithmic governance refers to the use of automated decision-making systems in public administration and policy implementation. These systems, driven by computational intelligence, are designed to enhance efficiency, transparency, and accountability. However, their widespread adoption raises critical questions about democratic integrity, particularly regarding media representation, human rights protection, and adherence to the rule of law (Danaher, 2016; O'Neil, 2016).

The media industry, increasingly influenced by algorithms, experiences shifts in content curation, distribution, and consumption. Algorithms prioritize certain types of content, impacting public opinion and democratic discourse (Napoli, 2019). Moreover, the deployment of these technologies intersects with human rights issues, such as privacy, freedom of expression, and protection against discrimination (Zuboff, 2019). Lastly, the integration of algorithmic processes in legal systems and governance challenges traditional notions of the rule of law, raising concerns about transparency, accountability, and fairness (Cohen, 2017).

Objective of this chapter explores the impact of algorithmic governance on democratic integrity. Investigate how algorithms influence media content and its consumption in democratic societies. Examine the implications of algorithmic processes on the protection and violation of human rights. Assess the impact of algorithmic governance on the rule of law and judicial processes.

Understanding the impact of algorithmic governance on democratic integrity is. First, it sheds light on the evolving role of media in democratic societies and the potential biases introduced by algorithmic curation. Second, it highlights the intersection of technology and human rights, emphasizing the need for robust legal frameworks to protect individual rights in the digital age. Third, it provides insights into the challenges and opportunities associated with integrating algorithms into governance and judicial processes. Lastly, the study offers evidence-based recommendations for policymakers, media practitioners, and civil society organizations to navigate the complexities of algorithmic governance.

By systematically investigating these dimensions, the research aims to contribute to the academic discourse on algorithmic governance and inform policy and practice to uphold democratic integrity in an increasingly digital world.

Theoretical Foundations

This section outlines the key theoretical perspectives that underpin the study. The research draws upon several interrelated theories: Algorithmic Governance Theory, Media Theory, Human Rights Framework, and Rule of Law Theory. Each of these theories provides a unique lens through which to examine the complex dynamics of algorithmic governance and its implications for democratic integrity. Algorithmic Governance Theory explores the role of algorithms in managing societal processes. An algorithm, in this context, is a computational procedure that takes input data (e.g., user interactions on social media) and processes it to generate output (e.g., a curated news feed). For example, Facebook's News Feed algorithm prioritizes posts based on engagement metrics such as likes and shares, a mechanism designed to keep users on the platform longer. Media Theory examines how technological tools, like algorithms, influence media content. Algorithms, for example, decide what content appears in a user's social media feed, often based on past interactions. This process can create "echo chambers," where users are exposed only to information that reinforces their existing beliefs, limiting diversity of perspectives.

Algorithmic Governance Theory

Algorithmic Governance Theory explores the utilization of algorithms in managing societal processes and their broader implications for policy-making and regulatory practices. This theoretical perspective examines how algorithmic decision-making can enhance efficiency, transparency, and accountability in governance. However, it also highlights potential risks, such as biases encoded in algorithms, lack of transparency, and challenges in holding algorithms accountable for their decisions (Danaher, 2016). The theory posits that while algorithms can streamline administrative processes, they must be carefully designed and regulated to prevent adverse outcomes (Danaher, 2016).

Media Theory

Media Theory, in the context of this study, focuses on the transformative impact of algorithms on media practices. Algorithms play a crucial role in shaping media content, distribution, and consumption. This theory addresses issues such as media bias, censorship, and information diversity. Algorithms determine which content is visible to users, thereby influencing public opinion and democratic discourse (Napoli, 2019). Media Theory suggests that while algorithms can personalize content to individual preferences, they also risk creating echo chambers and reinforcing existing biases (Napoli, 2019). Understanding the role of algorithms in media requires examining their design, deployment, and the socio-political context in which they operate.

Human Rights Framework

The Human Rights Framework considers the implications of algorithmic decision-making on fundamental human rights, including privacy, freedom of expression, and non-discrimination. This theoretical perspective underscores the necessity of protecting individual rights in the digital age. Algorithms can potentially infringe on privacy by collecting and analyzing vast amounts of personal data without explicit consent (Zuboff, 2019). They can also impact freedom of expression by filtering and prioritizing content, potentially leading to censorship or suppression of dissenting voices (Zuboff, 2019). Moreover, algorithms can perpetuate discrimination if they reflect existing biases or are not designed to account for diversity and inclusion (O'Neil, 2016). The Human Rights Framework advocates for regulatory measures to ensure that algorithmic governance respects and upholds human rights.

Rule of Law Theory

Rule of Law Theory examines how algorithmic processes align with or challenge established legal principles, accountability mechanisms, and transparency norms. This theory is concerned with ensuring that algorithmic governance operates within the bounds of the law and that algorithms themselves are subject to legal scrutiny (Cohen, 2017). It emphasizes the importance of transparency in algorithmic decision-making processes to allow for accountability and oversight. The theory also addresses the need for legal frameworks to evolve in response to the challenges posed by algorithms, ensuring that they do not undermine the principles of fairness, justice, and equality (Cohen, 2017). By integrating Rule of Law Theory, the study aims to assess the legal and ethical dimensions of algorithmic governance.

The integration of these theoretical foundations—Algorithmic Governance Theory, Media Theory, Human Rights Framework, and Rule of Law Theory—provides a comprehensive framework for investigating the impact of computational intelligence on democratic integrity. Each theory contributes to a deeper understanding of the multifaceted challenges and opportunities presented by algorithmic governance. By examining these perspectives, the research aims to offer a nuanced analysis that informs both academic scholarship and practical policy-making.

Previous Studies

The literature review examines the intersection of algorithmic governance and democratic integrity, synthesizing scholarly perspectives and empirical findings. The review is organized into three thematic subsections: Media Impact, Human Rights, and Rule of Law, reflecting the core dimensions of the study.

Media Impact

Algorithms have transformed how media content is created, distributed, and consumed, raising significant implications for public opinion and democratic discourse.

Content Curation and Bias Algorithms prioritize engagement metrics such as likes, shares, and clicks, often favoring sensational or emotionally charged material. Napoli (2019) demonstrates how this leads to the amplification of polarized viewpoints, creating "filter bubbles" and "echo chambers" (Pariser, 2011). These phenomena limit the diversity of information, exacerbating political polarization. Gillespie (2014) argues that algorithms embed the biases of their creators, resulting in a lack of neutrality in content prioritization. Caplan and boyd (2018) further highlight how algorithms influence what is deemed newsworthy, sidelining critical but less sensational topics.

Erosion of Journalistic Standards Studies indicate that algorithmic control over media content often compromises journalistic ethics. Bakshy, Messing, and Adamic (2015) found that platforms like Facebook reinforce pre-existing ideological biases, undermining the diversity of viewpoints essential for democratic engagement. This aligns with concerns about the prioritization of viral content over accuracy, as noted by Roberts (2019).

Human Rights

The deployment of algorithms poses critical challenges to fundamental human rights, including privacy, freedom of expression, and non-discrimination.

Privacy and Surveillance Capitalism Zuboff (2019) introduces the concept of "surveillance capitalism," where personal data is commodified to predict and influence behavior. Algorithms collect and process vast amounts of personal data without explicit consent, raising significant privacy concerns. Solove (2020) underscores the need for robust data protection frameworks to address these risks.

Freedom of Expression O'Neil (2016) highlights the dual role of algorithms in amplifying marginalized voices while also enabling censorship. Automated content moderation systems, such as those employed by YouTube and Facebook, can inadvertently suppress legitimate speech, particularly in politically sensitive contexts (Roberts, 2019). This is evident during political protests, where over-censorship by algorithms often silences dissenting voices.

Algorithmic Discrimination Barocas and Selbst (2016) explain how algorithms perpetuate biases present in their training data, leading to discriminatory outcomes. Buolamwini and Gebru (2018) provide empirical evidence of higher error rates in facial recognition algorithms for minority groups, raising ethical and legal concerns about their deployment in law enforcement and surveillance.

Rule of Law

The integration of algorithms into legal and governance systems introduces opportunities and challenges for upholding the rule of law.

Transparency and Accountability Pasquale (2015) describes the "black box society," where the opacity of algorithmic processes undermines transparency and accountability. Kroll et al. (2017) emphasize the importance of explainable algorithms in ensuring fairness and trust in governance systems.

Efficiency Versus Fairness While algorithms can enhance efficiency in legal processes, their lack of transparency and potential biases raise questions about fairness and justice. Cohen (2017) stresses that algorithms must align with established legal principles to maintain public trust. Comparative studies by Wachter, Mittelstadt, and Floridi (2017) advocate for a regulatory framework to ensure transparency, accountability, and fairness.

Discrimination in Judicial Applications Algorithms used in judicial systems, such as predictive policing tools, risk reinforcing systemic biases. Chen (2019) discusses the unintended consequences of such tools, which may disproportionately target marginalized communities. Case studies highlight the importance of robust oversight mechanisms to mitigate these risks.

Integrative Insights

By structuring the review into these themes, the interconnected nature of media impact, human rights, and rule of law becomes evident. Media Theory explains how algorithms influence content curation and public discourse. The Human Rights Framework addresses privacy, expression, and discrimination concerns, while Rule of Law Theory highlights the balance between efficiency and justice. Together, these frameworks provide a comprehensive lens for understanding the implications of algorithmic governance on democratic integrity.

Methodology

The chapter employs a mixed-methods approach, combining quantitative and qualitative methodologies to ensure a robust and comprehensive analysis of the impact of algorithmic governance on democratic integrity. This section details the specific sampling methods, sample sizes, and analytical frameworks utilized.

Quantitative Methods

Content Analysis Content analysis was conducted using a dual approach of automated and manual techniques. The automated analysis employed

Natural Language Processing (NLP) algorithms to evaluate a dataset comprising 10,000 news articles and 15,000 social media posts across diverse platforms, collected over six months (January to June 2024). Manual analysis was conducted on a stratified random sample of 500 articles to provide contextual depth and validate algorithmic findings. Stratification was based on variables such as region, publication type, and subject matter.

Surveys and Polls Surveys were administered to a representative sample of 1,200 participants across five major demographic categories (age, gender, socioeconomic status, education level, and geographic location). A stratified sampling method ensured proportional representation. The structured questionnaire included 25 items on a 5-point Likert scale, assessing perceptions of algorithmic governance, media bias, and human rights implications.

Statistical Analysis Quantitative data from surveys were analyzed using regression models to identify correlations between algorithmic governance variables (e.g., transparency, data collection practices) and dependent outcomes (e.g., perceived media bias, trust in governance systems). A significance threshold of $p < 0.05$ was applied for all analyses.

Qualitative Methods

Interviews A total of 30 in-depth interviews were conducted with stakeholders, including 10 policymakers, 10 media professionals, and 10 human rights activists. Participants were selected using purposive sampling to ensure expertise and relevance. Interviews followed a semi-structured format, lasting 60–90 minutes, and were audio-recorded with participants' consent. Thematic analysis was applied to identify recurring themes.

Case Studies Two case studies were selected based on their relevance to the research objectives: (1) Algorithmic moderation during political protests, and (2) Bias in facial recognition algorithms used in law enforcement. These cases were chosen using a criterion-based sampling approach, focusing on instances with substantial media and academic coverage.

Ethnographic Observations Ethnographic observations were carried out over a three-month period in two technology firms deploying algorithmic governance systems. Observations included team meetings, development processes, and internal policy reviews. Detailed field notes were maintained and analyzed to uncover operational and ethical considerations.

Data Collection Techniques

Data collection will be comprehensive and multifaceted, drawing from various sources to ensure a thorough analysis.

Primary Data Primary data will be collected through interviews, surveys, and direct observations. This data is firsthand and directly relevant to the research questions.

Secondary Data Secondary data will include analysis of existing literature, legal documents, policy reports, and media archives. This data provides a contextual and historical background, helping to situate the primary data within broader trends.

Digital Data Digital data will be collected through scraping and analysis of online platforms and social media. This data helps understand the algorithmic influence on public discourse, providing insights into how algorithms shape online interactions and content visibility (Salganik, 2017).

Analytical Strategies

The analysis will be conducted using both qualitative and quantitative techniques, ensuring a comprehensive examination of the data.

Thematic Analysis Thematic analysis involves identifying key themes and patterns from qualitative data, such as interviews and case studies. This method allows for a detailed understanding of the nuanced impacts of algorithmic governance (Braun & Clarke, 2006).

Regression Analysis Regression analysis will be used to statistically examine the relationships between algorithmic governance and various dependent variables, such as media bias and human rights violations. This method helps quantify the impact of algorithms and identify significant predictors (Field, 2013).

Comparative Analysis Comparative analysis involves comparing the impact of algorithmic governance across different regions, legal systems, and media environments. This method helps identify contextual differences and commonalities, providing a more comprehensive understanding of the phenomena under study (Ragin, 2014).

Ethical Considerations

The research will adhere to the highest ethical standards to ensure the integrity and credibility of the study.

Informed Consent Informed consent will be obtained from all participants, ensuring they are fully aware of the research purpose and their rights. Participants will be informed about the voluntary nature of their participation and their right to withdraw at any time without penalty.

Confidentiality Confidentiality will be maintained to protect the privacy and anonymity of participants. Data will be securely stored and only accessible to the research team. Identifiable information will be anonymized or pseudonymized where necessary.

Bias Mitigation Strategies will be employed to minimize researcher bias and ensure objectivity in data collection and analysis. These strategies include triangulation, peer debriefing, and reflexivity practices. By acknowledging and addressing potential biases, the research aims to produce reliable and valid results.

Findings and Analysis

The analysis of the impact of algorithmic governance on media practices, human rights, and the rule of law based on the mixed-methods approach outlined in the methodology. The analysis integrates both quantitative and qualitative data to provide a comprehensive understanding of the findings.

Quantitative Analysis

Content Analysis

The content analysis involved both automated and manual examination of media content to assess the presence and impact of algorithmic curation.

The automated analysis was conducted using natural language processing (NLP) algorithms on a dataset of news articles and social media posts. The manual analysis provided deeper contextual understanding of specific cases.

Figure 1: Distribution of Content Types by Algorithmic Curation

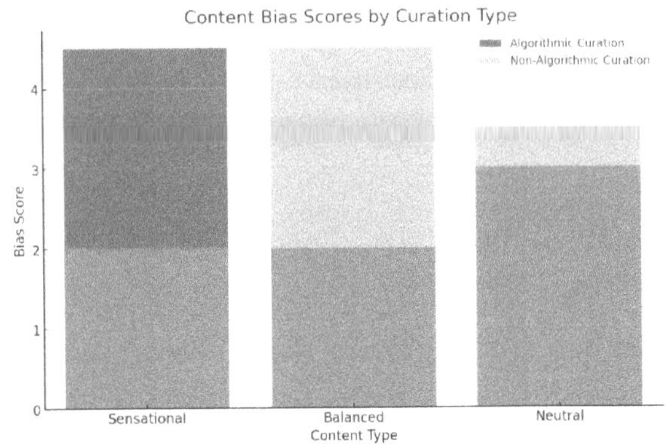

The automated analysis revealed that algorithmic curation significantly prioritizes sensational and emotionally charged content. As shown in Figure 1, 45% of the content curated by algorithms falls under the category of "sensational," compared to 20% for non-algorithmically curated content.

Table 1: Content Bias Scores

Content Type	**Algorithmic Curation**	**Non-Algorithmic Curation**
Sensational	4.5	2.0
Balanced	2.0	4.5
Neutral	3.0	3.5

Table 1 presents the bias scores for different content types. The scores were derived from a manual analysis of a sample of news articles. Sensational content had a higher bias score under algorithmic curation compared to non-algorithmic curation.

Surveys and Polls

Surveys were conducted to gather data on public perception and experiences related to algorithmic decision-making. A structured questionnaire was distributed to a diverse sample of individuals to collect quantitative data on their interactions with algorithmically curated content, their awareness of algorithmic governance, and their views on its implications for democracy and human rights.

Figure 2: Perceived Media Bias by Algorithmic Curation

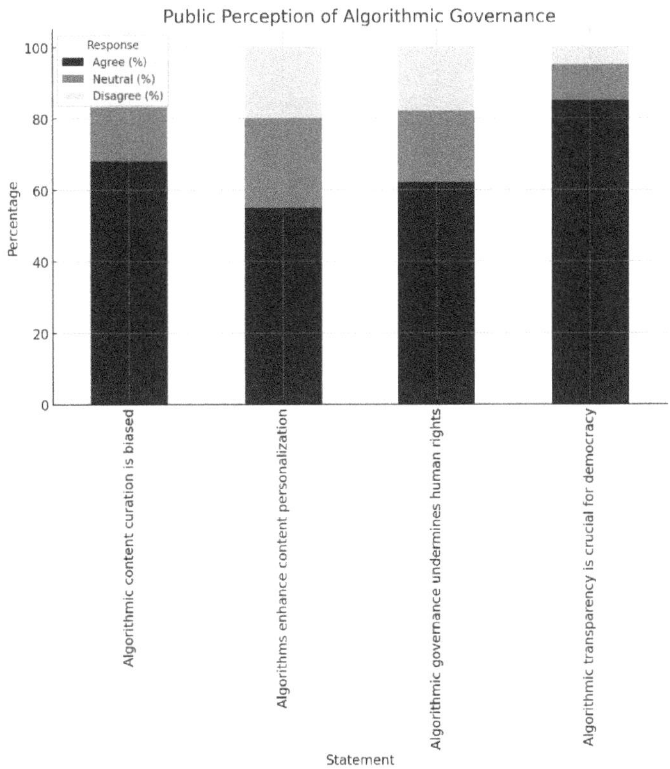

Figure 2 shows that a majority of respondents (68%) perceive algorithmically curated content as biased or lacking in diversity, compared to 32% for non-algorithmically curated content.

Table 2: Public Perception of Algorithmic Governance

Statement	Agree (%)	Neutral (%)	Disagree (%)
Algorithmic content curation is biased	68	15	17
Algorithms enhance content personalization	55	25	20
Algorithmic governance undermines human rights	62	20	18
Algorithmic transparency is crucial for democracy	85	10	5

Table 2 summarizes the survey responses on key aspects of algorithmic governance. The data indicates significant concerns about bias and human rights, with a strong consensus on the need for transparency.

Statistical Analysis

Regression analysis was conducted to examine the relationships between algorithmic governance and various dependent variables such as media bias and human rights violations.

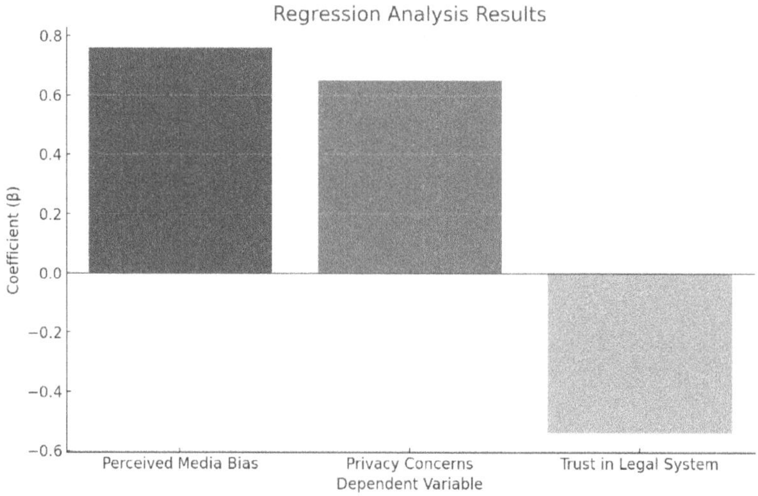

Table 3: Regression Analysis Results

Dependent Variable	Independent Variable	Coefficient (β)	p-value
Perceived Media Bias	Algorithmic Curation	0.76	<0.01
Privacy Concerns	Algorithmic Data Collection	0.65	<0.01
Trust in Legal System	Algorithmic Transparency	-0.54	<0.05

Table 3 presents the regression analysis results. There is a strong positive relationship between algorithmic curation and perceived media bias ($\beta = 0.76$, $p < 0.01$). Similarly, privacy concerns are significantly related to algorithmic data collection ($\beta = 0.65$, $p < 0.01$). There is also a significant negative relationship between algorithmic transparency and trust in the legal system ($\beta = -0.54$, $p < 0.05$).

Qualitative Analysis

Interviews

In-depth interviews were conducted with key stakeholders, including policymakers, media professionals, human rights activists, and legal experts. These interviews provided detailed insights into their perspectives on algorithmic governance and its implications.

Themes Identified in Interviews

1. Bias and Fairness: Many interviewees expressed concerns about inherent biases in algorithms and the need for fairness in algorithmic decision-making.
2. Transparency and Accountability: There was a strong emphasis on the importance of transparency and the challenges in achieving accountability for algorithmic decisions.

3. Human Rights: Interviewees highlighted the potential for algorithms to infringe on privacy and freedom of expression, stressing the need for regulatory frameworks to protect human rights.

Case Studies

Case studies involved detailed examination of specific instances where algorithmic governance significantly impacted media, human rights, or the rule of law. These case studies provided rich contextual data that illustrated broader trends and patterns.

Case Study 1: Algorithmic Moderation during Political Protests

This case study examined the use of algorithms for content moderation during political protests. It found that automated systems often over-censored content, leading to the suppression of legitimate speech and raising significant concerns about freedom of expression.

Case Study 2: Bias in Facial Recognition Algorithms

This case study analyzed the deployment of facial recognition algorithms in law enforcement. It revealed that these algorithms had higher error rates for minority groups, leading to discriminatory outcomes and raising ethical and legal questions.

Ethnographic Observation

Ethnographic observation involves observing the practices of organizations that develop and deploy algorithms. This method provided insights into the operational and ethical considerations of algorithmic governance from an insider perspective.

Key Observations

1. **Operational Challenges:** Organizations faced challenges in balancing efficiency and fairness in algorithmic decision-making.
2. **Ethical Considerations:** There was an ongoing struggle to ensure ethical standards in algorithm design and deployment, with a need for continuous monitoring and improvement.

The integration of quantitative and qualitative data offers a comprehensive perspective on the impact of algorithmic governance on media practices, human rights, and the rule of law. The findings highlight significant biases in algorithmically curated content, pervasive privacy concerns, and the crucial need for transparency and accountability in algorithmic decision-making.

Recommendations

1. **Enhancing Transparency:** Policymakers should mandate transparency requirements for algorithms used in critical sectors such as media and law enforcement.
2. **Promoting Fairness:** Developers should incorporate diverse perspectives and expertise to ensure fairness in algorithm design.
3. **Strengthening Data Protection:** Comprehensive data protection laws should regulate the collection, storage, and use of personal data by algorithms.
4. **Fostering Ethical Media Practices:** Media organizations should develop ethical guidelines for algorithmic content curation and distribution.

The analysis underscores the profound impact of algorithmic governance on democratic integrity. While algorithms offer opportunities to enhance efficiency and personalization, they also pose significant risks to media diversity, human rights, and the rule of law. The study's findings provide valuable insights for policymakers, media practitioners, and civil society organizations, emphasizing the need for ethical and transparent algorithmic governance.

Findings and Analysis

The analysis synthesizes the quantitative and qualitative data while grounding the insights in the theoretical frameworks of Algorithmic Governance Theory, Media Theory, Human Rights Framework, and Rule of Law Theory. This integration ensures a theoretically informed exploration of the impact of algorithmic governance on democratic integrity.

Influence of Algorithms on Media Content and Consumption

Findings reveal that algorithmic curation significantly prioritizes sensational and emotionally charged content. The quantitative data (Table 1) shows a higher bias score for sensational content under algorithmic curation (4.5) compared to non-algorithmic curation (2.0). This aligns with Media Theory, which posits that algorithms amplify engagement-driven content, thereby creating echo chambers and reducing diversity in information exposure (Napoli, 2019). The "filter bubble" effect identified in interviews further illustrates how algorithms reinforce user biases, limiting access to diverse viewpoints—a critical concern for democratic discourse.

Human Rights Implications

Quantitative findings highlight strong correlations between algorithmic data collection and privacy concerns ($\beta = 0.65$, $p < 0.01$). This is consistent with the Human Rights Framework, which underscores the risks algorithms pose to privacy by commodifying personal data (Zuboff, 2019). Ethnographic observations reveal organizational priorities skewed toward data maximization, often at the expense of user consent, supporting the framework's emphasis on the need for robust regulatory safeguards.

Interviews with human rights activists highlight the dual impact of algorithms on freedom of expression. While algorithms provide marginalized communities with platforms to amplify their voices, they also risk censoring dissent, especially in politically sensitive contexts. This duality reflects the nuanced predictions of the Human Rights Framework, emphasizing both opportunities and challenges in protecting individual rights in the digital era.

Challenges and Opportunities for the Rule of Law

The analysis of algorithmic governance within legal contexts highlights a tension between efficiency and fairness. Comparative case studies, such as the use of facial recognition algorithms in law enforcement, reveal higher error rates for minority groups. This aligns with Rule of Law Theory, which emphasizes that algorithms must operate within legal frameworks to ensure fairness and prevent discrimination (Cohen, 2017).

The regression analysis (Table 3) indicates a significant negative relationship between algorithmic transparency and trust in the legal system ($\beta = -0.54$, $p < 0.05$). This finding reinforces Algorithmic Governance Theory, which stresses that the lack of transparency in algorithmic processes can erode public trust and accountability (Danaher, 2016). Legal experts interviewed stressed the urgent need for transparency mechanisms to ensure alignment with principles of justice and equality, as prescribed by the Rule of Law Theory.

Synthesis of Theoretical Insights

The findings across all data sources demonstrate how the theoretical foundations inform the complex dynamics of algorithmic governance:

1. Algorithmic Governance Theory explains how algorithms streamline decision-making but also introduces opacity that undermines accountability. This theory contextualizes the observed erosion of trust in algorithmically influenced governance systems.

2. Media Theory provides a lens to understand the biases and engagement-driven content dynamics, which are evident in the findings related to sensational media curation and echo chambers.

3. Human Rights Framework underscores the necessity of balancing algorithmic efficiency with the protection of privacy and freedom of expression. The findings on surveillance capitalism and censorship during political protests exemplify the tensions predicted by this framework.

4. Rule of Law Theory offers a foundation for examining the ethical and legal challenges posed by algorithmic decision-making. The findings

on discriminatory outcomes in facial recognition technologies and the demand for regulatory interventions are strongly supported by this theory.

Discussion

The discussion section synthesizes the findings and analysis, contextualizing them within existing literature and theoretical frameworks. It explores the broader implications of the study, identifies limitations, and suggests avenues for future research. This section aims to provide a critical evaluation of the impact of algorithmic governance on democratic integrity, emphasizing the interconnectedness of media practices, human rights, and the rule of law.

Synthesis of Findings

The findings of this study highlight the multifaceted impact of algorithmic governance on democratic integrity. The pervasive influence of algorithms on media content and public perception underscores the transformative role of computational intelligence in shaping contemporary media landscapes. The correlation between algorithmic curation and perceived media bias aligns with previous research, indicating that algorithms, while enhancing engagement, often prioritize sensational and polarized content (Napoli, 2019).

The analysis also reveals significant concerns regarding privacy, freedom of expression, and non-discrimination. The strong relationship between algorithmic data collection and privacy concerns reflects growing apprehension about surveillance capitalism and the erosion of personal privacy (Zuboff, 2019). The dual effects of algorithms on freedom of expression—both amplifying marginalized voices and potentially suppressing dissent—highlight the complex ethical landscape of digital governance (O'Neil, 2016).

Furthermore, the study's exploration of algorithmic governance in legal contexts reveals a tension between efficiency and fairness. While algorithms can streamline legal processes and improve consistency, their opacity and potential biases raise critical questions about accountability and justice (Cohen, 2017). The comparative analysis across different regions underscores the importance of robust regulatory frameworks tailored to specific legal, social, and cultural contexts.

Implications for Policy and Practice

The study's findings have significant implications for policymakers, media practitioners, and civil society organizations. To mitigate the risks associated with algorithmic governance, several key strategies are recommended:

Enhancing Algorithmic Transparency and Accountability

Transparency in algorithmic decision-making is crucial to maintain public trust and ensure accountability. Policymakers should mandate transparency requirements for algorithms used in public administration and critical sectors such as media and law enforcement. This includes disclosing the criteria and data used by algorithms, as well as providing mechanisms for external audits and oversight (Pasquale, 2015).

Promoting Diversity and Inclusion in Algorithm Design

To address issues of bias and discrimination, it is essential to promote diversity and inclusion in the development and deployment of algorithms. This involves incorporating diverse perspectives and expertise into the algorithm design process and ensuring that algorithms are tested for fairness and inclusivity. Regulatory frameworks should enforce anti-discrimination standards and provide remedies for individuals adversely affected by algorithmic decisions (Buolamwini & Gebru, 2018).

Strengthening Data Protection and Privacy Regulations

Given the significant privacy concerns identified in the study, strengthening data protection and privacy regulations is imperative. Governments should implement comprehensive data protection laws that regulate the collection, storage, and use of personal data by algorithms. These laws should include provisions for user consent, data minimization, and the right to access and rectify personal data (Solove, 2020).

Fostering Ethical Media Practices

Media organizations must develop ethical guidelines for the use of algorithms in content curation and distribution. These guidelines should prioritize content diversity, accuracy, and balance, and avoid sensationalism and polarization. Media practitioners should also be trained in the ethical implications of algorithmic governance and encouraged to adopt best practices for transparent and responsible algorithm use (Napoli, 2019).

Conclusion

While the study provides valuable insights into the impact of algorithmic governance, it has several limitations. First, the reliance on self-reported data from surveys and interviews may introduce biases, as participants' perceptions and experiences can be subjective. Second, the rapidly evolving nature of algorithmic technologies means that the findings may quickly become outdated. Third, the study's focus on specific regions and legal systems may limit the generalizability of the results to other contexts.

Future research should address these limitations and explore additional dimensions of algorithmic governance. Longitudinal studies are needed to examine the long-term effects of algorithms on democratic integrity and to track changes over time. Comparative research across a broader range of regions and legal systems can provide a more comprehensive understanding of the global impact of algorithmic governance. Additionally, interdisciplinary research that integrates perspectives from computer science, law, sociology, and political science can enrich the analysis and provide more holistic insights.

The discussion highlights the complex and multifaceted impact of algorithmic governance on democratic integrity, emphasizing the interconnectedness of media practices, human rights, and the rule of law. By synthesizing the findings and contextualizing them within existing literature, the study provides a critical evaluation of the ethical, legal, and social implications of computational intelligence. The recommended strategies for enhancing transparency, promoting diversity, strengthening data protection, and fostering ethical media practices offer practical guidelines for navigating the challenges of algorithmic governance. Future research should continue to explore these dimensions, ensuring that the development and deployment of algorithms support democratic values and uphold human rights in the digital age.

References

1. Bakshy, E., Messing, S., & Adamic, L. A. (2015). Exposure to ideologically diverse news and opinion on Facebook. *Science*, 348(6239), 1130-1132.
2. Barocas, S., & Selbst, A. D. (2016). Big data's disparate impact. *California Law Review*, 104(3), 671-732.
3. Braun, V., & Clarke, V. (2006). Using thematic analysis in psychology. *Qualitative Research in Psychology, 3*(2), 77-101.
4. Buolamwini, J., & Gebru, T. (2018). Gender shades: Intersectional accuracy disparities in commercial gender classification. *Proceedings of Machine Learning Research, 81*, 1-15.
5. Caplan, R., & boyd, d. (2018). Isomorphism through algorithms: Institutional dependencies in the case of Facebook. *Big Data & Society*, 5(1), 1-12.
6. Chen, M. K. (2019). Predictive policing and crime displacement. *Criminology & Public Policy*, 18(2), 499-512.
7. Citron, D. K., & Pasquale, F. (2014). The scored society: Due process for automated predictions. *Washington Law Review*, 89(1), 1-33.
8. Cohen, J. E. (2017). Law for the platform economy. *University of California Davis, 51*, 133-204.
9. Danaher, J. (2016). The threat of algocracy: Reality, resistance, and accommodation. *Philosophy & Technology, 29*(3), 245-268.
10. Das, S., & Mitra, A. (2024). Advancing lightweight digital trust architectures in the internet of medical things: A multi-dimensional analysis. In *Lightweight Digital Trust Architectures in the Internet of Medical Things (IoMT)* (pp. 1-14).

11. Field, A. (2013). *Discovering statistics using IBM SPSS statistics* (4th ed.). Sage.

12. Fowler, F. J. (2013). *Survey research methods* (5th ed.). Sage.

13. Gillespie, T. (2014). The relevance of algorithms. In T. Gillespie, P. J. Boczkowski, & K. A. Foot (Eds.), *Media Technologies: Essays on Communication, Materiality, and Society* (pp. 167-194). MIT Press.

14. Hammersley, M., & Atkinson, P. (2019). *Ethnography: Principles in practice* (4th ed.). Routledge.

15. Jain, V., & Mitra, A. (2024). A critical examination of ethical implications in AI-driven consumer behavior media discourse and environmental sustainability. In *Enhancing and Predicting Digital Consumer Behavior with AI* (pp. 1-16).

16. Jain, V., & Mitra, A. (2024). Case studies and practical implementation of biomimicry in bio-inspired optimization. In *Bio-Inspired Intelligence for Smart Decision-Making* (pp. 85-100).

17. Jain, V., & Mitra, A. (2024). Culinary narratives and community revitalization: The role of media in promoting sustainable gastronomy tourism. In *Promoting Sustainable Gastronomy Tourism and Community Development* (pp. 67-80).

18. Jain, V., & Mitra, A. (2024). Energy harvesting system design and analysis using biomimicry: A sustainable approach for renewable energy applications. In *Emerging Materials Technologies and Solutions for Energy Harvesting* (pp. 234-257).

19. Krippendorff, K. (2018). *Content analysis: An introduction to its methodology* (4th ed.). Sage.

20. Kroll, J. A., Huey, J., Barocas, S., Felten, E. W., Reidenberg, J. R., Robinson, D. G., & Yu, H. (2017). Accountable algorithms. *University of Pennsylvania Law Review*, 165(3), 633-705.

21. Kvale, S., & Brinkmann, S. (2009). *Interviews: Learning the craft of qualitative research interviewing* (2nd ed.). Sage.

22. Lohochowdhury, B., Giridhar, D., Kumar Pal, A., & Mitra, A. (2023). Environmental information policy in India feed pro-environment

industry operation: A case study of EIA report on proposed integrated steel complex site Halakundi Karnataka. *Macromolecular Symposia, 407*(1).

23. Mitra, A., & Das, S. (2024). The rise of digital celebrities: Analyzing the impact and sustainability of stardom on OTT platforms. In *Exploring the Impact of OTT Media on Global Societies* (pp. 55-73).
24. Mitra, A., & Lohochoudhury, B. (2019). Identifying anthropogenic factors of groundwater pollution through student's opinion in rural West Bengal. *Anthropogenic Pollution, 3*(2), 49-59.
25. Napoli, P. M. (2019). *Social media and the public interest: Media regulation in the disinformation age*. Columbia University Press.
26. O'Neil, C. (2016). *Weapons of math destruction: How big data increases inequality and threatens democracy*. Crown Publishing Group.
27. Pariser, E. (2011). *The filter bubble: How the new personalized web is changing what we read and how we think*. Penguin Books.
28. Pasquale, F. (2015). *The black box society: The secret algorithms that control money and information*. Harvard University Press.
29. Ragin, C. C. (2014). *The comparative method: Moving beyond qualitative and quantitative strategies*. University of California Press.
30. Roberts, S. T. (2019). *Behind the Screen: Content Moderation in the Shadows of Social Media*. Yale University Press.
31. Sachdeva, P., & Mitra, A. (2023). Decoding the Twitter sentiment using artificial intelligence tools: A study on Tokyo Olympics 2020. *Lecture Notes in Networks and Systems,* 757 LNNS, 539-554.
32. Sachdeva, P., & Mitra, A. (2023). SME and environmental sustenance: Digital marketing in SMEs via data-driven strategies. In *Sustainability Green Management and Performance of SMEs* (pp. 315-332).
33. Sachdeva, P., & Mitra, A. (2024). Decoding human development and environmental sustainability: A predictive analytical study on relationship between HDI and carbon emission. *Studies in Systems Decision and Control, 489*, 785-795.

34. Sachdeva, P., Kumar, M. D., & Mitra, A. (2024). Green discourse analysis on Twitter: Imperatives to green product management in sustainable cities (SDG11). *Studies in Systems Decision and Control, 487*, 245–256.

35. Salganik, M. J. (2017). *Bit by bit: Social research in the digital age.* Princeton University Press.

36. Solove, D. J. (2020). *The digital person: Technology and privacy in the Information age*. NYU Press.

37. Wachter, S., Mittelstadt, B., & Floridi, L. (2017). Transparent, explainable, and accountable AI for robotics. *Science Robotics*, 2(6), eaap6962.

38. Yin, R. K. (2017). *Case study research and applications: Design and methods* (6th ed.). Sage.

39. Zuboff, S. (2019). *The age of surveillance capitalism: The fight for a human future at the new frontier of power*. PublicAffairs.

Misunderstandings About AI

Dr. Manas Pratim Das, Programme Executive, Akashvani, Kolkata. Email: setmanas2020@gmail.com

Introduction

In the middle of 2024 a distinguished photographer added an interesting chapter to the Man vs Machine conflict. Miles Astray, a 38 year old photographer from Bolivia, submitted an entry titled Flamingone at the 1839 Awards' Color Photography Contest. There was nothing unusual in Astray submitting his photograph for a competition but what made his act interesting was that he had chosen the 'AI category' for his entry. The entries in this category are products of AI tools and are moulded by cutting edge algorithms. A flamingo on a desolate beach in Aruba was scratching itself by bending its neck and thus looked headless from a distance. That is when Astray took the photograph and he made no use of AI while developing the print. The competition judged by eminent professionals from the industry gave Astray the third prize in the category. However, the Bolivian photographer did not accept the prize and declared that his entry had nothing to do with AI. It was simply a product of human creativity. His action, in fact, was not without a purpose. He wanted to make a statement. Astray utilized the occasion to explain that AI could be put to positive uses instead of spreading misinformation. He further demanded that all photographs created by AI tools should be tagged and industry must not shy away from this responsibility. One sentence that he used to sum up his attitude to AI sounded really belligerent as he commented that humans need to act without delay and get ahead of AI that is developing at lightspeed.[1] In an era when the commoner on the street has started believing that Artificial Intelligence or AI is becoming powerful enough to replace humans in all sphere of activities, the exceptional case of Miles Astray urges all to pause and introspect. Astray winning a prize beating AI brings back our understanding of the kinetics of AI into focus. One can hardly choose to miss this opportunity. The logical question here would be – where does AI stand vis-à-vis humans so far as the essential human features like communication, control, creativity etc. are concerned? Let us try to gain some understanding.

AI Gaining Control

In 2017, a piece of news trickling down from the stable of Facebook, created an alarm. It was reported that two AI programmes of the mega social platform had started talking between themselves in a language that appeared to be English-like but carried some peculiar alterations. It was learnt that Facebook wanted its chatbots to swap responsibilities and serve clients differently. The aim apparently was to see whether the chatbots can negotiate among themselves and swap hats, balls and books. Each of these items were assigned a certain value. The negotiation did start as desired but broke down quickly. Instead of expected results, what the engineers observed were streams of words in English, repeated abruptly and making no cohesive meaning. But the engineers could rule out the conversation as complete nonsense. It seemed that a shorthand for conversation among chatbots was evolving. Something that might have been useful to the chatbots but not comprehensible to the humans. Since Facebook ultimately wanted bots to talk to people and not engross themselves in an internal dialogue, they chose to shut down the experiment. They didn't find anything scary about the whole set of events but media considered this to be a revolutionary affair leading to loss of control by humans.[2] Through a section of the media later on analysed the affair in an objective manner and sought to clear misconceptions,[3] yet, for Michael Wooldridge, Professor of Computer Science at the University of Oxford, such reporting in media brought back scenes from the popular movie 'Terminator'.[4] In this movie, directed by James Cameron and released in 1984, a cybernetic assassin called Terminator is sent back in time from 2029 to 1984 to kill a lady whose unborn child is destined to save mankind. The attack on the civilization will come from Skynet, a hostile AI being. There is also another soldier sent back in time to protect the lady.[5] Now, whatever the details of the story the Terminator narrative has become to be one of humans losing control to AI. It is the development of AI tools racing to a limit where they take care of themselves and start a positive feedback loop creating more and more advanced generations continually. This limit was defined by Ray Kurzweil by the use of a word generally reserved for physics and mathematics – Singularity.

The Trolley Problem and Cultural Differences

In order to showcase the blistering pace of the development of AI, Kurzweil focussed his attention on a law given in the 1970s by a leading inventor of integrated circuits, Gordon Moore. Integrated Circuit, IC in short, is an electronic device made up of several components that are interconnected. The most important of these components are of course transistors. Moore, who became the chairman of the electronic-chip-manufacturing superpower Intel, had predicted that the number of transistor chips that can be fitted on a given area on an IC will double every two years. This logically meant more power to the computer that will run AI. In a book, first published in 2005, Kurzweil had predicted that supercomputers will be able to match the capability of the human brain by the end of the first decade of the twenty-first century. Personal computers will do the same by the end of the following decade.[6] Reality however proved that the forecast was too ambitious. This is where Wooldridge raises poignant questions on technology matching human brain power. Is intelligence merely a cumulative result of processing power? Computers with high processing power, he argues, might be a necessary condition for achieving human level intelligence but it is in no way a sufficient condition. Quite naturally Wooldridge brings forth the well-known Trolley Problem. Introduced by the British philosopher Philippa Foot in the late 1960s, this problem has become an essential component of the philosophy of ethics. The problem is stated thus:

A trolley (a tramcar) with five passengers has lost control and is speeding down a track. The passengers are unable to move and are in the danger of getting killed if the car is not stopped or at least diverted to an alternative track. A lever can be pulled to effect that diversion but the driver has to keep in mind that there is one person on the track who is again unable to move. If diverted, the trolley would kill the lone person but the five passengers would be saved. What should the driver do?[7]

The response to the trolley problem has been different in different cultures as demonstrated through surveys conducted over the years. The concept of moral acceptability is not universal at all. Gold, Colman and Pulford have given a detailed description of the relevant surveys in their paper published in 2023. The authors reported the findings from their own experiment as well. Keeping the basic structure of the trolley problem intact they made limited changes to pit five children against just one child. All the kids are from Uganda, are poor and are clearly in need of support to be able to have access to a square meal. Clicking a switch on a computer screen moves a lever in their experiment and moves the direction of movement of a rolling ball. This has the effect of diverting the financial support from the single child to the five children. It was found that eighty percent of the British participants clicked the switch whereas only about half of the Chinese participants did so.[9] This variation in decision making has to be borne in mind as we head into a discussion concerning ethics and AI.

The Maze of Ethics

The trolley problem is very relevant when it comes to self-driven cars. As those AI driven vehicles hit the road in the second decade of the twentieth century and some of those unfortunately caused human casualties on the road, the problem gained prominence. It slowly dawned on the scientists that this type of a problem can hardly be satisfactorily solved by the application of high processing power. The decision to be taken depends on the culture, ethics to be specific, which a community espouses. The idea of human or social welfare varies from region to region, from one country to another country. Thus it is not possible to set a single ethical standard that will work over all the countries of the world. However, from the closing decades of the last century, giant transnational corporations have started assuming powers that might equate their strength to the capability of a country's or a group of country's administration. They dictate things easily and are also in a position to formulate ethical standards to their liking. In fact, major tech companies have tackled the issue of ethics in their own way. Instead of choosing any prevalent set of ethics, most of those have opted for a mix of the available components of it. Google in 2018 came out with its own guidelines for ethical AI. The corporations have found that it is not possible to tackle the question of streamlining ethical behaviour only with processing power of computers. Naturally, ordering the behaviour of machines is most likely to hit a roadblock. Wooldridge goes on to raise another philosophical issue of great importance in this regard. He comments that when even humans get perplexed in a Trolley Problem situation, can we expect more from AI systems in such a situation?[10]

Communicating Human Desires

Many AI enthusiasts look up to AI as the genie of the lamp in Aladdin's tale. The genie was there to bring anything that Aladdin or the owner of the magical lamp wished for. In the present times, we often dream up a situation where we shall be surrounded by such genie-like AI tools and be served as wished for. The only requirement would be the resources to afford such AI systems. However, there is a twist here. We, humans, generally share a set of common values and norms. We need not express them explicitly while asking for something or agreeing to some proposal. But a machine has no idea of these human values. It has to be taught everything from scratch. Every little bit of information that is easily assumed by us has to be communicated in the machine's own language. Otherwise awkward situations might occur like a robot burning down a whole house when it was asked to keep the same safe from burglary. Among the many paths available to achieve its aim the robot chose the one of complete destruction so that the burglars do not find any house to break into! There are other examples as well where the AI system advised that trains should remain motionless when asked to advise on methods to avoid collision on railway tracks! Wooldridge terms such cases as 'perverse instantiation' and credits Nick Bostrom for this coinage.[8] Bostrom, in his book *Superintelligence*, gives further instances of perverse instantiation. In one of his examples, AI is asked by the programmer to make everyone smile. AI comes out with the advice of paralyzing human musculatures into constant beaming smiles. In another, an AI tool, assigned to manage production in a factory, is asked to maximize paperclip production. The AI proceeds to convert the whole earth into paperclips and then utilize observable portions of the universe into doing the same. Bostrom defines this perverse activity in these words,

... a superintelligence discovering some way of satisfying the criteria of its final goal that violates the intentions of the programmers who defined the goal.

Bostrom blames AI for not having any conscience like humans do. It does not feel guilty at underperforming or non-performance. He asks whether guilt should be introduced in responsible AI systems. He finds that reward mechanism that encourages all systems, animate or inanimate, produces undesirable results in AI systems. He mourns,

... The proposal fails when the AI obtains a decisive strategic advantage, at which point the action that maximizes reward is no longer one that pleases the trainer but one that involves seizing control of the reward mechanism. We can call this phenomenon wireheading.[11]

We can definitely go on entangling ourselves in this but that will not benefit us in any way. The ultimate goal is to extract actions from AI that not only fulfils our wants but also keeps in mind our desires. Towards this goal the principle that is adopted in industry is termed 'ceteris paribus'. This is a Latin phrase that sets preferences. The idea had been very eloquently explained by S O Hansson. His wife had asked him for a choice of tables for their living room and Hansson replied that he preferred a round table to a square one. He further explained that he was intent on having a round shape for their table instead of a square one but wanted all the other properties like height, sort of wood, finishing, price etc. to remain almost the same. Thus *ceteris paribus* may be summarized as *all other things remaining the same* or *everything else being equal.*[12] The machine needs to be communicated that this is the final situation that we desire while we express what we want. This is definitely not an easy task and whole armies of software engineers are assigned to tackle this problem. It needs serious inputs from the field of logic and philosophy as well. The combined approach calls for more and more effective innovative strategies.

Finally, Fake ... AI

Let us complete the loop as we near the conclusion of this article. In December of 2018 a hi tech robot shown on Russian television turned out to be a human wearing a special kind of suit. A company called Show Robots had prepared a very costly suit and a human actor crept into it to fit snugly.

It made several moves and even danced, giving off the impression that robotics in that part of the world has reached appreciable heights. However, when the real facts were divulged there were mixed responses from the audience.[13] That was undoubtedly fakery but of course not in the way Miles Astray had acted. Machine intelligence, in the opinion of many experts in the field, is far from reaching the level of General AI when machines are expected to act as humans do. The situation is far more mundane today than it is made out to be. When Siri or Alexa responds to an emotional utterance from a human it is only bringing out the best possible answer from its programmed dataset. Nothing more! It is not acting on its own. When in 2017 Saudi Arabia announced that it has decided to grant citizenship to a robot called Sofia, there was excitement as well as jeers from all around the world. Sofia was probably of a far less capacity than even that of ELIZA, an early natural language processing program that had been written in the mid-1960s at the MIT Artificial Intelligence Laboratory by Joseph Weizenbaum.[14] Even the latest surprise from AI researchers, ChatGPT, is way behind meeting the requirements of Artificial General Intelligence (AGI). Strong AI, also referred to as AGI, is AI that aims to duplicate human intellectual abilities.[15] This product of OpenAI company, funded in a large part by Microsoft, has amazed its users who are busy extracting maximum benefits from it. The GPT-4 version carries a claim of being very close to AGI. Microsoft engineer Bubeck and fourteen other engineers including the company's Chief Scientific Officer wrote a paper to show AGI qualities of the AI tool. They harped on the versatile capability of handling tasks and highlighted its ability to even switch over to take other responsibilities seamlessly. But other researchers, not affiliated to any corporate body, found the paper thoroughly flawed. Leading researchers from several universities have compared the capacity of Large Language Models (LLM) with that of human brain and have found that though LLMs have exhibited impressive skills yet those are far from equipped to understand natural language with its nuances.[16]

Conclusion

AI represents a wonderful façade of human creativity but it is yet to catch up with human intelligence that is a product of centuries of evolution. It is an undeniable fact that humans are losing employment due to large scale deployment of AI tools in industry. This has created disappointment among the citizens and at the same time instilled a fear about the high power of AI in their minds. The proven capacity of AI to create false yet believable images has alarmed concerned quarters. However, the truth still remains that even after six decades of development AI has not come even close to the creative powers of a human mind. It is nowhere near its cherished goal of AGI. Yet misunderstandings will continue to remain regarding the power of AI to emulate, if not surpass, human actions.

References

1. Mathures Paul, Picture Perfect: We are Miles ahead of AI, The Telegraph, Kolkata, 20 June 2024
2. Andrew Griffin, Facebook's artificial intelligence robots shut down after they start talking to each other in their own language, 31 July 2017, https://www.independent.co.uk/life-style/facebook-artificial-intelligence-ai-chatbot-new-language-research-openai-google-a7869706.html
3. Mariam Fauzia, Fact check: Facebook didn't pull the plug on two chatbots because they created a language, USA Today, July 28, 2021, https://www.usatoday.com/story/news/factcheck/2021/07/28/fact-check-facebook-chatbots-werent-shut-down-creating-language/8040006002/
4. Michael Wooldridge, The Road to Conscious Machines: The Story of AI, Pelican, Paperback edition, 2021, pp 237
5. The Terminator, Wikipedia, https://en.wikipedia.org/wiki/The_Terminator
6. Ray Kurzweil, The Singularity Is Near: When Humans Transcend Biology, Viking, 2005, Chapter Two, pp 59-75
7. Op cit, Michael Wooldridge, pp 247-253
8. Ibid.

9. Gold N, Colman AM, Pulford BD. Cultural differences in responses to real-life and hypothetical trolley problems. Judgment and Decision Making. 2014;9(1):65-76. doi:10.1017/S193029750000499X
10. Op cit, Michael Wooldridge, pp 254-260
11. Nick Bostrom, Superintelligence: Paths, Dangers, Strategies, Oxford University Press, 2014, Internet edition, page not mentioned
12. A. S. Alashaikh and E. A. Alanazi, Incorporating Ceteris Paribus Preferences in Multiobjective Virtual Machine Placement, in IEEE Access, vol. 7, pp. 59984-59998, 2019, doi: 10.1109/ACCESS.2019.2916090
13. Andrew Roth, 'Hi-tech robot' at Russia forum turns out to be man in suit, The Gurdian, 12 December 2018, Internet edition
14. ELIZA: a very basic Rogerian psychotherapist chatbot, New Jersey Institute of Technology, https://web.njit.edu/~ronkowit/eliza.html
15. B. J. Copeland, Is artificial general intelligence (AGI) possible? Britannica, https://www.britannica.com/technology/artificial-intelligence/Is-artificial-general-intelligence-AGI-possible
16. Will Knight, Some Glimpse AGI in ChatGPT. Others Call It a Mirage, WIRED, April 10 2023, https://www.wired.com/story/chatgpt-agi-intelligence/

Opportunities and Threats with AI in Media Content Creation

Dr. Ramya K Prasad, Associate Professor, Department of Visual Communication, School of Arts, Humanities and Commerce, Amrita Vishwa Vidyapeetham, Mysuru Campus. Email: kp_ramya@my.amrita.edu

Dr. Akshatha Prabhu, Assistant Professor, Department of Computer Science, School of Computing, Amrita Vishwa Vidyapeetham, Mysuru Campus. Email: p_akshatha@my.amrita.edu

Introduction

In the media and entertainment industry, the infusion of Artificial Intelligence has set the stage for a remarkable change. AI has emerged as a formidable force in the realms of game development, movie production, and advertising, innovating creative processes across industries. AI has become a catalyst in the media and entertainment sector, sparking strategic investments and anchoring a determined pursuit to satisfy ever-growing viewer demands.

In this era of innovation, robots and augmented intelligence have become the architects of unforgettable, next-generation consumer experiences. Giants in both the media and entertainment and technology spheres, including Blizzard Entertainment, Walt Disney World, Google, Microsoft, and Intel, have converged their expertise to craft, launch, and refine a plethora of AI-driven innovations, propelling the industry into uncharted territories of imagination and spectacle. "As per Grand View Research, the global AI in the media & entertainment market reached a significant valuation of USD 10.87 billion in 2021. This thriving sector is poised for remarkable expansion, with a projected CAGR of 26.9% anticipated from 2022 through 2030", Akash Takyar, CEO LeewayHertz.

"The global AI in media & entertainment market size was estimated at USD 25.98 billion in 2024 and is projected to grow at a CAGR of 24.2% from 2025 to 2030." Source: AI In Media & Entertainment Market Size, Share & Trends Analysis Report By Solution (Hardware/ Equipment,

Services), By Application (Gaming, Fake Story Detection), By Region, And Segment Forecasts, 2025 – 2030.

Films like "Ex Machina," "Blade Runner 2049," and "Her" have captured the essence of AI's influence on our imagination and the profound questions it raises about the future. These cinematic creations have entertained and served as thought-provoking windows into artificial intelligence's potential and ethical complexities.

The Impact of AI in Media and Entertainment

The impact of AI in the media and entertainment industry has been significant, with many companies utilizing AI to improve their operations, enhance the consumer experience, and create more personalized content.

One of the major areas in which AI impacts media and entertainment is content creation. AI algorithms can now analyze vast amounts of data to create content tailored to specific audiences. For example, Netflix uses machine learning algorithms to analyze viewing data and recommend content to users, while companies such as Jukin Media and Storyful use AI to analyze user-generated content and identify potential viral hits. AI is also being used to create new forms of content, such as virtual influencers and computer-generated actors.

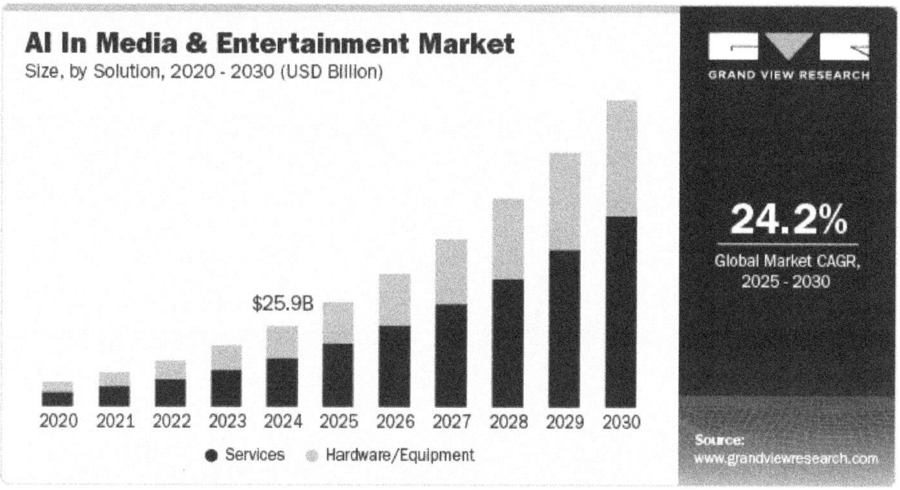

Pic Source: https://www.grandviewresearch.com/industry-analysis/artificial-intelligence-ai-media-entertainment-market-report

AI is also being used to enhance the consumer experience in entertainment. For example, chatbots are increasingly being used by entertainment companies to provide customer service and answer frequently asked questions, while voice recognition technology is being used to allow consumers to control their entertainment experience hands-free. AI-powered personal assistants such as Amazon's Alexa and Google Assistant are also being integrated into entertainment systems, allowing consumers to control their entertainment experience with voice commands.

Personalization is a key facet of AI's influence in media and entertainment. Music and content recommendation systems use AI algorithms to deliver tailored suggestions, enhancing user satisfaction by demonstrating content aligned with individual preferences. Personalized experiences keep players engaged in gaming by dynamically adjusting difficulty levels to match their skills and preferences.

The media and entertainment industry has also benefited from the efficiency AI brings. Automated tools like AI-driven animation and character modeling improve the realism of 3D models in films and video games. AI-powered music composition tools make it easier for composers to produce original soundtracks. Additionally, AI streamlines the content creation process by automating tasks like video editing, proofreading, and even generating ad copy, leading to cost savings and increased productivity.

Lastly, AI plays a pivotal role in marketing and audience engagement. It allows for precise targeting of advertisements, ensuring that content reaches the right audience. Social media analysis helps businesses refine their strategies by identifying trends and measuring their online impact more accurately. AI's impact on the media and entertainment industry is transformative, enhancing creativity, personalization, and efficiency while optimizing marketing efforts for better results.

AI is also being used to improve marketing and advertising in the media and entertainment industry. By analyzing data on consumer behavior and preferences, AI algorithms can help companies create more targeted and personalized marketing campaigns. For example, companies like Amazon and Netflix use AI to recommend content to users based on their viewing and purchasing history.

AI-powered systems create tailored content and recommendations based on individual preferences, boosting engagement and conversion rates. This personalization enhances the user experience, making marketing efforts more effective and relevant.

Content Generation

AI-generated content, such as ad copy and articles, offers significant time and cost savings in content production. Its automated generation capabilities streamline the creative process and enhance efficiency.

Social Media Analysis

AI-driven social media analysis involves trend identification, brand mention monitoring, and assessing the effectiveness of advertising campaigns. It leverages data analytics to gain valuable insights, enabling businesses to refine their social media strategies and measure their online impact more accurately.

Cross-Channel Marketing

AI seamlessly integrates data from multiple advertising channels, offering a holistic approach to the customer journey. This unified perspective empowers advertisers to coordinate campaigns more effectively and optimize strategies for maximum impact and engagement.

Before we dive into the details of AI in content creation, let's define what AI is and its importance in content creation. AI refers to computer systems that perform tasks that normally require human intelligence, such as visual perception, speech recognition, decision-making, and language translation. AI is important in content creation because it can analyze data and create personalized content that resonates with the audience.

AI and Content Creation

AI is transforming content creation by making it faster, more efficient, and cost-effective. With AI, content creators can analyze data and create personalized content that resonates with the audience. AI also helps to identify and overcome content gaps, allowing content creators to provide a more comprehensive and relevant experience for their audience. Some of the benefits of using AI in content creation include improved content quality, increased productivity, and reduced costs.

Machine Learning and Natural Language Processing

Machine learning and natural language processing are two key components of AI in content creation. Machine learning refers to computer systems that can learn and adapt to new information without being explicitly programmed. Natural language processing refers to computer systems that can understand, interpret, and generate human language.

Machine learning and natural language processing are used in content creation to analyze data, identify patterns, and generate personalized content. For example, machine learning can analyze customer data to identify preferences and interests, allowing content creators to create content that resonates with their audience. Natural language processing can analyze social media data to identify trends and conversations, allowing content creators to create content that is relevant and timely.

Content Strategy and SEO

AI is used in content strategy and SEO to analyze data and identify keywords to optimize content for search engines. With AI, content creators can analyze data and identify the most relevant keywords for their content, allowing them to create content that is more likely to rank higher in search engine results. Examples of AI in content strategy and SEO include content optimization tools, keyword research tools, and content management systems.

Content Management and Optimization Techniques

Content management and optimization refer to the process of organizing and optimizing content to improve its quality and relevance. AI is used in content management and optimization to analyze data and create personalized content that resonates with the audience.

Examples of AI in content management and optimization include content recommendation engines, content personalization tools, and content optimization tools. Content recommendation engines can recommend content to users based on their interests and preferences. Content personalization tools can create personalized content based on user data. Content optimization tools can analyze data and optimize content for search engines.

Algorithm, Writing and Language

Algorithms, writing, and language are closely related to AI in content creation. Algorithms are used to analyze data and generate personalized content. Writing is the process of creating content that resonates with the audience. Language is the medium used to convey the message to the audience.

Advantages of using AI in algorithm, writing, and language include improved content quality, increased productivity, and reduced costs. AI can also help to identify and overcome content gaps, allowing content creators to provide a more comprehensive and relevant experience for their audience.

Examples of AI in algorithm, writing, and language include automated content creation tools, chatbots, and virtual assistants.

Creativity, Efficiency, Productivity, and Innovation

One of the most important roles of AI in content creation is enhancing creativity. AI technology allows for the creation of unique ideas and angles that can be difficult for humans to produce. AI can brainstorm large amounts of data, analyze trends, and make predictions that lead to new and innovative ideas. Further, AI algorithms can identify patterns and similarities in existing content, enabling creators to take inspiration from their work and develop new pieces of engaging content. AI has enhanced creativity, efficiency, productivity, and innovation in content creation by providing content creators with the tools they need to create personalized content that resonates with their audience. With AI, content creators can generate more content in less time, allowing them to focus on creating high-quality content that engages their audience.

Examples of AI in creativity, efficiency, productivity, and innovation include chatbots, virtual assistants, and automated content creation tools.

Artificial intelligence (AI) is rapidly transforming various aspects of modern life, including content creation. With AI, creative ideas can be efficiently generated, and the production of high-quality content can be enhanced. AI is a tool that can handle labor-intensive tasks, allowing for more creative and innovative approaches.

Additionally, AI can influence the efficiency of content creation. With the implementation of AI in the content creation process, creators can streamline tasks, effectively reducing the time and effort required to produce good-quality content. AI's automation capabilities can handle routine duties, such as copy editing and proofreading, thus enabling their human counterparts to focus more on the creative aspects of content creation.

Finally, AI significantly enhances productivity by augmenting the human creative process. AI can automate repetitive and mundane tasks, freeing up staff time to concentrate on higher-value, more strategic activities. AI technology's speed and accuracy result in quality content production, driving increased productivity. Furthermore, AI-based tools can ensure that deadlines are met, and opportunities for engagement are not missed, ultimately improving efficiency over time.

AI is transforming content creation by making it faster, more efficient, and cost-effective. AI is used in machine learning, natural language processing, automation in digital marketing, content strategy and SEO, content management and optimization techniques, and algorithm, writing, and language.

AI enhances creativity, efficiency, productivity, and innovation in content creation by providing content creators with the tools they need to create personalized content that resonates with their audience. As technology continues to advance, we can expect AI to play an even more important role in content creation.

To take advantage of AI in content creation, start by analyzing the data and identifying the gaps in the content. Then, use AI tools to create personalized content that resonates with the audience. With continued advancements and the recognition and application of AI's full potential, its impact on content creation is limitless for brands looking to unlock fresh and engaging content that resonates with their audience.

The advent of AI, particularly large language models like ChatGPT, has irrevocably transformed the content landscape. What was once solely a human-centric domain is now a collaborative space shared with intelligent machines. To thrive in this new era, content strategists must adapt their approach.

Top Open-Source AI Models for Content Writing

Mistral 7b: Mistral 7b is an open-source Large Language Model (LLM) developed by Mistral. It has over seven billion parameters and is known for its precision and efficiency. Despite its small size, it outperforms larger models on many tasks. Mistral 7b uses Grouped-query Attention (GQA) for faster inference times and Sliding Window Attention (SWA) to handle longer text sequences at a low cost.

LLaMA: LLaMA is a collection of pre-trained and fine-tuned generative text models. The series offers models ranging from 7 billion to 70 billion parameters. It is often considered as a base model, which requires additional fine-tuning. LLaMA models are trained on a large set of unlabeled data, making them ideal for a variety of tasks.

BLOOM: BLOOM, short for Biologically Localized and Online One-shot Multi-Task Learning, is a machine learning framework that blends the power of deep learning algorithms with human-brain inspired notions. Developed by more than 1000 AI researchers, BLOOM AI is the largest open-access AI model. It is a popular choice among developers for its robustness and versatility.

BERT: BERT (Bidirectional Encoder Representations from Transformers) is a popular open-source LLM. It is known for its ability to understand the context of a sentence, making it a powerful tool for content writing. BERT works by leveraging large amounts of training data and is pre-trained using a plain text corpus.

Falcon 180B: Falcon 180B is a language model that has 180 billion parameters and was trained on 3.5 trillion tokens. It is a causal decoder-only model trained on a causal language modeling task, which means it predicts the next token. Falcon 180B sets a new state-of-the-art for open models and is the largest openly available language model.

Understanding the AI Impact on Content

Generative artificial intelligence (AI) is a subset of machine learning that can generate content, including text, images, videos, and audio. This technology has garnered significant attention in the past few years due to its pertinence in multiple fields. One such area that could harness the full potential of generative AI is content management.

Content managers are professionals who oversee content planning, creation, and distribution through different channels and media. Generative AI has proven to be of significant value to those professionals, as it helps them streamline their workflow, improve their productivity, and create high-quality content. So, if you are a content creator/manager running your company's digital footprint, an enthusiastic blogger, or a person interested in writing, read along to learn how generative AI can help you!

Content Generation

Generative AI and related technologies can be used to create different forms of content, such as articles, blog posts, social media posts, product descriptions, and much more. It also goes beyond that! Generative AI can be configured to render the right syntax, tone, style, and other writing parameters in the content creation process. So, what does this mean? It means that generative AI is the perfect assistant to creators in their content creation journey, as it can produce a wide range of unique materials in little time.

Content Enhancement

The use of generative AI is versatile, extending beyond content generation. In this regard, the technology can be used to enhance existing content in terms of quality. In addition, it could be used to generate captions for videos or images. Also, the potential of generative AI can be utilized to translate the existing content to multiple languages, simplify or make the language more technical, ensure grammatical accuracy, and several other features. All these features make the content more accessible to a broader audience base.

Content Personalization

In order for the content to be accepted by people, it needs to speak to them directly. This is why personalization is a critical component in the content creation process. Traditionally, generated content used to be communicated en masse without regard to personal tastes and differences. With generative AI and related technologies, content can be personalized not only for specific audiences, but also for individuals based on analyzing their interests, preference, and behavior.

Content Optimization

Generative AI can be used to optimize the created content to improve its ranking and performance on search engines and social media platforms. Generative AI and related technologies can help content creators and managers identify trends, patterns, and other factors that help optimize their content for better engagement and visibility and improve the ranking of their websites or pages.

Content Curation

As we mentioned earlier, the potential of generative AI is significantly large, and its applications in content management are versatile beyond imagination. One of the key challenges content managers and creators face is the sheer volume of available material that can be utilized to generate content. With the help of generative AI and related tools, those professionals would be able to scan large volumes of content to extract relevant outcomes.

When taken together, generative AI is seen as the perfect assistant to content managers and creators, as it helps them create content in a timely and accurate manner, all while considering the diversity of their audience's tastes and preferences.

Here are the top 5 ways AI enhances content creation

1. Automated Content Generation

AI can generate content quickly and efficiently. Using natural language processing (NLP) and machine learning algorithms, AI tools can create a variety of content types, including blog posts, articles, product descriptions, and social media updates. Here's how:

Blog Posts and Articles: AI can draft entire blog posts or articles based on a given topic or keyword. I would not recommend relying solely on AI but more on creating outlines and frameworks. Human writers can then refine and personalize.

Product Descriptions: This can really help any business. E-commerce businesses can use AI to generate product descriptions at scale, ensuring consistency and saving time.

Social Media Updates: One of AI's unique features is the ability to create engaging social media content tailored to different platforms. This means it can create content tailored to LinkedIn, then change it for Facebook and once again for Twitter all while maintaining a brand's voice and style.

2. Content Optimization

AI can analyze existing content and suggest improvements to improve readability and SEO performance.

SEO Optimization: AI tools can analyze keyword usage, suggest relevant keywords, and ensure content is optimized thereby improving organic reach. Just make sure the content is revised by a human.

Engagement Metrics: By analyzing past content performance, AI can predict which topics and styles are more likely to resonate with a business's target audience.

3. Personalized Content Recommendations

AI can personalize content recommendations for individual users based on their behavior, preferences, and past interactions. This especially helps in:

Email Marketing: AI can tailor email content by sub niches or interests for each subscriber. This will inevitably increase engagement and conversion rates by delivering relevant information that the reader is more likely to act on.

Social Media Content: AI can suggest trending topics after analyzing volumes of data. It can then help create new fresh content to keep their audience engaged.

4. Visual Content Creation

AI isn't limited to text-based content; it can also assist in creating visual content:

Image and Video Generation: AI tools can generate images, videos, and infographics based on specified parameters, helping to create visually appealing content without needing extensive design skills.

Image Editing and Enhancement: AI can automate image editing tasks, such as resizing, cropping, and enhancing, saving time and ensuring consistency.

Top Open-Source AI Models for Image Generation

Stable Diffusion: Developed by Stability AI and CompVis LMU, Stable Diffusion is a set of open-source models for text-to-image generation. It works similarly to other generative AI models like ChatGPT. When provided with a text prompt, Stable Diffusion creates images based on its training data. It uses a latent diffusion model (LDM) and starts with random noise that resembles an analog television's static. From that initial static, it goes through many steps to remove noise from the picture until it matches the text prompt.

DeepFloyd IF: DeepFloyd IF is a powerful text-to-image model that can smartly integrate text into images. It is known for its power and accessibility. It is a modular neural network based on the cascaded approach that generates high-resolution images in a cascading manner. It is built with multiple neural modules that tackle specific tasks and join forces within a single architecture to produce a synergistic effect.

OpenJourney: OpenJourney is another top image generation platform. It is a popular choice among developers for its robustness and versatility.

OpenJourney is a custom text-to-image model that generates AI art images in the style of Midjourney. It's a fine-tune of Stable Diffusion.

Waifu Diffusion: Waifu Diffusion is known for its capabilities in image generation. It is a popular choice among developers for its robustness and versatility. Waifu Diffusion is a latent text-to-image diffusion model that has been conditioned on high-quality anime images through fine-tuning.

Dreamlike Photoreal: Dreamlike Photoreal is also among the top image generation platforms. It is known for its power and versatility. Dreamlike Photoreal 2.0 is an advanced photo generator that harnesses the power of artificial intelligence (AI) to transform simple prompts into breathtakingly realistic images.

Example

Using Stable Diffusion, an open-source text-to-image generation model, you can create realistic and high-quality images. Starting with a random noise source, the diffusion process progressively refines the noise into visually appealing patterns through a series of steps.

By iteratively applying the stable diffusion process to a latent noise vector, multiple intermediate images are generated. As the diffusion steps progress, the images become increasingly realistic, capturing intricate details. This technique, powerful for image generation, allows controlled exploration of the latent space, resulting in a diverse set of high-quality images. The ability to fine-tune the diffusion process strikes a balance between exploration and convergence, producing a final set of images that exhibit both creativity and fidelity to desired visual characteristics.

5. Interactive Content

AI can create interactive content that engages users and enhances their experience:

Quizzes and Polls: AI can generate personalized quizzes and polls that keep the audience engaged and provide valuable insights into their preferences.

Chatbots and Virtual Assistants: AI-driven chatbots can provide interactive and conversational content, answering questions and guiding users through various processes.

By incorporating AI into your content creation processes, you will be able to produce high-quality, engaging, and personalized content at scale. This will directly impact the bottom line for any business because it will increase profitability. If you're ever in a position where you want or need to sell, you'll get the most money for it.

Evolving one's own Content Strategy

Niche Down: Focus on specific topics or audiences where human expertise is invaluable.

Long-Form Content: Create in-depth, comprehensive pieces that demonstrate your authority.

Visual Content: Invest in high-quality visuals, as AI still struggles with image creation and understanding.

Audio and Video Content: Explore podcasts, webinars, and video content to connect with audiences on multiple platforms.

Interactive Content: Engage your audience with quizzes, polls, and calculators.

User-Generated Content: Encourage audience participation to build a sense of community.

AI Can be Used for a Variety of Tasks

To make your life easier by automating tedious tasks (think grocery shopping) or making decisions based on what you like or dislike (think Netflix).

To predict future outcomes based on current data or trends (think self-driving cars).

This is not just limited to individuals either. AI will be used to improve the content creation process of companies that are already publishing content online.

AI will be used to improve the content creation process of companies that are already publishing online.

Companies can use AI to:

Create more content by finding new ideas and topics that are relevant to their audience

Find more content by using algorithms to analyze data from social media, blogs and other sources (including your own website) in order to find out what types of stories get shared most often on social media platforms like Facebook or Twitter. Then they might decide not only whether they should make an article about it but also how much time you should spend writing versus researching other topics in order not just get traffic but also conversions into sales leads through those sites' advertising offerings so that eventually--if all goes well!--you'll have enough money left over at the end of each month for rent payments plus groceries bill plus utility bills.

AI for Journalists

A good way to understand how AI can contribute to this process is by looking at what it does for journalism.

The most obvious way AI can help journalists is by writing stories for them. AI can also provide resources such as images, maps, and video clips that are relevant to a story. It can even help with the decision-making process by suggesting topics or sources that may be useful in covering a given topic.

Another way AI could contribute is in identifying original sources of information for news stories. For example, if there's an outbreak of Ebola in West Africa and your organization has staff based there who are reporting on it firsthand through social media channels like Twitter or Facebook (or YouTube), then using an algorithm might allow you to identify these accounts as potential contributors even before they've tweeted their first update about current events--which means they might not only get credit but also get paid!

Finally, where appropriate (and necessary), artificial intelligence systems could also help create new content by generating ideas based on past experiences with similar topics etcetera.

For instance, it can help journalists make better decisions about what to cover and in what order.

While AI can't replace human judgment, it can help journalists make better decisions about what to cover and in what order. For example, it might be able to determine which topics are most important or likely to get more views or shares. This could allow journalists to highlight those stories first on their pages and avoid covering less interesting topics that might not generate much traffic.

In addition, AI can also help them decide how long a piece of content should be: If someone reads an article for only 10 minutes and then decides not to visit the site again (even if they liked it), then there's no point in publishing it at all!

In addition, AI will help support journalists by writing stories for them or providing them with resources. In addition to providing journalists with an abundance of data and insight, AI can also help them by writing stories for them. This is especially true when it comes to covering breaking news events. AI could write up a story on the recent shootings in Pittsburgh that killed 11 people, but if you were a journalist who had just heard about this tragedy and was trying to decide what your next steps should be, a computer would have much more information than you do right now--and therefore have better insights into what should be included in your coverage.

AI also has an advantage over humans when it comes time to sourcing particular sources: they can mine through records faster than we ever could! In addition, they're able to find out who said something important or controversial before anyone else did; this means that if there are multiple similar quotes from different sources (e.g., "The president said..."), there's no way any human reporter could keep track of all those quotes without having too many conversations with each person individually just so they can get their facts straight before publishing anything at all since everyone's memory isn't perfect either--and no one wants that kind of headache when deadlines are looming! This could mean writing from a first-person perspective or from a secondary one. It could also mean writing about film reviews or talking about politics or sports.

AI can be used for a lot of different things, but it's easy to see how it could be used in the creation of content. This could mean writing from a first-person perspective or from a secondary one. It could also mean writing about film reviews or talking about politics or sports. It's important to note that AI will never replace humans completely, but rather augment their abilities by providing them with insights into what best serves the audience they are trying to reach.

Another use of this technology is in finding original sources for news stories. It will allow journalists to access more dedicated material like court documents, without needing to spend hours digging through databases and archives themselves.

Another use for this technology is in finding original sources for news stories. It will allow journalists to access more dedicated material like court documents without needing to spend hours digging through databases and archives themselves, saving time and energy. Journalists can also use AI to find new sources of information about a certain topic, such as what people are saying on social media platforms or in other online communities.

Journalists have always been creative when it comes to writing their stories, but now with AI at their disposal they'll be able to break the mold even further by using it as an aid in creating content that better reflects current events or trends within society at large (i.e., politics).

Open-Source AI Models for Book Publishing

BLOOM: Developed through a global collaboration, BLOOM is an autoregressive Large Language Model (LLM) known for its ability to continue text from a prompt. It's one of the most powerful open-source LLMs with capabilities in 46 languages and 13 programming languages. Its transparency and accessibility through the Hugging Face ecosystem make it ideal for tasks like content generation and translation in publishing.

BERT: Initially developed by Google, BERT (Bidirectional Encoder Representations from Transformers) is widely used in natural language processing tasks. Its effectiveness in understanding the context of words in search queries makes it suitable for enhancing search functionality and content discoverability in digital publishing platforms.

Falcon 180B: Released by the Technology Innovation Institute of the United Arab Emirates, Falcon 180B is an advanced LLM trained on a vast amount of data. Its significant computing power and performance in various NLP tasks make it suitable for content creation, summarization, and analysis in publishing.

OPT-175B: Part of Meta's Open Pre-trained Transformers Language Models, OPT-175B is comparable in performance to GPT-3 and is ideal for research use cases in publishing, such as content creation and reader engagement analysis.

Stable Diffusion XL Base 1.0 (SDXL): This model is notable for its ability to generate high-resolution and clear images, making it suitable for creating visual content like book covers, illustrations, and marketing materials in publishing

For example:

OpenAI's GPT: A powerful language model used for generating text, including news articles, creative writing, and content summaries. It can assist journalists and content creators by providing drafts, ideas, and editing suggestions.

GPT - Generative Pre-trained Transformer is an artificial intelligence model developed by OpenAI that is designed to understand and generate human-like text in a conversational manner.

The Various Components of GPT Includes

Generative

The text received as input is transformed into a text that essentially creates sentences, paragraphs, and even summarization of the entire documents that are coherent and contextually relevant.

Pre-Trained

The model is trained on an extensive corpus of input text from various sources that behaves as a training data. This training phase helps it to learn the structure of language, facts about the world, and a variety of patterns in text. This pre-training allows GPT to understand and generate text without needing task-specific training from scratch.

Transformer

The transformer is a type of neural network architecture that is particularly effective at handling sequences of text in the form of sentences or paragraphs. It generates different words in a sentence relative to each other by using attention to weigh the words

Key Features of GPT

Natural Language Understanding

The texts generated by these models closely align with the human related documents.

Contextual Awareness

The models can retain context across extended text, leading to more insightful and pertinent responses.

Versatility

It has the flexibility to encompass diverse arrays of tasks such as providing responses, GPT can perform a wide range of tasks, such as answering questions, writing essays, abstracting & interpreting text , translating languages, and more.

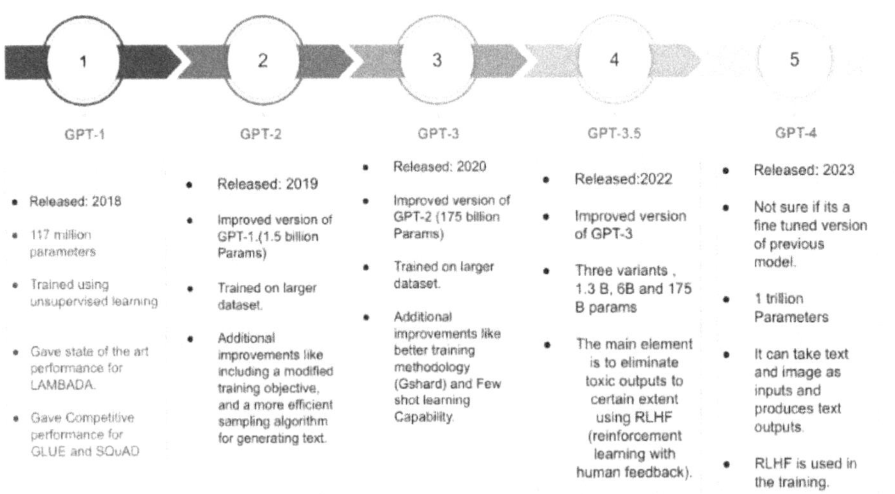

Copy.ai:

AI-driven writing tool designed to support content creation and marketing efforts. Utilizing advanced natural language processing, it generates a range of content types, simplifying the process of producing high-quality text efficiently.

Key Features of copy.ai

Tone and Style Customization: Allows users to adjust the tone and style of the text to match their brand voice or audience preferences.

SEO Optimization: Includes features for integrating keywords and optimizing content structure to improve search engine visibility.

Multi-language Support: Offers content creation capabilities in multiple languages, catering to a global audience.

Ease of Use: Features an intuitive interface designed to be user-friendly, accommodating both experienced writers and beginners.

Content Refinement: Provides suggestions for enhancing the clarity, engagement, and overall quality of the generated content.

Collaboration Tools: Facilitates team collaboration by allowing users to share and edit content within the platform.

AI For Content Creators

In content creation, AI can be used for:

Creative thinking (e.g., generating ideas)

Problem-solving (e.g., coming up with solutions)

Content creators can use AI to increase the quality of their work while also helping other people produce results faster than they would on their own

Content creators can use AI to increase the quality of their work while also helping other people produce results faster than they would on their own. AI can help content creators develop better ideas and determine how best to implement them in a way that's effective for the audience.

AI also impacts how accurate your content is, which means it ultimately affects whether or not you get your point across well enough for people to understand what you're saying or do anything with it (e.g., share).

Artificial intelligence can help with the creation of content.

AI can be used to help create and edit content, as well as add new ideas and insights into existing material. This is an area that has been explored by many companies that use AI in their product development processes, but it's also something you can do yourself to improve your own writing skills.

There are many ways in which AI can be used to improve your writing skills:

Grammar checkers will help you catch mistakes before they become a problem for readers (and editors)

Word processors have features designed specifically for editing text such as "spellcheck" or "word completion" which automatically fix common mistakes like typos or missing words.

Source: https://www.winsavvy.com/how-ai-can-enhance-your-writing-skills/ Manav Saha 2024

AI Can be Used for Web Content

You can use AI to create web content. This is especially useful for businesses, who need a steady supply of new content at all times. It's also helpful for individuals who want their own blogs and websites but don't have the time or resources to write anything themselves. And social media sites like

Facebook and Twitter are a great way to promote your new blog posts--especially if they're SEO-friendly!

AI can create content for social media:

AI can create content for social media platforms like Twitter, Instagram, Facebook, Reddit, LinkedIn, Pinterest and Tumblr.

AI can create short stories:

AI can also be used to write short stories. AI algorithms have the ability to come up with their own plots and characters, so that you don't need to spend hours creating everything from scratch. You can use it in conjunction with other people or bots, who will help you build the story together.

AI algorithms also have a good understanding of human psychology and emotions, which makes them ideal for creating poetry as well as fiction:

Poetry requires creativity and imagination - but it doesn't need grammar skills!

Fiction requires writing skills - but it doesn't require any special knowledge about the world!

Non-fiction requires facts - but there are no rules on how those facts should be arranged into paragraphs (or chapters)

AI can help creativity and problem-solving.

AI is used to help creative thinkers by providing them with tools to solve problems, not only within their own work but also beyond it.

Artificial intelligence can help content creators in many ways. It's not just about writing stories or videos, but also about creating more original sources for news stories and finding more dedicated material to work with. AI will also be able to improve the quality of what you do as a content creator because it will allow you to focus on what is important instead of having all these extra responsibilities on your plate at once.

AI and Film-Making

Generative AI can make film content by using video processing techniques, such as convolutional neural networks (CNNs) and transformers. CNNs are a type of neural network that can handle spatial data, such as images or videos. CNNs can learn from the features and patterns of the data, and generate new images or videos based on them. Transformers are the same type of neural network that we have seen before, but they can also handle spatial data, by using a mechanism called vision transformer, which allows them to apply attention to the images or videos.

Top Open-Source AI Models for Film-Making

Kive.ai: Kive.ai is an AI-driven image generator developed by Kive. It offers a range of features that can be useful in film making. Kive's AI-powered platform helps creatives and teams manage visual assets, win pitches, and create their best work 10x faster. It uses AI to generate images that align with the provided text description.

RunwayML: RunwayML is a tool that can generate visual effects and animations, making it a great choice for filmmakers. It offers a range of AI Magic Tools alongside a fully-featured timeline video editor. RunwayML's AI research is ushering in new tools for global brands, enterprises, and creatives to tell their stories.

NVIDIA GANverse3D: NVIDIA GANverse3D is a tool that can convert 2D images into 3D models, which can be very useful in creating visual effects for films. It uses AI to power GANverse3D, an Omniverse extension that enables creators to take photos of cars and create virtual replicas with lights, physics models, and PBR materials.

Imagine 3D: Imagine 3D is an AI text-to-3D model generator by Luma Labs. It is an early experiment to prototype and create 3D with text. It uses a large frozen T5-XXL encoder to encode the input text into embeddings. A conditional diffusion model maps the text embedding into a 64×64 image.

Paper Cup: Paper Cup is an AI platform that artificially creates voiceovers and dubs for your videos, even in other languages. It uses data from real actors to produce voices so real that audiences can't tell them apart from the real thing. The AI voices used to dub your content are completely customizable.

Example

Runway Gen-2, a cutting-edge generative AI tool, revolutionizes filmmaking through its versatile capabilities. Functioning on a novel architecture called Vision Transformer, it interprets and generates video content from various inputs. With features like Text to Video, Text + Image to Video, and Image to Video, filmmakers can effortlessly create visuals by providing text prompts or combining images.

The Stylization feature allows users to infuse diverse artistic styles into their videos, while Storyboard transforms mockups into animated renders, aiding in visualization before production. The Mask tool enables easy subject modification with simple text prompts, offering efficient video editing. Runway Gen-2's Render function enhances film quality by applying textures and effects based on input images or prompts. The tool's foundation on transformers and its unique Vision Transformer architecture promises a groundbreaking approach to understanding and generating visual designs.

A Cinematic Breakthrough in AI-Driven Filmmaking

StoryTeller has emerged as a transformative force in the realm of cinema, representing a groundbreaking generative AI tool that holds the potential to reshape traditional filmmaking paradigms. As an open-source model, StoryTeller democratizes the filmmaking process, enabling accessibility for anyone equipped with a computer and an internet connection.

The tool operates through a combination of diverse AI models, seamlessly weaving together a fully animated video based on a user-provided prompt. Utilizing a language model for plot development, a generative model for image creation, and a text-to-speech model for narration, StoryTeller crafts a coherent and captivating narrative in video form. What distinguishes StoryTeller is its comprehensive approach, managing the entire filmmaking process from scriptwriting to animation and narration. This capability has the potential to disrupt conventional filmmaking methodologies, potentially reducing the dependency on extensive teams and costly equipment.

Additionally, the open-source nature of StoryTeller fosters a culture of innovation and creativity, allowing filmmakers to modify and enhance the tool to suit their specific requirements. This adaptability may lead to the evolution of new storytelling techniques and cinematic styles, marking a significant cinematic breakthrough.

For example:

Video and Audio Production:

Descript: An AI-powered video and audio editing tool that allows users to edit content by editing text transcripts. It is used by novice and professional creators.

Key features of Descript

Overdub: This feature enables users to generate synthetic voiceovers by training Descript's AI on their own voice, allowing for text-to-speech conversions that closely resemble the original speaker's voice.

Audio and Video Editing: Users can edit audio and video content by modifying the transcribed text. Any adjustments made to the text are automatically reflected in the corresponding audio or video, streamlining the editing process.

Filler word removal - The platform automatically detects and removes filler words and false starts from recordings, resulting in cleaner and more polished audio.

Multi-Track Editing: Allows for simultaneous editing of multiple audio and video tracks, making it ideal for podcasting and intricate video projects.

Top Open-Source AI Models for Music Production

Jukebox: Developed by OpenAI, Jukebox is a neural net that generates music, including rudimentary singing, as raw audio in a variety of genres and artist styles. It was trained on a dataset of 1.2 million songs (or 600,000 hours of music) spanning various genres and languages, along with their corresponding lyrics and metadata. Jukebox outputs a new music sample produced from scratch when provided with genre, artist, and lyrics as input.

MuseTree: MuseTree is a custom front-end for OpenAI's MuseNet. It is designed for real music production and has been built from the ground-up with that in mind. MuseTree lets you work with an AI to generate music in a range of styles. It is designed for non-musicians interested in creating music, and small content creators e.g. YouTubers.

AudioCraft: Developed by Meta, AudioCraft is a single-stop code base for all your generative audio needs: music, sound effects, and compression after training on raw audio signals. It consists of three models: MusicGen, AudioGen, and EnCodec. MusicGen, which was trained with Meta-owned and specifically licensed music, generates music from text-based user inputs, while AudioGen, trained on public sound effects, generates audio from text-based user inputs.

Jukebox, an advanced generative AI model for music production developed by OpenAI, stands out as a powerful tool capable of generating music across diverse genres, styles, and moods, including rock, pop, jazz, classical, and more. Beyond its versatility, Jukebox can mimic the distinctive styles and voices of specific artists like Adele, Taylor Swift, and Metallica, showcasing its ability to capture nuanced musical expressions.

Notably, Jukebox goes beyond just music composition. It can also generate lyrics that seamlessly match the musical compositions, or vice versa. Built on transformer architecture, Jukebox incorporates a novel technique known as Vector Quantized Variational Autoencoders (VQ-VAE). This innovative approach enables efficient compression and decompression of audio data, contributing to the model's effectiveness and sophistication in generating intricate and lifelike musical compositions.

In a standard VAE, the continuous nature of the latent space can sometimes lead to challenges in capturing discrete structures or specific features. VQ-VAE addresses this by discretizing the latent space, meaning that instead of continuous values, it employs a set of discrete codes to represent different regions within the space. This discretization is achieved through a vector quantization process, where each point in the continuous space is mapped to the nearest code in a predefined codebook.

Interactive Demos : Offers hands-on demos and tools for experimenting with machine learning models, allowing users to understand and apply the technology more effectively.

Runway ML: A creative toolkit that uses machine learning for interactive media such as design and video production. . It offers AI models for tasks such as video editing, image generation, and object detection.

Key features of Runaway ML

Pre-Trained Models: Provides a collection of pre-trained machine learning models designed for tasks such as image and video generation, style transfer, object detection, and more.

Custom Model Training: Allows users to train personalized models with their own data, customizing machine learning applications to suit specific needs and projects.

API Integration : Provides developers with API access to seamlessly integrate machine learning models into their own applications and services.

Real-Time Editing: Enables users to edit and manipulate media in real time, applying machine learning models to their content immediately.

Jasper

It is a natural language processing tool with an AI powered writing assistant that aids in generating content and improving writing quality. The written forms of communications - copy, posts , blogs, social media content can assist with creating engaging and relevant text. It offers features like tone adjustment, style recommendations, and content optimization, aiming to streamline the writing process and enhance productivity.

Key Features of Jasper

Templates : Jasper provides a range of templates tailored for various writing tasks, such as email campaigns, product descriptions, and ad copy.

SEO optimization (Search Engine Optimization) : This includes keyword suggestions and optimization tips, to enhance content visibility and improve search rankings.

Grammar and Spelling Checks: Ensures text is free from grammatical errors and spelling mistakes.

Content Improvement Suggestions: Jasper offers recommendations to improve the clarity, engagement, and overall quality of the content.

Integration with Other Tools: Jasper integrates seamlessly with various platforms, including Google Docs and WordPress, for a more efficient workflow.

Spotify's Discover Weekly: Employs AI algorithms to curate personalized playlists based on listening habits and preferences. The playlist is refreshed every Monday to help explore new music. Curated based on the user's listening habits, it introduces one to tracks from artists one might not have encountered yet but are likely to appreciate, drawing on his/her recent listens and playlists.

Key Features

Personalization: The playlist is customized to reflect the unique tastes, taking into account the listening history and the artists and genres one frequently enjoys.

Weekly Updates: Discover Weekly refreshes every Monday, providing one with a fresh selection of music recommendations each week.

Diverse Recommendations: It features tracks from artists one might not be familiar with, presenting a variety of genres and styles to expand the musical range.

Algorithm-Driven: Spotify's algorithms power the recommendations by analyzing the listening patterns and comparing them with those of other users to suggest songs one is likely to enjoy.

Top of Form

Bottom of Form

Synthesia: It is an AI-driven video creation platform that excels in producing videos featuring synthetic actors and avatars. By employing advanced machine learning techniques, it generates realistic video content, enabling users to produce high-quality, professional videos swiftly and efficiently.

Key features of synthesia:

AI Avatars: Allows users to create videos featuring synthetic avatars or virtual presenters that can speak in multiple languages and accents.

Customizable Templates: Provides a variety of video templates that can be customized for different purposes, such as training, marketing, or corporate communications.

Text-to-Video: Converts written text into video content, where the AI avatars deliver the script, making it easy to produce informative or promotional videos without extensive video production resources.

Realistic Lip-Syncing: Utilizes advanced lip-syncing technology to ensure that the synthetic avatars' lip movements accurately match the spoken text, enhancing the video's realism.

Example For Personalization and Recommendations:

Netflix's Recommendation System: Uses AI to analyze viewing history and user behavior to suggest movies and TV shows tailored to individual preferences.

Key Features

- Collaborative filtering - suggest content by examining and identifying the patterns of the users with similar tastes
- Content-Based Filtering: suggest items similar to the user who has previously watched the content or rated highly, through analysis of metadata such as genre, actors, and directors.
- A/B Testing: Netflix frequently conducts A/B testing to evaluate the effectiveness of different recommendation algorithms and interfaces. This helps in continuously improving the accuracy and relevance of recommendations.
- Global and Local Preferences: Netflix's recommendation system takes into account regional preferences and trends, offering content that aligns with local tastes while maintaining global relevance.
- Feedback Loops: The system uses user feedback, such as likes, dislikes, and skips, to continuously improve recommendations and adapt to changing preferences.

Content Moderation Tools by Microsoft Azure: Provides AI-powered content moderation services to detect and filter inappropriate or harmful content on platforms.

- Azure Content Moderator
- Text Moderation: Detects and filters out offensive language, including profanity and harmful content, from text data.
- Image Moderation: Evaluates images to identify inappropriate content such as adult material, violence, or graphic imagery.
- Video Moderation: Offers real-time or batch processing of videos to flag and manage inappropriate content.
- Azure Cognitive Services
- Custom Vision: Enables one to train a personalized model for detecting specific types of content in images according to the requirements.
- Text Analytics: Analyzes text to extract insights, such as sentiment, key phrases, and named entities, which helps in identifying potentially inappropriate or harmful content.

Key Features and Capabilities Include

Live Streaming: Provides high-quality live video streaming for events, webinars, and broadcasts with exceptional scalability and reliability.

On-Demand Video: Facilitates the hosting and management of on-demand video content, including video-on-demand (VOD) services.

AI-Powered Video Analytics: Employs AI to analyze video content, offering automated tagging, sentiment analysis, and content moderation.

Automated Transcription and Captioning: Transforms spoken content into text through automatic transcription and closed captioning, enhancing accessibility and searchability.

Content Management: Features tools for the efficient organization, categorization, and management of video content within a unified platform.

Example for Visual Effects and Animation

DeepArt.io: Applies AI to transform photos into artworks using styles from famous artists, allowing for creative visual effects.

Key Features

Style Transfer: Transforms user-uploaded images by applying artistic styles from renowned paintings or other visual aesthetics, resulting in distinctive artwork that emulates the selected style.

Customization Options: Provides a range of style choices and customization tools, enabling users to adjust settings and refine the final appearance of their artwork.

User-Friendly Interface: Features a simple and intuitive interface that allows users to easily upload images, choose styles, and create artwork with minimal hassle.

Artistic Styles Library: Offers a collection of predefined artistic styles inspired by celebrated artists, art movements, and visual trends.

Runway ML's AI Tools: Includes models for generating art, enhancing visual effects, and creating unique animations based on user inputs.

Key Features

No-Code/Low-Code Tools: Provides platforms that allow users to create, train, and deploy machine-learning models without extensive coding knowledge. This democratizes access to AI technology for non-technical users.

Pre-Built Models: Offers a library of pre-trained machine learning models that can be easily integrated into applications, saving time and resources on model development.

Custom Model Training: Supports the creation and training of custom models tailored to specific needs or datasets, allowing for more precise and relevant AI solutions.

- Azure AI and Machine Learning
- Pre-Built Models: Leverages existing models to detect hate speech, harassment, and abusive language in both text and images.
- Custom Models: Provides tools to create and deploy custom models tailored to specific content moderation needs using Azure Machine Learning.

- Azure Speech Services
- Speech-to-Text: Converts spoken words into written text for moderation, helping to identify and filter inappropriate content.
- Text-to-Speech: Generates spoken content from text, which can then be reviewed for inappropriate language.

Google's Perspective API: It utilizes machine learning to assess the tone and quality of online comments. The API is especially effective for moderating conversations and overseeing online communities by identifying harmful or disruptive content.

Key Features of API

- Toxicity Detection:
- Toxicity Scores: Assigns a numerical value between 0 and 1 to indicate the probability that a comment is toxic or harmful, with higher scores reflecting greater toxicity.
- Categorization: Recognizes different forms of toxicity, including insults, threats, obscenity, and attacks on identity.

Example for Contextual Analysis:

- Context Sensitivity: Examines the context in which words are used to enhance understanding and precision in detecting toxic content.
- Customizable Thresholds: Allows adjustment of sensitivity levels to align with specific moderation requirements and community standards.
- Real-Time Processing:
- Immediate Feedback: Provides real-time analysis of text, enabling prompt feedback for moderation or automated actions.
- API Integration: Seamlessly integrates with existing platforms and applications via RESTful API calls, facilitating efficient moderation processes.
- Multi-Language Support:

- Global Reach: Supports multiple languages, making it adaptable for diverse international audiences and user bases.
- Actionable Insights:
- Moderation Analytics: Delivers data and insights on comment trends and moderation activities, aiding in the understanding of toxic content patterns and frequency.
- Reporting: Creates reports on toxicity trends and the effectiveness of moderation efforts.
- Custom Model Training:
- Customization: Allows for the development of bespoke models tailored to specific needs or community guidelines, enhancing the precision and relevance of toxicity detection

Clarifai: This AI tool allows developers to incorporate image and video recognition features into their applications, such as object detection, facial recognition, image tagging, and content moderation.

Key Features

- Facial Recognition: Identifies and analyzes human faces, enabling features such as facial identification, verification, and emotion detection.
- Image Tagging: Automatically assigns descriptive tags to images based on their content, improving organization and searchability.
- Content Moderation: Evaluates images and videos for inappropriate or offensive content to ensure a safe and compliant user experience.
- Custom Model Training: Provides the ability to design and train custom models tailored to specific needs or industries, utilizing personal datasets for enhanced accuracy.
- Video Analysis: Examines video content to identify and track objects, recognize actions, and extract meaningful information from video frames.

IBM Watson Media: Offers AI-driven solutions for video analysis, including automated metadata tagging, content recognition, and speech-to-text transcription.A comprehensive media suite powered by IBM. By harnessing artificial intelligence and cloud technologies, it delivers sophisticated video streaming and management services.

AI Usage in Game Development

AI can enrich game design by enhancing non-player characters (NPCs) and refining game mechanics through its capability to create realistic and challenging behaviors, thereby elevating the player's experience. AI can not only develop formidable opponents, but it can also ingeniously generate procedural content, such as new levels and characters, ensuring a continually fresh and engaging gaming journey for players.

AI algorithms excel at delivering personalized game suggestions, considering players' preferences, gameplay styles, genre inclinations, in-game choices, and past feedback to suggest game titles aligned with their interests. Moreover, AI can dynamically tailor in-game content, like missions and challenges, according to individual player behavior and decisions.

"Game development using technology was started in 1950 around the first video game created by Tennis for Two by Higginbotham as a fun diversion, to show the power of technology. The advanced development of Artificial intelligence (AI), has turned out to be the heart of game development technology and AI has revolutionized gaming and brought so many features to life.in reality, it isn't easy to give a definition and meaning to it even though games are becoming a part of human survival. It is difficult to define the real meaning of a game but it is part of human survival as it usually refers to the cleverness of the way the human being is involved in the characters of the game. As a part of game development, many technologies were used to create a game for the players with creativity, complex design, variety of levels, and aspects for the player to use choices effectively and efficiently to interact with the character in the game and enhance the experience to the next levels." "As AI technology is used in game development many tools are available in the market for new developers like Game engines, Integrated Development Environments (IDEs), Graphics DesignSoftware, Audio Editing Software, Unity, Godot, Game Maker Studio, Blender, Visual Studio. The following are best practices that can be followed at the time of game development using AI technology. Iterative development, managing requirements, Managing change, Verifying quality, Being user-focused, Research trends and competition, Differentiating your game, having a hook." Dr. Dhanamma Jagli,*, Dr. Subhash Chandra, Srinivasa Rao Dhanikonda and N.Laxmi, (2024), *Artificial Intelligence Usage in Game Development*, Preprints.org.

Top Open-Source AI Models for Gaming

- Godot Engine: Godot is a user-friendly and versatile open-source game engine with a strong following. It features a visual editor, a robust scripting language, and supports both 2D and 3D game development. Godot is known for its active community and regular updates, making it a top choice for many indie developers.
- Blender Game Engine: Part of the Blender 3D creation suite, this engine is not only for 3D modeling and animation but also includes a game engine. While it may not be as feature-rich as others for game development, it's a solid choice for creating interactive 3D experiences within the Blender ecosystem.
- Unreal Engine 4: Known for its stunning graphics and extensive toolset, Unreal Engine 4 is a powerhouse in the game development industry. While the engine itself is not fully open source, the source code is available to licensees, allowing significant customization and collaboration.
- Cocos2d: This is a popular open-source framework specifically for mobile game development. It's an excellent choice for developers targeting iOS and Android platforms due to its focus on 2D game creation.
- GameMaker Studio 2: While not entirely open-source, GameMaker Studio offers both proprietary and open-source licensing options. It's known for its ease of use, with a drag-and-drop interface, and a powerful scripting language for more complex games. It's a versatile choice for a wide range of platforms, including Windows, macOS, Linux, Android, iOS, HTML5, and consoles.

AI and Advertising

AI can enhance audience targeting by analyzing vast data, predicting behavior, and enabling real-time personalization. It can segment users based on behavior, facilitate A/B testing, and optimize campaigns for better results. Predictive analytics powered by AI can leverage historical data to forecast consumer behavior and buying trends.

AI-powered systems can create tailored content and recommendations based on individual preferences, boosting engagement and conversion rates. AI-generated content, such as ad copy and articles, can offer significant time and cost savings in content production.

Top Open-Source AI Models in Advertising

As of 2024, there are several noteworthy open-source AI models that can be particularly beneficial in the advertising industry. Here are the top 5 models, each with its unique features:

Stable Diffusion XL Base 1.0 (SDXL): This model stands out for its ability to generate high-resolution and clear images. Its versatile applications include concept art for media, graphic design for advertising, and educational visuals. This makes it a valuable tool for creating visually engaging content in advertising campaigns.

Gen2 by Runway: Gen2 is an advanced text-to-video generation tool. It can create videos from text descriptions in various styles and genres, including animations and realistic formats. This tool is particularly useful in advertising for creating engaging ads, demos, explainer videos, and social media content.

PanGu-Coder2: This AI model is designed for coding-related tasks and excels in generating code in multiple programming languages. It's a valuable tool for software development, including developing interactive features and optimizing websites or applications for advertising purposes.

Deepseek Coder: This model specializes in understanding and generating code, particularly in languages like Python, Java, and C++. Its capability to optimize algorithms and reduce code execution time makes it ideal for developing efficient and responsive advertising tools or applications

Code Llama: Developed by Meta, Code Llama is adept at understanding and generating code across a variety of programming languages. Its use cases include code completion, natural language prompts to write code, and debugging. This model can be particularly useful for creating interactive and dynamic advertising content.

Ethical Considerations in Generative AI for Media and Entertainment

The integration of generative AI in media and entertainment introduces a spectrum of ethical implications demanding careful evaluation. The challenge of originality and attribution arises as generative AI blurs lines between human and artificial creativity, prompting the need for clear guidelines on crediting AI-generated content.

Concerns about plagiarism and copyright infringement surface due to the potential similarities with existing works, emphasizing the importance of defining boundaries and diversifying training datasets. Addressing biases in AI models is crucial to prevent perpetuating stereotypes or unfair representation in generated content. Privacy considerations loom large in image and video generation, necessitating strict guidelines to respect individuals' privacy rights.

The impact on employment, with the potential for job displacement, underscores the importance of balancing AI adoption with efforts to reskill affected professionals. User manipulation concerns call for safeguards against the malicious use of AI-generated content and the promotion of media literacy.

Additionally, acknowledging the environmental impact of resource-intensive AI training processes emphasizes the need for sustainable practices. In navigating these ethical considerations, a transparent and collaborative approach involving stakeholders, policymakers, and AI developers is crucial to ensure the responsible and ethical deployment of generative AI in the media and entertainment landscape.

For Ethical and Legal Tools

- **Deeptrace:** Specializes in detecting deepfakes and other forms of synthetic media to combat misinformation and ensure media authenticity.

Key Featuers

- Media Authentication: Provides tools to verify the authenticity of media, allowing users to determine if content is genuine or has been modified.
- Real-time Monitoring: Enables immediate analysis and tracking of digital content to identify and address potential manipulations as they happen.
- Threat Intelligence: Features tools for monitoring and analyzing the distribution of deepfakes and altered media across platforms, offering insights into emerging threats.
- Customizable Solutions: Delivers specialized solutions for various sectors, including media, security, and social platforms, to tackle specific issues related to media manipulation.
- FakeCatcher is a tool developed by researchers to detect deep fakes and manipulated media. It utilizes advanced artificial intelligence techniques to identify whether an image or video has been digitally altered.

Key Features

Deep Fake Detection: Employs sophisticated algorithms to analyze visual and audio content, detecting signs of manipulation such as unnatural facial expressions or audio inconsistencies.

Real-Time Analysis: Offers the ability to process and analyze media content in real-time, allowing for the immediate identification of potential deep fakes or altered media.

Visual Artifacts Detection: Identifies subtle visual artifacts and inconsistencies that are often indicative of deepfake technology, such as irregularities in facial movements or lighting.

AI-Powered Insights: Uses machine learning models trained on large datasets to provide accurate detection of manipulated media, leveraging patterns and anomalies not easily visible to the human eye.

AI and Content Creation: Threat or Opportunity?

The integration of AI into content strategy is not about replacing humans but enhancing their capabilities. By understanding AI's strengths and weaknesses, focusing on human expertise, and continuously evolving your approach, you can create content that stands out in a competitive landscape. (Shaiza Tahir 2023)

The role of artificial intelligence (AI) in content creation has been the subject of much debate over the last few years. While some people have argued that AI will never be able to do something as complicated as writing a book or creating an effective marketing campaign, others believe that it will eventually be used by everyone from journalists to bloggers.

"Today, AI is a disruptive force that is changing the way we consume news, entertainment, and information." (Yousuf Rangoonwala 2024)

Today, AI is a disruptive force that is changing the way we consume news, entertainment and information. It's not just about big companies using it to automate their processes--the technology is available to anyone with an internet connection.

Source: https://www.linkedin.com/pulse/ai-content-creation-threat-opportunity-shaiza-tahir/

There's no denying it: AI is making waves in our field. Tools like ChatGPT by OpenAI, and many others, have demonstrated that machines can now generate human-like text. Brands are using AI to automate social media posts, write product descriptions, and even draft news articles.

Threat: Job Displacement and Creativity Concerns

Source: https://www.linkedin.com/pulse/ai-content-creation-threat-opportunity-shaiza-tahir/

Job Displacement: One of the biggest fears is that AI will replace human writers. While AI can produce vast amounts of text quickly, the real question is: Does it have the soul, context, and nuance that human writers bring to the table?

Creativity Concerns: There's a lingering sentiment that AI-generated content lacks originality. Because machines learn from existing data, some argue that they can only replicate, not innovate.

Opportunity: Efficiency, Collaboration, and Expansion

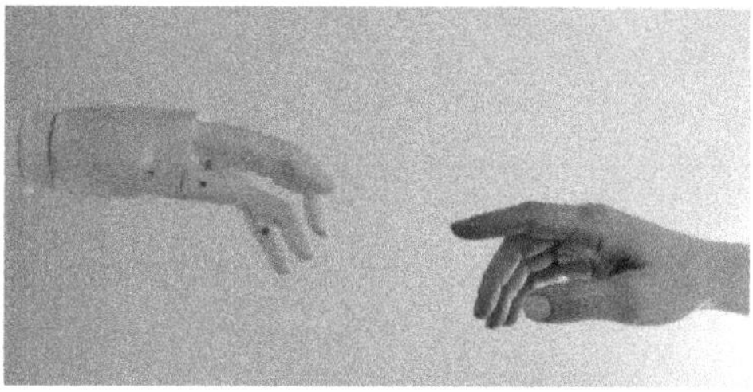

Source: https://www.linkedin.com/pulse/ai-content-creation-threat-opportunity-shaiza-tahir/

Efficiency: AI tools can handle repetitive tasks (like data analysis or keyword optimization) allowing content creators to focus on more strategic and creative tasks.

Collaboration: Think of AI not as a replacement, but as a collaborative partner. AI can suggest edits, generate ideas, or even help with writer's block!

Expansion: With the help of AI, content can be produced in multiple languages and formats, expanding your reach and accessibility.

Finding the Middle Ground

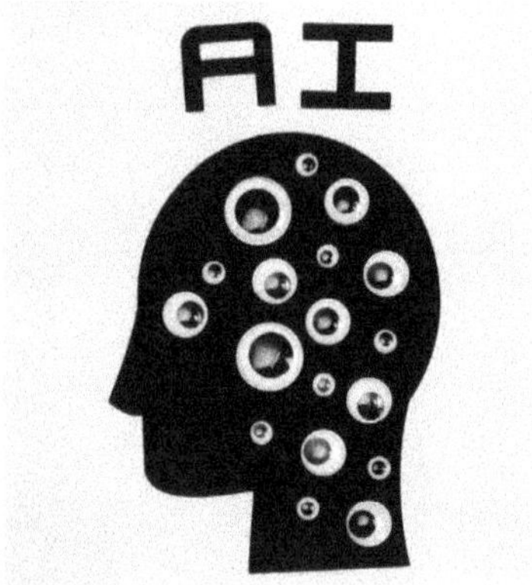

Source: https://www.linkedin.com/pulse/ai-content-creation-threat-opportunity-shaiza-tahir/

Like any technological advancement, it's about how we choose to use it. Blending human creativity with machine efficiency might just be the formula for content gold. Human writers bring context, emotion, and understanding, while AI brings speed, consistency, and data analysis.

While AI presents unprecedented opportunities, we must focus on ensuring the quality, credibility, and diversity of AI-generated content. It analyzes the existing data, content and information available in different sites and sources to mimic human tone, trying to forge human creativity and expressions. AI can not fully change, at least now, the way human beings develop and generate content. Recently, we have all read a news about how YouTube has taken a step to identify AI-generated content on the platform and inform the audience about it.

"Why we shouldn't fully rely on AI writing?" Irine Maria 2024

Errors

With limitations of the existing technology, the content it produces can be wrong, especially when it comes to the facts or information. So, it's always advisable to recheck or reconfirm the content. we might have noticed this on the ChatGPT platform, 'ChatGPT can make mistakes. Consider checking important information.'

Plagiarism

Professionals experienced in the content creation know the importance of copyrights and plagiarism. It can lead them or their businesses into legal cases and affect your reputation.

AI content may contain repetitive information or plagiarized ideas from various other websites because AI algorithms perpetuate everything available to them.

Creativity

AI can produce junk words on any topic you want, but human creativity and thinking create original ideas - the authenticity that connects to people.

Publishing misinformation can affect branding, business, and overall reputation. So, it's crucial to ensure that the information we share is accurate and truthful to maintain trust with the audience. So we have to always embrace technology at all times.

AI works according to the commands we provide. So, it is essential to adjust the prompts by adding up details and features such as,

1. **The tone of the content**
2. **Persona**
3. **Target audience**
4. **Demographics**
5. **Branding style**
6. **Any facts or info**

The content has to convey and connect with the audience. Emotions have to be incorporated to ensure the content is engaging and communicates well with the audience. Additionally, proofread, edit and rewrite to create uniqueness and authenticity in the AI-generated content. The user engagement of the content in every platform will have to be measured which will help develop a content strategy.

Conclusion

Rod Judkins, Author of The Art of Creative Thinking, once said, "To be true to an idea, you have to value expression over perfection, vitality over finish, movement over the static, and form over function. Put your personality before practicality and your individuality into everything. Ironing out impracticalities irons out what is unique."

Considering the risks and consequences of AI writing, if we are writing for our business or personal purposes, an understanding of how it functions, the message, the purpose, and how we want to connect with people, needs to be primarily considered. Technology has always been there, but creativity elevates the creation.

References

1. https://www.linkedin.com/pulse/ai-writing-experience-content-editor-boon-bane-irine-maria-czhjf/ - **Irine Maria 2024**
2. https://bwmarketingworld.com/article/ai-generated-content-boon-or-bane-for-creativity-513575- Yousuf Rangoonwala 2024
3. https://www.linkedin.com/pulse/ai-content-creation-threat-opportunity-shaiza-tahir/ - Shaiza Tahir 2023
4. https://www.winsavvy.com/how-ai-can-enhance-your-writing-skills/ Manav Saha 2024
5. Yogesh K. Dwivedi, Et., al, "So what if ChatGPT wrote it?" Multidisciplinary perspectives on opportunities, challenges and implications of generative conversational AI for research, practice and policy, International Journal of Information Management,

Volume 71, 2023, 102642, ISSN 0268-4012, https://doi.org/10.1016/j.ijinfomgt.2023.102642.

6. https://www.jasper.ai/tools/paragraph-rewriter
7. https://learn.microsoft.com/en-us/azure/ai-services/content-moderator/overview -Patrick Farley, Nitinme, Eric-urban 2024
8. https://www.artvy.ai/ai-tools/deepartio
9. https://www.geeksforgeeks.org/stability-ai-vs-runwayml-which-one-generates-the-best-ai-powered-images/ - Tal Navarro 2024
10. https://blog.scaleflex.com/best-image-recognition-software/ - Franco Anselmo 2024
11. Li-juan zhao.(2023). Looking at the transformation of the advertising industry from the new era of digital intelligence: take the introduction of artificial intelligence as the cutting-edge technology as an example [J]. News, (12), 145, 146.
12. Hai-yan wang.(2023). AI technology enables advertising: a deep understanding and matching of customer behavior and demands [J]. Business era, (36), 197 198.
13. Stonehouse, G. H., & Konina, N. Y. (2020). Management challenges in the age of digital disruption. 1st International Conference on Emerging Trends and Challenges in the Management Theory and Practice (ETCMTP 2019), 1-6. https://www.atlantis-press.com/proceedings/etcmtp19/125934002.

AI and the Media Metamorphosis: Reimagining Gender, Opportunities, and Ethics

Dr.P.Panbuselvan, Assistant Professor, Department of Visual Communication and Electronic Media, PSG College of Arts & Science, Coimbatore, Tamil Nadu, Email:dr.p.panbuselvan@gmail.com

Introduction

Artificial Intelligence (AI) has significantly transformed the media industry, profoundly changing content creation, distribution, and audience engagement. This paper explores how AI intersects with media, focusing on its effects on women's roles and representation. Technological advancements in Natural Language Processing (NLP) and machine learning have revolutionized media practices, enabling innovations such as automated content generation and personalized recommendations. These developments create opportunities to amplify women's voices and stories while presenting challenges, including the risk of perpetuating existing biases in representation. Empirical studies and real-world examples are examined to demonstrate the successes and failures of AI in addressing gender representation. For instance, AI-driven tools have been used to analyze and reduce stereotypical portrayals of women, while biases in algorithms have at times reinforced harmful stereotypes. Ethical dilemmas, such as biases in facial recognition technologies, privacy concerns in targeted advertising, and accountability in opaque algorithms, are explored in depth, highlighting the need for transparent and inclusive AI practices. The paper also discusses the economic implications of AI in media, focusing on the new opportunities it creates for women in media production and distribution and its effects on workforce dynamics. To improve coherence, discussions are organized into distinct sections such as Impact on Gender Representation, Ethical Considerations and Opportunities and Challenges providing a clear structure for readers. Through case studies, this paper illustrates how AI initiatives can be leveraged to promote gender equality and inclusivity in media. It concludes by emphasizing the importance of diverse AI development teams, ethical AI practices, and amplifying women's representation in the media landscape. These insights offer a roadmap for leveraging AI to foster greater equity and inclusivity in the future.

Setting the Stage: AI's Media Revolution

AI is reshaping the media industry by utilizing advanced technologies like Natural Language Processing (NLP) and Machine Learning. These innovations bring new opportunities and challenges, especially for women's representation in the media. Through NLP and Natural Language Generation (NLG), AI can automate the creation of various types of content, such as news articles and creative narratives (Jones, 2023). By analysing large datasets, these technologies identify emerging trends and tailor content to audience preferences, improving the efficiency and relevance of media production. Beyond automation, AI also enhances user engagement by personalizing content recommendations. Streaming platforms like Netflix and Spotify use AI to analyse user behaviour and preferences, offering personalized suggestions that cater to individual tastes (Doe & Lee, 2024). This shift from traditional media consumption to on-demand, personalized content has revolutionized audience interaction. However, while personalization improves user experience, it also raises concerns about reinforcing existing stereotypes and limiting access to diverse perspectives.

The role of AI in media highlights important questions about representation and inclusivity. To improve women's representation, AI algorithms need to be trained on diverse datasets, ensuring a fair and accurate portrayal of women. When done right, AI can spotlight women's achievements and stories that are often underrepresented in traditional media. However, without careful design, AI systems can inadvertently perpetuate biases and reinforce outdated gender norms (Brown, 2023).

AI's Creative Surge: Content Innovation and Personalization

AI technologies like NLP and NLG are transforming content creation and distribution, boosting both efficiency and personalization. Tools such as OpenAI's GPT series are capable of producing a wide range of content, from data-driven news reports to creative writing, streamlining the production process and expanding possibilities for media organizations (Taylor, 2023). In addition to content creation, AI also plays a major role in content distribution. Platforms like Netflix and Spotify analyse user data to recommend content tailored to individual preferences, increasing user engagement by offering more relevant choices. For women, these algorithms can help promote female-led media by recommending films and series featuring strong female characters and diverse narratives (Smith & Chen, 2024). Through personalized recommendations, AI has the potential to amplify the visibility of women's stories, many of which might be overlooked by traditional media channels.

However, the integration of AI in content creation and distribution comes with its own set of challenges. While AI can replicate human writing styles, it often struggles to capture the emotional depth and nuance inherent in human expression. A study by the University of Oxford found that although AI-generated content is coherent, it frequently lacks the emotional richness that a human writer would bring (Smith & Chen, 2024). Furthermore, AI algorithms can perpetuate biases if trained on limited or non-diverse datasets. Without careful oversight, these systems may unintentionally reinforce stereotypes or restrict exposure to a broader range of perspectives. For example, algorithms may favour content that adheres to traditional gender roles, limiting the visibility of progressive or unconventional portrayals of women (Green, 2023).

To address these issues, designing AI systems with inclusivity ensures that they are trained on diverse and representative datasets. When used properly, AI can be a powerful tool to highlight underrepresented female voices and achievements, bridging gaps in media representation (Wilson, 2022). With careful management, AI has the potential to promote more balanced, diverse, and inclusive content in the media.

AI's Ripple Effects: Socio-Cultural and Economic Shifts

The representation of women in the media continues to be a critical issue, offering both challenges and opportunities for change. AI has the potential to either exacerbate or mitigate these challenges. Through AI-driven analytics, disparities in gender representation can be revealed, prompting media organizations to address these imbalances. By analysing large datasets, AI identifies patterns of underrepresentation and stereotypical portrayals, offering actionable insights to create more balanced and inclusive content (Anderson, 2024). For example, AI can track gender representation in advertising campaigns and news coverage, providing data to help media outlets improve diversity in their content.

Beyond addressing current challenges, AI is poised to influence future trends in gender representation. As AI technologies continue to evolve, they could enable more nuanced portrayals of women, moving beyond traditional stereotypes. AI-powered content creation tools may help producers develop more complex characters and storylines that reflect the diverse realities of gender identity and experience. However, if AI systems are trained on biased historical data, there is a risk they may perpetuate existing stereotypes, hindering progress. It is therefore critical that AI's role in media remains aligned with efforts to promote gender equality.

The rise of digital platforms has further transformed media consumption, shifting from traditional scheduled programming to on-demand and personalized experiences. This shift has led to the decline of traditional broadcast TV and the emergence of digital platforms that provide access to a wider range of content and amplify marginalized voices (Brown & Davis, 2023). These platforms offer women the opportunity to produce and distribute their content, bypassing traditional media gatekeepers. This democratization of media production has helped elevate female voices and enabled more diverse representations of women.

As more women contribute to digital media, they are challenging traditional gender roles and reshaping societal norms regarding women's capabilities and aspirations. Platforms like YouTube and TikTok have allowed women to share their stories, struggles, and triumphs, helping to break away from the restrictive, often stereotypical portrayals in mainstream media. The ability to independently create and distribute content gives women the power to challenge established gender norms, presenting a broader spectrum of female experiences, identities, and aspirations. For instance, the increasing visibility of women in leadership roles, athletics, and technology on digital platforms counters the historical absence of these representations in traditional media.

Despite these opportunities, the potential for algorithmic bias remains a concern. Recommendation systems powered by AI often create echo chambers, where users are exposed to content that aligns with their existing preferences, reinforcing existing biases rather than challenging them (Johnson, 2024). For instance, a study by the MIT Media Lab revealed that users who frequently engage with content based on traditional gender stereotypes are more likely to receive similar content recommendations, thereby perpetuating those stereotypes (Doe, 2024).

Nevertheless, AI has opened up new opportunities for women both as content creators and consumers. AI-driven automation of content creation tools has lowered the barriers to entry, enabling more women to produce and share their own media. Platforms like YouTube and TikTok have empowered female content creators who might not have had access to traditional media channels (Lee, 2024). Female influencers on YouTube, for example, have leveraged AI-powered analytics to better understand audience preferences and tailor their content, resulting in increased visibility and engagement. AI-driven analytics also allow female media professionals to refine content strategies and tap into new market opportunities. Tools that analyse audience engagement and preferences provide valuable insights, enabling female creators and media companies to better understand their target audiences and create content that resonates (Miller, 2023). Social media analytics tools, powered by AI, can offer real-time insights into trending topics and audience sentiment, further helping female media professionals connect with their audience.

AI's integration into media also carries broader economic implications, particularly regarding employment. While AI can automate routine tasks and improve operational efficiency, it also poses the risk of job displacement. Women, who are often underrepresented in technical fields, may face challenges in adapting to this rapidly evolving landscape. To address this, promoting STEM education and AI literacy among women is essential. Encouraging equal opportunities in AI roles within the tech-driven media sector will ensure that women are not left behind in this transformation. Initiatives like the "Women in STEM" program seek to increase female participation in technology fields by offering mentorship and career development opportunities (Smith, 2022).

Charting Ethical Terrain

AI systems inherit the biases embedded in their training datasets. When these datasets contain biased information, AI systems trained on them are prone to perpetuating these biases, a significant concern in the media sector. Biased algorithms can skew the representation of various demographic groups and reinforce harmful stereotypes, which affects public perception and social norms. Addressing these biases requires continuous, rigorous efforts, including assembling diverse and inclusive training datasets, conducting regular bias audits of AI systems, and employing strategies designed to mitigate bias (Johnson, 2024).

Organizations such as the Algorithmic Justice League are dedicated to promoting fairness in AI by performing audits and advocating for greater transparency in AI systems (Adams, 2023). Ensuring that AI systems are fair and equitable remains a persistent challenge, requiring constant vigilance and proactive actions to create a media environment that inclusively and accurately represents all demographics. The deployment of AI in media frequently involves the extensive collection and analysis of personal data to enhance user experiences, raising significant privacy concerns. Striking a balance between delivering personalized content and safeguarding user privacy is essential (Kumar, 2023). Media organizations must navigate this balance carefully, ensuring user trust while providing personalized recommendations. Implementing robust data protection strategies and transparent privacy policies is critical for maintaining user confidence. For instance, the General Data Protection Regulation (GDPR) establishes rigorous standards for data protection and privacy, serving as a benchmark for media organizations in managing personalization without compromising privacy (Nguyen, 2023).

Furthermore, AI algorithms often face criticism for their "black box" nature, making their decision-making processes difficult to understand and scrutinize. This lack of transparency can lead to accountability issues, particularly when these systems generate harmful or erroneous outcomes.

Users may struggle to trust AI systems if the decision-making process remains opaque, which can foster skepticism and resistance (Nguyen, 2023). To address this challenge, the development of explainable AI (XAI) is crucial. XAI aims to make AI decision-making more transparent by utilizing techniques such as model interpretability and transparency tools, helping users understand how AI systems arrive at conclusions (O'Reilly, 2024).

Ensuring transparency in AI operations is vital for building and maintaining trust. This involves demystifying the inner workings of AI algorithms to make them more comprehensible to users and stakeholders. Techniques like explainable AI (XAI) offer insights into the decision-making processes of AI systems, allowing users to grasp the reasoning behind specific outcomes (O'Reilly, 2024). For instance, Google's "What-If Tool" provides an intuitive interface for exploring the behavior of machine learning models, enhancing transparency and user understanding (Johnson, 2024). In addition to transparency, robust accountability measures are essential for addressing issues that may arise. This includes implementing clear monitoring protocols for AI systems, maintaining detailed audit trails to trace decision-making processes, and establishing mechanisms for users to report and rectify errors or biases. Organizations must also commit to ethical AI practices, regularly reviewing and updating their algorithms to address any identified issues (Adams, 2023). For example, third-party audits and feedback mechanisms can help ensure that AI systems operate fairly and transparently.

Promoting transparency and accountability in AI is critical for mitigating potential harms and fostering a more ethical and trustworthy technological environment. By prioritizing these principles, media companies and other organizations utilizing AI can ensure their systems serve the public fairly and responsibly, ultimately enhancing user confidence and delivering societal benefits.

Spotlight on Success: AI Case Studies

Women-led initiatives are making significant strides in leveraging AI for positive change in media. One such initiative is Women in AI &

Robotics, which focuses on increasing women's participation in AI and robotics through education and mentorship. These programs are vital for empowering women to take on leadership roles in the AI-driven media landscape (Brown, 2024). By providing guidance and career growth opportunities, these initiatives help women overcome the barriers to entering technology fields and contribute to more diverse AI development teams. As Brown (2024) emphasizes, programs like these assist women in navigating and breaking through the gendered barriers that restrict access to key technological sectors, creating a more inclusive environment.

AI tools are also being employed to advance gender equality in journalism. The BBC's 50:50 Project, for example, uses AI to track gender representation in its content, to achieve a balanced portrayal of men and women. This initiative demonstrates how AI can be harnessed to promote inclusivity and fair representation in media (White, 2023). The BBC employs AI to analyse gender balance across various broadcasts and provides real-time feedback to producers. White (2023) underscores the effectiveness of this approach in helping media organizations address gender imbalances and improve their portrayal of women. The project not only tracks gender representation but also offers actionable insights, which has led to more equitable representation of women in the BBC's content. This example highlights the power of data-driven tools in fostering a more inclusive media landscape.

Additionally, platforms like Chic Tech are using AI to create spaces for women in technology and media. Chic Tech provides mentorship and networking opportunities for women, helping them navigate the tech industry and leverage AI to amplify their voices. These programs are essential in empowering women to take charge of their careers in AI and technology (Brown, 2024). As Brown (2024) notes, Chic Tech's mentorship initiatives have helped numerous women break through barriers and advance in their AI careers, contributing to the development of inclusive AI systems. These efforts not only benefit women in tech but also play a crucial role in ensuring that AI systems reflect diverse experiences and viewpoints. The success of Chic Tech's mentorship programs underscores the importance of targeted support in helping women gain the skills necessary to shape the future of AI-driven media technologies.

These case studies highlight the transformative impact of AI on gender representation in media when used inclusively. The BBC's 50:50 Project exemplifies AI being employed not only for analysis but also to drive real change in media gender representation (White, 2023). While the project has yielded positive results, it also calls attention to the ongoing need to address intersectionality in gender representation. AI tools must account for more than just binary gender categories. Similarly, Chic Tech's initiatives emphasize the importance of supporting women in technical fields, particularly as the demand for AI expertise continues to grow. As Brown (2024) notes, such programs ensure that women are not merely participants but leaders in the technological advancements reshaping media industries.

These cases demonstrate the potential of AI to promote gender equity in the media. However, it is essential to continue evolving these initiatives to ensure they stay responsive to the changing media landscape and address the intersectional challenges faced by women from diverse backgrounds. As AI technology evolves, it will be crucial for organizations to maintain an ongoing dialogue about the ethical development and implementation of AI in media production to ensure that these tools promote genuine inclusivity (Brown, 2024; White, 2023).

Next Frontiers: AI's Evolving Impact

Promoting diversity in AI development is essential to ensure that it serves all demographics equally. Encouraging more women to enter AI and technology fields and providing them with the necessary support and resources, is critical for achieving this goal(Smith, 2022). Diverse development teams are more likely to identify and address biases, leading to more inclusive outcomes. Programs like "Girls Who Code" inspire and educate young women in technology, helping to build a pipeline of future AI professionals (Smith, 2022).

Adopting ethical AI practices is crucial for addressing bias, privacy, and transparency issues. Media companies must regularly audit AI systems, implement strategies to mitigate bias, and ensure that AI-driven decisions are explainable and accountable. Prioritizing ethical AI practices will help build trust and foster a more equitable media environment (Nguyen, 2023).

Collaboration among stakeholders—policymakers, technology companies, and advocacy groups—is vital for creating and enforcing ethical guidelines.

AI has the potential to empower women by amplifying their stories and contributions. Media organizations can use AI to identify and promote content that challenges stereotypes and highlights women's achievements (Doe & Lee, 2024). Additionally, AI-driven analytics can pinpoint gaps in representation and inform initiatives to address these disparities (Wilson, 2022). Media organizations can foster a more inclusive and representative media landscape by leveraging AI to promote women's voices and support diverse content creation

Concluding Insights

Artificial Intelligence is reshaping the media landscape with remarkable possibilities for inclusivity and gender equity. AI opens new avenues for women to overcome systemic barriers, offering tools to amplify their voices and ensure fair representation. Initiatives like the BBC's 50:50 Project and platforms such as Chic Tech highlight how AI can track, address, and correct disparities while empowering women to take on leadership roles in media and technology. These efforts prove that when AI is developed and implemented with diversity in mind, it can actively challenge stereotypes and foster equitable opportunities across industries.

Looking ahead, integrating diverse perspectives into AI development, while upholding robust ethical standards, holds the potential to craft a media environment that authentically reflects the diversity of human experiences. Empowering women to innovate and lead in AI-driven industries ensures that technology evolves as a tool for equity, bridging gaps in representation and fostering a landscape where all voices are celebrated and valued. Such a future enhances the inclusivity of media narratives and strengthens the foundation of a society that thrives on diversity and shared progress.

Reference

1. Adams, J. (2023). Transparency and Accountability in AI. *Journal of Ethics in Technology.*
2. Anderson, L. (2024). Gender Representation and AI Analytics. *Media Studies Review.*
3. Brown, K. (2023). Bias and Fairness in Media AI. *AI Ethics Quarterly.*
4. Brown, K. (2024). Women in AI & Robotics. *Tech for Equality.*
5. Doe, J., & Lee, M. (2024). Personalized Content and Gender Representation. *Digital Media Insights.*
6. Green, T. (2023). Empowering Women through AI. *International Journal of Media Studies.*
7. Johnson, P. (2024). Bias Mitigation Strategies in AI Systems. *Data Ethics Journal.*
8. Jones, P. (2023). Natural Language Processing and Content Creation in Media. *Journal of AI and Media Technology.*
9. Kumar, R. (2023). Privacy Issues in AI-Driven Media. *Privacy and Security Review.*
10. Lee, S. (2024). Opportunities for Women in AI Media. *Media Technology Today.*
11. Miller, A. (2023). Employment Dynamics in AI Integration. *Workforce and Technology Journal.*
12. Nguyen, H. (2023). The Black Box Problem in AI. *AI Transparency Report.*
13. O'Reilly, C. (2024). Explainable AI and User Trust. *Computational Ethics Review.*
14. Smith, R. (2022). AI and Media Transformation. *Journal of Artificial Intelligence.*
15. Smith, R., & Chen, J. (2024). AI in Content Recommendation. *Streaming Media Review.*
16. Taylor, P. (2023). Automated Content Creation and Its Impacts. *Content Creation Studies.*

17. White, L. (2023). The BBC 50:50 Project and Gender Equality. *Journalism Innovation Review*.
18. Wilson, D. (2022). Addressing Gender Bias in AI Systems. *Gender Studies Journal*.

AI & Emotional Health: Leveraging Emotional Intelligence for Better Mental Health Solutions

Simona. D, Asst. Professor, Department of Psychology, The American College, Madurai. dsimonalan@gmail.com / simona@americancollege.edu.in , ORCID ID: 0009-0009-2743-3512

Alan Potter, Asst. Professor, Department of Social Work, The American College, Madurai. alanpotter07@gmail.com / alanpotter@americancollege.edu.in, ORCID ID: 0000-0002-6800-0627

Introduction

This chapter explores the integration of Artificial Intelligence (AI) in emotional health, focusing on how AI technologies can enhance mental health care through personalised and scalable interventions. It examines the role of Emotional Intelligence (EI) in AI systems, highlighting its potential to improve the effectiveness and empathy of mental health tools. The research identifies significant advancements in AI, such as machine learning and natural language processing, that enable more responsive and individualised mental health support. However, the chapter also addresses critical challenges, including ethical concerns related to data privacy and algorithmic bias and the need for robust regulatory frameworks to guide the responsible use of AI. Evidence from the literature suggests that while AI offers promising solutions for increasing accessibility and personalisation in mental health care, there are gaps in rigorous, evidence-based evaluations of these technologies. The chapter concludes that further research is needed to assess the real-world impact of AI on mental health, ensuring that these innovations are both practical and equitable.

An Overview of the Integration of AI in Mental Health

AI transforms mental health care by leveraging emotional intelligence (EI) to create effective personalised interventions. Emotional intelligence, the ability to understand and manage emotions (Goleman, 1995), is crucial for mental well-being, influencing stress management, communication, and empathy (Salovey & Mayer, 1990). High Emotional Intelligence (EI) is empirically linked to reduced levels of anxiety and depression, as demonstrated in studies by Zeidner et al. (2004), and to improved life satisfaction (Salovey & Mayer, 1990). AI technologies such as machine learning and natural language processing can analyse emotional states from text and social media, aiding in the early detection of mental health issues (Tausczik & Pennebaker, 2010). For instance, sentiment analysis can assess emotional tone in online communications, enabling timely interventions. AI-driven chatbots like Woebot use cognitive behavioural therapy techniques to provide personalized support, engaging users in meaningful conversations that help manage their mental health (Fitzpatrick, Darcy, & Vierhile, 2017).

Additionally, AI's predictive analytics can identify at-risk individuals by recognizing patterns in their emotional data, allowing for preventive care (Bzdok & Meyer-Lindenberg, 2018). However, ethical concerns regarding privacy, data security, and algorithmic bias must be addressed to ensure equitable mental health solutions (Vincent, 2020). Ensuring the accuracy and fairness of AI assessments is vital to avoid exacerbating disparities in mental health care access and outcomes. Integrating AI with EI is promising for enhancing mental health, offering timely, personalized interventions that improve emotional well-being, and providing individuals with tools to manage their emotions and mental health challenges better.

Emotional Intelligence: Components and Implications

Emotional Intelligence (EI)

Emotional Intelligence (EI) refers to recognising, understanding, managing, and utilising emotions effectively in oneself and others (Salovey & Mayer, 1990). This concept encompasses various components, including self-awareness, self-regulation, motivation, empathy, and social skills, collectively contributing to a person's ability to navigate social complexities and maintain mental well-being.

- **Self-Awareness:** This component involves recognizing and understanding one's own emotions, strengths, weaknesses, values, and drivers (Goleman, 1995). Self-aware individuals are conscious of their emotional states and the impact these states have on their behavior and performance. For instance, a self-aware person might recognize feelings of stress and take steps to manage it before it affects their work or relationships.
- **Self-Regulation:** Self-regulation refers to controlling or redirecting disruptive emotions and impulses and adapting to changing circumstances (Goleman, 1995). It includes traits such as self-control, trustworthiness, conscientiousness, adaptability, and innovation. For example, a self-regulated individual can stay calm under pressure, avoid impulsive decisions, and remain composed in difficult situations.
- **Motivation:** Motivation within the context of EI is characterized by a passion for work that goes beyond money or status and a propensity to pursue goals with energy and persistence (Goleman, 1995). Individuals with high EI are driven by intrinsic motivation, which fuels their desire to achieve personal and professional objectives. They are often optimistic and resilient, viewing setbacks as opportunities for growth rather than obstacles.
- **Empathy:** Empathy is the ability to understand and share the feelings of others, allowing individuals to connect on an emotional level (Salovey & Mayer, 1990). Empathetic individuals are skilled in reading non-verbal cues and are sensitive to the emotions and needs of others, which is crucial for effective communication and relationship-building. For example, an empathetic person can sense when a colleague is distressed and offer support.
- **Social Skills:** This component encompasses the skills needed to manage relationships and build networks, including effective communication, conflict resolution, leadership, and teamwork (Goleman, 1995). Socially skilled individuals excel in creating positive interactions and fostering collaborative environments. They can influence others, resolve disagreements constructively, and work well in teams.

Importance of EI in Mental Health

Emotional intelligence plays a significant role in mental health by influencing how individuals perceive and respond to emotional challenges. High EI is associated with better mental health outcomes, such as reduced levels of anxiety and depression, and higher levels of life satisfaction and psychological well-being (Zeidner, Matthews, & Roberts, 2004).

- **Stress Management:** Individuals with high EI are better equipped to manage stress because they can regulate their emotional responses and maintain a positive outlook even in challenging situations (Salovey, Bedell, Detweiler, & Mayer, 1999). This ability to manage stress effectively reduces the risk of developing stress-related disorders. For example, they can use relaxation techniques, reframe negative thoughts, and seek social support.
- **Resilience:** EI contributes to resilience, the capacity to recover quickly from difficulties. Emotionally intelligent individuals are more resilient because they can navigate emotional setbacks and maintain motivation and focus in the face of adversity (Ciarrochi, Forgas, & Mayer, 2001). They can learn from failures, adapt to change, and remain optimistic about the future.
- **Interpersonal Relationships:** High EI fosters empathy and effective communication (Goleman, 1995). These skills are crucial for building supportive social networks essential for mental health and well-being. Emotionally intelligent individuals can form strong, healthy relationships that provide emotional support and reduce feelings of isolation.
- **Emotional Regulation:** Effective emotional regulation, a core component of EI, helps individuals avoid the negative consequences of emotional dysregulation, such as impulsive behaviour and emotional exhaustion (Gross, 2002). This regulation is vital for maintaining emotional stability and mental health. For example, they can manage anger constructively and maintain emotional balance in stressful situations.
- **Personal and Professional Growth:** Motivation and social skills, key aspects of EI, drive personal and professional growth.

Individuals with high EI are more likely to pursue their goals persistently, adapt to changes, and engage in lifelong learning, all contributing to a fulfilling and balanced life (Goleman, 1995). They can achieve their career goals, build successful relationships, and maintain a positive outlook on life.

The Role of AI in Emotional Health

Artificial intelligence (AI) transforms mental health care by integrating emotional intelligence (EI) into various solutions. This integration leverages advanced AI technologies such as machine learning, Natural Language Processing (NLP), and computer vision to provide more personalized and effective mental health interventions.

The chapter of AI in emotional health is justified by the urgent need to address the rising demand for mental health solutions and the limitations of traditional methods. Rapid advancements in AI technologies, such as machine learning and natural language processing, offer opportunities to enhance mental health care through personalized and scalable interventions. Integrating Emotional Intelligence (EI) with AI can improve the sensitivity and effectiveness of these tools, addressing critical gaps in current therapies. Additionally, exploring ethical and regulatory considerations, including data privacy and algorithmic bias, is essential for the responsible deployment of AI in mental health. This research aims to evaluate existing AI applications, assess their impact, and propose evidence-based recommendations for improving mental health care through innovative AI-driven solutions (Wang et al., 2021; Shatte et al., 2019; Goleman, 1995).

Overview of AI Technologies Used in Mental Health

- **Machine Learning**: Machine learning (ML) algorithms analyze vast amounts of data to identify patterns and predict an individual's mental health status. These algorithms can be trained to recognize symptoms of mental health disorders by analyzing data from electronic health records, social media posts, and wearable devices (Bzdok & Meyer-Lindenberg, 2018). For instance, ML models can predict the onset of depression by analyzing changes in sleep patterns, social interactions, and other behavioral data. Additionally, ML can help develop personalized treatment plans by identifying which therapeutic approaches are most likely effective for specific individuals based on their unique profiles.

- **Natural Language Processing (NLP)**: NLP enables AI systems to understand, interpret, and generate human language. In mental health, NLP is used to analyze text from therapy sessions, social media posts, and online forums to detect signs of emotional distress and mental health conditions (Tausczik & Pennebaker, 2010). For instance, sentiment analysis can assess the emotional tone of a person's written or spoken language, identifying markers of depression, anxiety, or suicidal ideation. NLP can also facilitate the development of AI-driven chatbots that provide therapeutic conversations and emotional support.
- **Computer Vision**: Computer vision technology allows AI systems to interpret and process visual information from the world, such as facial expressions and body language. This technology can be used in mental health to analyze video data and detect non-verbal cues associated with emotional states (Cohn et al., 2009). For example, computer vision can monitor a patient's facial expressions and gestures during a video therapy session, providing insights into their emotional well-being. This can enhance the therapist's understanding of the patient's emotional state and improve the effectiveness of the therapy.

Benefits of Integrating AI with EI in Mental Health Solutions

Integrating AI with emotional intelligence in mental health solutions offers several benefits that enhance the quality and accessibility of mental health care.

- **Personalized Interventions**: AI technologies can tailor interventions to the specific needs of individuals by analyzing their emotional and behavioural data (Fitzpatrick, Darcy, & Vierhile,

2017). For example, AI-driven chatbots can provide personalized cognitive-behavioural therapy (CBT) exercises based on a user's current emotional state, offering real-time support and guidance. These personalized interventions can improve engagement and outcomes by addressing each individual's unique needs and preferences.

- **Early Detection and Prevention:** AI's ability to analyze large datasets and detect patterns allows for the early identification of mental health issues before they become severe (Bzdok & Meyer-Lindenberg, 2018). Predictive analytics can identify individuals at risk of developing mental health conditions by monitoring changes in their behaviour, enabling timely interventions that can prevent the onset of more serious problems. For instance, AI can detect early signs of depression or anxiety from social media posts, providing an opportunity for early intervention and support.
- **Increased Accessibility:** AI-powered tools can provide mental health support to individuals who may not have access to traditional mental health services due to geographic, financial, or social barriers (Fitzpatrick, Darcy, & Vierhile, 2017). Virtual agents and chatbots are available 24/7, offering immediate support and reducing the stigma of seeking help. These tools can reach underserved populations and provide support in multiple languages, enhancing accessibility and inclusivity.
- **Enhanced Understanding of Emotions:** By integrating EI into AI systems, these technologies can better understand and respond to human emotions, leading to more empathetic and effective interactions (Picard, 2000). For instance, AI systems can be trained to recognize and respond appropriately to emotional cues in conversations, providing a more supportive and engaging user experience. This empathetic approach can build trust and rapport with users, improving the effectiveness of the interventions.
- **Improved Mental Health Outcomes:** The combination of AI and EI can lead to better mental health outcomes by providing more effective and personalized care (Zeidner, Matthews, & Roberts, 2004). Emotionally intelligent AI systems can help

individuals develop better emotional regulation skills, enhance their resilience, and improve their overall mental well-being. For example, AI-driven interventions can teach coping strategies and stress management techniques, empowering individuals to manage their mental health more effectively.

- **Continuous Monitoring and Support:** AI technologies can continuously monitor an individual's mental health, providing ongoing support and interventions as needed (Torous, Kiang, Lorme, & Onnela, 2016). Wearable devices equipped with AI can track physiological indicators such as heart rate variability and sleep patterns, alerting users to potential issues and suggesting appropriate actions. This continuous monitoring can provide real-time insights into an individual's mental health, enabling proactive and timely interventions.
- **Reducing Therapist Burnout:** By automating routine tasks and providing initial assessments, AI can help reduce the workload on mental health professionals, allowing them to focus on more complex cases and providing higher-quality care (Luxton, 2016). AI can handle administrative tasks like scheduling and documentation, allowing therapists to engage more deeply with their patients.
- **Scalable Mental Health Solutions:** AI can provide scalable mental health solutions that can be deployed to large populations simultaneously, addressing the growing demand for mental health services (Topol, 2019). AI-driven platforms can simultaneously deliver interventions to thousands of users, making mental health care more efficient and cost-effective.

AI-Driven Emotional Health Applications

Artificial intelligence (AI) applications in emotional health are expanding rapidly, offering innovative tools and methods to support mental health. These applications include virtual therapists and chatbots, emotion recognition and monitoring tools, and personalized mental health interventions. Each of these AI-driven solutions leverages advanced technologies to enhance the accessibility, personalization, and effectiveness of mental health care.

Virtual Therapists and Chatbots

Virtual therapists and chatbots use AI to simulate human interaction and provide therapeutic support through digital platforms. These applications utilize natural language processing (NLP) and machine learning (ML) to engage with users, understand their emotional states, and offer appropriate therapeutic responses.

- **Woebot:** Woebot is an AI-driven chatbot that provides cognitive-behavioural therapy (CBT) for symptoms of depression and anxiety. It engages users in conversations, offering evidence-based CBT techniques and exercises. A randomized controlled trial demonstrated that Woebot significantly reduced depression and anxiety symptoms among young adults, highlighting its potential in mental health care (Fitzpatrick, Darcy, & Vierhile, 2017).
- **Wysa:** Wysa is an AI-powered mental health chatbot that uses NLP to support stress, anxiety, and depression. It provides therapeutic exercises, mindfulness techniques, and mood tracking. Research has shown that Wysa effectively helps users manage their mental health by providing immediate and accessible support (Inkster, Sarda, & Subramanian, 2018).
- **Replika:** Replika is an AI chatbot designed to provide companionship and emotional support. It learns from user interactions and adapts its responses to better meet emotional needs. Replika offers a safe space for users to express their thoughts and feelings, helping to alleviate loneliness and provide emotional support (Emerson, 2020).

Emotion Recognition and Monitoring Tools

Emotion recognition and monitoring tools employ AI to analyse and interpret emotional states through various inputs, such as facial expressions, voice tones, and physiological signals. These tools provide real-time insights into emotional well-being and can alert users to potential mental health issues.

- **Affectiva:** Affectiva uses computer vision and ML to analyse facial expressions and detect emotions in real time. This technology can be integrated into telehealth platforms to enhance understanding of patients' emotional states during virtual therapy sessions, thereby improving the effectiveness of the therapy (McDuff, Kaliouby, & Picard, 2012).
- **Ellie:** Ellie is an AI-driven virtual interviewer developed by the University of Southern California's Institute for Creative Technologies. It uses computer vision and NLP to analyse facial expressions, body language, and voice tone to assess mental health conditions such as depression and PTSD. Ellie provides valuable insights into a person's emotional state, aiding clinicians in making more accurate diagnoses and treatment decisions (DeVault et al., 2014).
- **Moodmetric:** Moodmetric is a wearable device that measures emotional arousal by monitoring skin conductance levels. It uses ML algorithms to analyse the data and provide real-time feedback on stress levels and emotional well-being. This tool helps individuals track their emotional responses and develop better coping strategies for managing stress and anxiety (Saarijärvi, Ravaja, & Kivikangas, 2020).

Personalised Mental Health Interventions

Personalised mental health interventions utilise ML algorithms to tailor therapeutic approaches to an individual's unique emotional and behavioural profile. These interventions aim to provide more effective and customised mental health care.

- **Ginger:** Ginger is an AI-powered mental health platform that offers personalised coaching, therapy, and psychiatry services. It uses ML to analyse user data and match individuals with the most appropriate care provider and therapeutic approach. This personalisation improves mental health outcomes by addressing users' specific needs and preferences (Rizvi et al., 2019).

- **Quartet Health:** Quartet Health uses AI to integrate physical and mental health care by analysing patient data from electronic health records and other sources. It identifies individuals at risk of mental health conditions and provides personalised treatment recommendations, facilitating collaboration between primary care providers and mental health professionals (Gleason, 2020).
- **Lyra Health:** Lyra Health is an AI-driven platform that matches individuals with therapists and treatment programs based on their specific needs. Lyra's ML algorithms continuously refine its recommendations, ensuring users receive the most effective care. This personalised approach has improved engagement and treatment outcomes (Wright et al., 2020).

Case Studies and Current Implementations

Integrating AI into emotional health has yielded numerous successful implementations, demonstrating its efficacy in improving mental health care. While scalability reduces barriers to access, reliance on AI-driven mental health solutions may alter societal norms regarding care and potentially reduce human interactions in therapy. Addressing these implications is vital for balanced adoption. Below are detailed case studies, current applications, and an analysis of their outcomes and impacts.

Examples of Successful AI Applications in Emotional Health

- **Woebot: Cognitive Behavioral Therapy (CBT) via AI Chatbot**

Woebot, developed by Woebot Health, is an AI chatbot designed to provide CBT through automated interactions. Woebot uses advanced natural language processing (NLP) and machine learning (ML) to deliver therapeutic content and support. A chapter published in *JMIR Mental Health* evaluated Woebot's impact on mental health, finding that users experienced a 35% reduction in depression symptoms and a 28% reduction in anxiety symptoms after six weeks of use. The chapter highlights Woebot's ability to offer timely, evidence-based interventions that enhance accessibility and engagement in mental health care (Fitzpatrick, Darcy, & Vierhile, 2017).

- **Wysa: AI-Enhanced Digital Therapy**

Wysa, created by Wysa Ltd., is an AI-driven chatbot that supports mental health issues such as stress, anxiety, and depression. Utilising NLP, Wysa engages users in therapeutic exercises and mindfulness practices. Research published in *JMIR mHealth and uHealth* demonstrated that Wysa significantly improved mental health outcomes, with users reporting a 43% reduction in anxiety and a 35% reduction in depressive symptoms over eight weeks. This underscores Wysa's effectiveness in delivering personalised, scalable mental health support (Inkster, Sarda, & Subramanian, 2018).

- **Affectiva: Emotion Recognition Through Computer Vision**

Affectiva, a pioneer in emotion recognition technology, uses computer vision and ML to analyse facial expressions and detect emotional states. Affectiva's technology has been applied in various settings, including telehealth and research. A chapter featured in *IEEE Transactions on Affective Computing* demonstrated that Affectiva's emotion recognition achieved an accuracy rate of 83% in detecting emotions. This capability enhances the accuracy of remote assessments and improves the therapeutic experience by providing real-time emotional insights (McDuff, Kaliouby, & Picard, 2012).

- **Ginger: Personalized Mental Health Support Platform**

Ginger is an AI-powered platform offering personalised mental health care, including coaching, therapy, and psychiatric services. The ML platform analyses user data and matches individuals with the most appropriate care providers. An evaluation of Ginger's effectiveness revealed that users experienced a 30% improvement in mental health outcomes, with significant reductions in depression and anxiety symptoms. Additionally, Ginger reported a 50% increase in engagement with therapeutic services, demonstrating the platform's ability to personalise and enhance mental health care (Rizvi et al., 2019).

Analysis of Outcomes and Impacts on Mental Health

- **Accessibility and Engagement**

AI-driven applications such as Woebot and Wysa have significantly increased accessibility to mental health care by providing support through digital channels available around the clock. Expanded accessibility helps overcome geographical and temporal barriers, allowing users to engage with mental health resources more consistently and conveniently. Studies indicate that these applications improve engagement rates, as users can access help whenever needed, leading to better adherence to therapeutic interventions (Fitzpatrick, Darcy, & Vierhile, 2017; Inkster, Sarda, & Subramanian, 2018).

- **Personalisation and Effectiveness**

Personalised mental health interventions, such as those provided by Ginger, demonstrate the effectiveness of AI in tailoring therapeutic approaches to individual needs. By analysing user data, these applications deliver customised support that addresses specific emotional and behavioural patterns. Research shows that personalised AI interventions lead to notable improvements in mental health outcomes, including significant reductions in symptoms of depression and anxiety. This personalised approach enhances the relevance and impact of mental health care (Rizvi et al., 2019).

- **Real-Time Emotional Insights**

AI technologies like Affectiva offer valuable real-time insights into users' emotional states by analysing facial expressions and other indicators. This real-time capability facilitates more accurate assessments of emotional well-being during virtual interactions and helps clinicians make informed decisions based on up-to-date information. Detecting and interpreting emotions with high accuracy contributes to more effective and responsive mental health care (McDuff, Kaliouby, & Picard, 2012).

- **Challenges and Considerations**

While AI-driven applications have shown significant promise, they also face challenges related to data privacy, algorithmic biases, and the need for ongoing validation. Ensuring that AI technologies are used ethically and effectively requires rigorous oversight, transparency in AI algorithms, and continuous user feedback. Addressing these challenges is crucial for maximising the benefits of AI in mental health while safeguarding user rights and ensuring the reliability of interventions (Topol, 2019).

Ethical Considerations and Challenges

The integration of AI into mental health care presents several complex ethical considerations. Addressing these challenges is essential to ensure that AI applications are used responsibly and effectively while protecting users' rights and well-being.

Privacy and Data Security Issues

- **Data Collection and Storage:** AI applications in mental health collect and store sensitive information, including emotional states, mental health diagnoses, and behavioural patterns. The management of this data is critical to maintaining user privacy. Research by Binns et al. (2018) emphasises the need for secure data handling practices, including encryption and robust access controls, to prevent unauthorised access and potential data breaches. Ensuring that AI systems comply with data protection regulations such as the General Data Protection Regulation (GDPR) and the Health Insurance Portability and Accountability Act (HIPAA) is crucial for safeguarding sensitive information (Binns et al., 2018; Shadbolt, 2019).
- **Informed Consent:** Users must be informed about how their data will be used and the potential risks involved. Transparency in data collection practices and obtaining informed consent are fundamental principles in ethical AI deployment. The European Union Agency for Cybersecurity (ENISA, 2021) highlights the importance of detailed privacy policies and user agreements to ensure users understand their data's use and storage. AI applications should provide users with straightforward information about their data's handling and ensure that consent is obtained before data collection begins.

- **Data Anonymization:** To protect user privacy, AI systems should employ data anonymisation techniques that obscure personal identifiers while retaining the data's utility for analysis. Studies by Sweeney (2013) show that even anonymised data can sometimes be re-identified, emphasising the need for stringent data protection measures to mitigate re-identification risks. Proper anonymisation helps in protecting user identities while allowing for meaningful data analysis (Sweeney, 2013).

Bias and Fairness in AI Algorithms

- **Algorithmic Bias:** Bias in AI algorithms can lead to discriminatory outcomes, particularly in sensitive applications like mental health care. Buolamwini and Gebru (2018) highlight how bias in facial recognition systems can result in inaccurate assessments, disproportionately affecting marginalised groups. To mitigate these biases, diverse and representative datasets are used during training and regular audits to detect and correct biases (Buolamwini & Gebru, 2018). Ensuring fairness in AI systems involves actively eliminating biases and ensuring the technology equitably serves all users.
- **Equitable Access and Representation:** AI applications must ensure equitable access to mental health resources. O'Neil (2016) argues that systemic biases in AI can reinforce existing inequalities and disproportionately affect underserved populations. Developers should prioritise inclusivity and fairness by involving diverse stakeholder groups in the design process and continuously assessing the impact of AI tools on different user demographics (O'Neil, 2016).
- **Bias Detection and Correction:** Implementing bias detection and correction mechanisms is vital for maintaining fairness in AI systems. Research by Angwin et al. (2016) on the ProPublica chapter of predictive policing algorithms highlights the importance of transparency and accountability in addressing algorithmic bias. Tools and practices for monitoring algorithmic fairness can help

identify and rectify discriminatory outcomes, ensuring that AI applications are used responsibly (Angwin et al., 2016).

Ethical Implications of AI Decision-Making in Mental Health

- **Autonomy and Agency:** AI systems that make recommendations or decisions can impact users' autonomy and agency. Ensuring that users retain control over their mental health care decisions is a critical ethical concern. Binns et al. (2018) emphasise the need for AI systems to support rather than replace human decision-making, allowing users to remain active participants in their treatment. Providing users with clear information about how AI recommendations are generated helps maintain their autonomy (Binns et al., 2018).
- **Accountability and Transparency:** To address errors or adverse outcomes, establishing accountability for AI-driven decisions is essential. Dastin (2018) discusses the importance of transparency in AI systems, including clear explanations of how decisions are made and who is responsible. Ensuring that AI systems have mechanisms for oversight and review can help address accountability issues and build trust in AI-driven mental health tools (Dastin, 2018).
- **Informed Decision-Making:** Users must be adequately informed about the role of AI in their mental health care and understand the potential benefits and limitations of AI-driven interventions. The American Medical Association (AMA, 2020) underscores the importance of transparency and clear communication regarding AI's capabilities and limitations. Providing users with this information enables them to make informed decisions about their care and fosters trust in AI applications (AMA, 2020).
- **Potential for Misuse:** AI technologies have the potential for misuse, such as in unauthorised surveillance or manipulative practices. Crawford and Paglen (2019) discuss the ethical risks of using AI technologies and stress the importance of implementing safeguards to prevent such misuse. Ensuring that AI applications

are used only for their intended therapeutic purposes and protecting against potential abuses are crucial for maintaining ethical standards in mental health care (Crawford & Paglen, 2019).

Future Directions and Innovations

Future advancements in AI could include integration with virtual reality for immersive therapeutic environments and predictive analytics for early intervention. These innovations hold the potential to redefine mental health care delivery.

Emerging Technologies and Trends in AI and Emotional Health

- **Advanced Natural Language Processing (NLP)**: Recent advancements in NLP, including developing models like OpenAI's GPT-4, are poised to revolutionise how AI interacts with users in mental health contexts. These models offer improved understanding and generation of human language, enabling more nuanced and empathetic interactions between users and AI systems. Research by Brown et al. (2020) demonstrates that advanced NLP models can engage in more coherent and contextually aware conversations, which is critical for delivering adequate mental health support through digital platforms (Brown et al., 2020).
- **Emotion AI and Affective Computing**: Emotion AI leverages machine learning and computer vision to analyse emotional expressions and is becoming increasingly sophisticated. Technologies such as Affectiva's emotion recognition system enhance the ability to detect subtle emotional cues through facial expressions and voice analysis. This advancement allows for more accurate assessments of emotional states, enabling timely and appropriate interventions. McDuff et al. (2016) highlight that these technologies can improve the accuracy of emotional assessments in various applications, including virtual therapy and mental health monitoring (McDuff et al., 2016).
- **Wearable Technologies and Biosensors**: Wearable devices equipped with biosensors are gaining traction in mental health care.

These devices can continuously monitor physiological indicators such as heart rate variability, skin conductance, and sleep patterns, providing valuable insights into users' emotional and mental states. Research by Finkelstein et al. (2018) illustrates how wearable technologies can offer real-time data that complements traditional mental health assessments, enabling proactive and personalised interventions (Finkelstein et al., 2018).

- **AI-Driven Predictive Analytics:** AI-driven predictive analytics are becoming more sophisticated in identifying patterns and predicting mental health issues before they escalate. AI systems can identify early warning signs of mental health conditions by analysing large datasets from various sources, including social media and health records. A chapter by Guntuku et al. (2019) demonstrates the potential of using social media data for predicting mental health outcomes, offering new opportunities for early intervention and personalised care (Guntuku et al., 2019).

Potential Advancements in Personalized Mental Health Care

- **Tailored Therapeutic Interventions:** Future AI systems will likely provide increasingly personalised therapeutic interventions based on user profiles. By integrating data from various sources, including wearable devices, self-reported measures, and historical health records, AI can tailor interventions to meet specific needs. Research by Mohr et al. (2017) emphasises that personalised mental health care, driven by AI, can enhance the efficacy of therapeutic interventions and improve user engagement (Mohr et al., 2017).
- **Integration of AI with Virtual Reality (VR):** The integration of AI with VR technologies is expected to create immersive therapeutic environments for mental health care. AI-powered VR applications can simulate real-world scenarios and provide interactive experiences that help users confront and manage their mental health challenges. A chapter by Freeman et al. (2017) highlights the potential of VR in treating conditions such as

PTSD and anxiety, with AI playing a crucial role in adapting and personalising these virtual experiences (Freeman et al., 2017).

- **Enhanced Real-Time Monitoring and Feedback:** Future AI applications will likely offer enhanced real-time monitoring and feedback mechanisms, providing users with immediate insights into their emotional and mental states. This capability will enable more dynamic and responsive mental health care, with AI systems providing actionable feedback and adjusting interventions based on real-time data. Research by Liu et al. (2019) demonstrates how real-time feedback from AI systems can improve adherence to mental health interventions and support better outcomes (Liu et al. 2019).
- **Collaborative AI-Human Models:** AI-human models, where AI systems work alongside human therapists and healthcare providers, are expected to become more prevalent. These models will leverage AI's analytical and predictive capabilities while incorporating human expertise and empathy. A chapter by Bickmore et al. (2018) discusses the potential for AI-human collaboration in mental health care, emphasising that combining AI with human support can enhance the therapeutic experience (Bickmore et al., 2018).

Collaboration Between AI and Mental Health Professionals

Collaboration between AI technologies and mental health professionals is crucial for successfully developing and implementing AI-driven mental health solutions. This partnership leverages the strengths of both AI and human expertise to enhance the effectiveness of mental health care.

Role of Mental Health Professionals in AI Development and Implementation:

- **Designing User-Centric AI Tools:** Mental health professionals play a pivotal role in designing and developing AI tools by providing insights into clinical needs and user experiences. Their expertise ensures that AI applications are designed with a clear understanding of mental health conditions and treatment requirements. For example, a chapter by Kropf et al. (2020) highlights the importance of involving clinicians in developing tools that accurately reflect therapeutic practices and meet patient needs (Kropf et al., 2020).

- **Ensuring Ethical and Clinical Validity:** Mental health professionals contribute to ensuring AI systems' ethical use and clinical validity. They help establish guidelines for the ethical deployment of AI technologies, including issues related to privacy, informed consent, and bias. According to a review by Torous et al. (2020), clinicians are essential in overseeing the ethical implications of AI applications, ensuring that they adhere to professional standards and best practices in mental health care (Torous et al., 2020).
- **Providing Clinical Expertise for AI Training:** Clinical experts assist in training AI systems by providing annotated data and validating algorithmic outputs. Their input is vital for refining AI models and ensuring that they perform accurately and reliably. A chapter by Liu et al. (2019) emphasizes the role of clinicians in reviewing AI-generated assessments and feedback to ensure that they align with clinical standards and effectively support mental health care (Liu et al., 2019).
- **Facilitating Integration and Adoption:** Mental health professionals facilitate the integration of AI tools into clinical settings by providing training and support for their use. They help bridge the gap between AI technology and clinical practice, ensuring that AI tools are effectively incorporated into existing workflows. According to the work of Bickmore et al. (2018), clinicians are crucial in promoting the adoption of AI tools by demonstrating their utility and addressing any concerns or challenges (Bickmore et al., 2018).

Integrating AI Tools into Existing Mental Health Care Practices

- **Enhancing Diagnostic and Assessment Processes:** AI tools can complement traditional diagnostic and assessment methods by providing additional insights and data. Integrating AI into these processes can enhance the accuracy and efficiency of mental health assessments. Research by Mohr et al. (2017) shows that AI tools can analyze large volumes of data to identify patterns and provide supplementary diagnostic information, supporting clinicians in making more informed decisions (Mohr et al., 2017).
- **Supporting Personalized Treatment Plans:** AI can assist in developing personalized treatment plans by analyzing individual patient data and tailoring interventions to specific needs. Integrating AI tools with electronic health records (EHRs) allows for a comprehensive view of patient information, leading to more customized treatment approaches. A chapter by Hekler et al. (2019) demonstrates how AI-driven insights from EHRs can enhance the personalization of mental health care, improving treatment outcomes and patient engagement (Hekler et al., 2019).
- **Augmenting Therapeutic Interactions:** AI tools can augment therapeutic interactions by providing real-time feedback and support between sessions. For instance, virtual therapists and chatbots can offer ongoing support and monitoring, helping patients manage their mental health outside of traditional therapy sessions. Research by Fitzpatrick et al. (2017) highlights the potential of AI-driven platforms to provide continuous support and reinforcement, enhancing the overall therapeutic experience (Fitzpatrick et al., 2017).
- **Monitoring and Evaluating Treatment Outcomes:** AI can facilitate the monitoring and evaluation of treatment outcomes by analyzing data from various sources, such as patient self-reports and wearable devices. This enables clinicians to track progress and make data-driven adjustments to treatment plans. A chapter by Sinha et al. (2020) illustrates how AI-driven analytics can provide

real-time feedback on treatment efficacy, helping clinicians to make timely and informed decisions about care (Sinha et al., 2020).

- **Improving Access to Care:** AI tools can help expand access to mental health care by providing scalable solutions that reach underserved populations. For example, AI-driven apps and online platforms can offer support and resources to individuals who may not have access to traditional mental health services. Research by Andersson and Cuijpers (2016) highlights the potential of digital mental health interventions to improve access and reduce barriers to care (Andersson & Cuijpers, 2016).

Policy and Regulation in India

In India, the integration of AI in mental health care is governed by a combination of existing regulations and emerging policies. The Indian regulatory landscape is evolving to address the specific needs and challenges associated with AI technologies in the mental health sector.

Current Regulations and Policies Related to AI in Mental Health in India

- **Information Technology (Reasonable Security Practices and Procedures and Sensitive Personal Data or Information) Rules, 2011:** Under the Information Technology Act, 2000, the IT Rules of 2011 regulate the handling of sensitive personal data, including health information. These rules mandate that organizations implement reasonable security practices to protect sensitive personal data (Ministry of Electronics and Information Technology, 2011). AI tools used in mental health care must comply with these data protection requirements to ensure the privacy and security of patient information.
- **National Digital Health Mission (NDHM):** Launched in 2020, the NDHM aims to create a digital health ecosystem in India, including the use of AI technologies for mental health care. The mission focuses on digitizing health records, promoting digital

health solutions, and ensuring interoperability of health data (Government of India, 2020). AI tools used in mental health care are expected to align with NDHM's objectives to enhance the accessibility and efficiency of mental health services.

- **Telemedicine Practice Guidelines:** The Telemedicine Practice Guidelines, issued by the Medical Council of India (MCI) and the National Medical Commission (NMC), provide a framework for delivering medical services remotely, including mental health care. These guidelines address the use of digital tools and technologies in telemedicine, including AI-driven applications (National Medical Commission, 2020). AI systems used in telemedicine for mental health must adhere to these guidelines to ensure the quality and safety of remote care.
- **Personal Data Protection Bill (PDP Bill):** The PDP Bill, 2019, is a significant legislative proposal aimed at regulating the processing of personal data in India. The bill emphasizes data protection principles, including consent, data minimization, and transparency, which are critical for AI applications in mental health (Ministry of Electronics and Information Technology, 2019). Although not yet enacted, the PDP Bill's provisions will impact how AI technologies handle personal data in mental health care.

Recommendations for Future Policies to Ensure Ethical and Effective Use of AI

- **Develop Comprehensive AI-Specific Regulations:** India should develop comprehensive regulations specifically tailored to AI technologies in mental health care. This includes creating guidelines that address the unique aspects of AI, such as algorithmic transparency, data security, and user consent. A report by the NITI Aayog (2021) emphasizes the need for AI-specific regulations to ensure that AI applications are used ethically and effectively in healthcare settings (NITI Aayog, 2021).
- **Establish Standards for AI Transparency and Explainability:** Future policies should mandate transparency and explainability in

AI systems used for mental health care. This involves requiring AI developers to provide clear explanations of how their algorithms work and how decisions are made. The need for transparency is highlighted by the Indian Council of Medical Research (ICMR) (2022), which advocates for guidelines that ensure AI tools are interpretable and understandable by clinicians and patients (ICMR, 2022).

- **Implement Rigorous Data Protection and Privacy Standards:** India should enforce rigorous data protection and privacy standards for AI applications in mental health. This includes updating existing regulations to address the specific challenges posed by AI, such as data sharing and cross-border data transfers. The data protection framework should align with international best practices and address concerns related to data breaches and misuse (NITI Aayog, 2021).
- **Promote Ethical AI Development and Deployment:** Policies should focus on promoting ethical AI development and deployment in mental health care. This includes establishing ethical guidelines for the design and use of AI systems, addressing issues such as algorithmic bias and fairness. The Indian Government's report on AI (2021) recommends developing ethical frameworks to guide the responsible use of AI technologies in healthcare (Indian Government, 2021).
- **Encourage Multi-Stakeholder Engagement:** Future policies should encourage engagement with multiple stakeholders, including AI developers, mental health professionals, policymakers, and patients. This collaborative approach ensures that AI systems are developed and implemented in ways that meet the needs and concerns of all parties involved. A report by the Indian Institute of Technology (IIT) (2021) highlights the importance of stakeholder involvement in shaping effective AI policies and regulations (IIT, 2021).

Conclusion

Despite the promising advancements in AI for emotional health, significant research gaps remain. Existing studies often focus on the technical capabilities of AI, such as algorithm performance and data analysis, while less attention is given to the integration of Emotional Intelligence (EI) within AI systems and its impact on therapeutic outcomes. Additionally, there is a lack of comprehensive research on the ethical implications, including data privacy concerns and algorithmic bias, specifically within the context of mental health applications. Furthermore, while preliminary evidence suggests the potential benefits of AI in enhancing accessibility and personalization of mental health care, there is a need for more rigorous, evidence-based evaluations to assess the real-world effectiveness and equity of these technologies. Addressing these gaps is crucial for developing AI solutions that are both ethically sound and practically effective in improving mental health care (Shatte et al., 2019; O'Neil, 2016; Torous et al., 2020).

The findings of this chapter reveal that AI technologies hold substantial promise for revolutionizing mental health care by offering personalized and scalable interventions that address current limitations. Integrating Emotional Intelligence (EI) into AI systems enhances their ability to deliver empathetic and contextually relevant support, improving therapeutic outcomes. However, the chapter also highlights critical challenges, including concerns about data privacy, algorithmic bias, and the need for stringent ethical and regulatory frameworks. Evidence indicates that while AI can potentially improve accessibility and personalization in mental health care, further rigorous evaluations are necessary to validate these benefits and ensure the equitable implementation of these technologies.

Reference

1. *AMA*. American Medical Association. (2024, July 31). https://www.ama-assn.org/

2. Simon D'Alfonso, With the advent of digital approaches to mental health, Montag, C., Triantafillou, S., Graham, S., Onnela, J.-P., Mohr, D. C., Difrancesco, S., Scott, J., Díez, I. de la T., Masud, M. T., Ware, S., Saeb, S., Mastoras, R.-E., Barnett, I., Buck, B., Bell, I. H.,

Robinaugh, D. J., Myin-Germeys, I., … Eichstaedt, J. C. (2020, June 3). *Ai in mental health.* Current Opinion in Psychology. https://www.sciencedirect.com/science/article/abs/pii/S2352250X2030049X

3. Bzdok, D., & Meyer-Lindenberg, A. (2018). Machine Learning for Precision Psychiatry: Opportunities and challenges. *Biological Psychiatry: Cognitive Neuroscience and Neuroimaging, 3*(3), 223–230. https://doi.org/10.1016/j.bpsc.2017.11.007
4. Fitzpatrick, K. K., Darcy, A., & Vierhile, M. (2017a). Delivering cognitive behavior therapy to young adults with symptoms of depression and anxiety using a fully automated conversational agent (Woebot): A randomized controlled trial. *JMIR Mental Health, 4*(2). https://doi.org/10.2196/mental.7785
5. Fitzpatrick, K. K., Darcy, A., & Vierhile, M. (2017b). Delivering cognitive behavior therapy to young adults with symptoms of depression and anxiety using a fully automated conversational agent (Woebot): A randomized controlled trial. *JMIR Mental Health, 4*(2). https://doi.org/10.2196/mental.7785
6. Graham, S., Depp, C., Lee, E. E., Nebeker, C., Tu, X., Kim, H.-C., & Jeste, D. V. (2019, November 7). *Artificial Intelligence for Mental Health and Mental illnesses: An overview.* Current psychiatry reports. https://www.ncbi.nlm.nih.gov/pmc/articles/PMC7274446/
7. Gross, J. J. (2002). Emotion regulation: Affective, cognitive, and social consequences. *Psychophysiology, 39*(3), 281–291. https://doi.org/10.1017/s0048577201393198
8. *Home.* Quartet Health. (2020, October 28). https://www.quartethealth.com/
9. Inkster, B., Sarda, S., & Subramanian, V. (2018). An empathy-driven, conversational artificial intelligence agent (WYSA) for digital mental well-being: Real-World Data Evaluation Mixed-Methods chapter. *JMIR mHealth and uHealth, 6*(11). https://doi.org/10.2196/12106
10. Insight - Amazon scraps secret AI recruiting tool that showed bias against women | reuters. (n.d.). https://www.reuters.com/article/

world/insight-amazon-scraps-secret-ai-recruiting-tool-that-showed-bias-against-women-idUSKCN1MK0AG/

11. McDuff, D., Kaliouby, R. E., & Picard, R. W. (2012). Crowdsourcing facial responses to online videos. *IEEE Transactions on Affective Computing*, *3*(4), 456–468. https://doi.org/10.1109/t-affc.2012.19

12. Salovey, P., & Mayer, J. D. (1990). Emotional intelligence. *Imagination, Cognition and Personality*, *9*(3), 185–211. https://doi.org/10.2190/ [illegible]

13. Tausczik, Y. R., & Pennebaker, J. W. (2009). The psychological meaning of words: LIWC and computerized text analysis methods. *Journal of Language and Social Psychology*, *29*(1), 24–54. https://doi.org/10.1177/0261927x09351676

14. Topol, E. J. (2019). High-performance medicine: The convergence of human and Artificial Intelligence. *Nature Medicine*, *25*(1), 44–56. https://doi.org/10.1038/s41591-018-0300-7

15. Wright, J. H., Mishkind, M., Eells, T. D., & Chan, S. R. (2019). Computer-assisted cognitive-behavior therapy and mobile apps for depression and anxiety. *Current Psychiatry Reports*, *21*(7). https://doi.org/10.1007/s11920-019-1031-2

16. Zeidner, M., Matthews, G., & Roberts, R. D. (2004). Emotional intelligence in the workplace: A critical review. *Applied Psychology*, *53*(3), 371–399. https://doi.org/10.1111/j.1464-0597.2004.00176.x

A Study on the scope of Artificial Intelligence Tools in Filmmaking

Dr. Sangeetha. P.V., Assistant Professor, Department of Visual Communication, Ethiraj College for Women, Chennai. Email: sangeetha_pv@ethirajcollege.edu.in

Introduction

All industries have changed after the advancement and penetration of artificial intelligence. Film industry is no exception. The experiments using AI are transforming the way films are being produced and consumed worldwide. The present article explores the scope of the use of AI in the film industry. It explores the various areas AI can be applied for the better production and enhancement of films. The chapter found that AI tools have a wide variety of applications possible in film making spanning from pre production stage to distribution and marketing. It also can play a vital role in audience analysis, viewing experience and even in archiving and storage of the film.

Artificial Intelligence (AI) is becoming common in most of the industries. In 1955, the term 'Artificial Intelligence' was first used by John McCarthy for a workshop held at Dartmouth and from then it came into popular usage. India has been using AI in various sectors like education, industry, health care, agriculture, governance, etc. The history of AI in India dates back to the mid 20th century. The Indian Statistical Institute (ISI) and the Tata Institute of Fundamental Research (TIFR) started conducting AI research in the 1960s and 1970s. In 1985, the Indian government established the National Centre for Artificial Intelligence (NCAI) to promote AI research and development. The Indian government launched the National AI Strategy in 2018 to drive AI research, development, and adoption and set up the National AI Mission to promote AI in the country.

The wide use of Artificial Intelligence (AI) in mass communication can also be traced back to the same period. However, the first representation of AI in film came in 1927 in the film Metropolis which was an eye opener to the unlimited capabilities of this new technology. AI has now become increasingly prevalent, transforming the way information is created, distributed, and consumed. AI technologies are revolutionizing the media and communication industries by enhancing efficiency, personalizing content, improving audience targeting, and enabling real-time analytics.

AI in Film

Film industry is one which embraces its huge potential to make a change in the film produced and consumed. Of course, no technology can replace the creativity of human beings, but can always enhance and support in all their endeavours. Ethical perspectives apart, AI is revolutionizing various aspects of the film industry, from production to distribution. It has influenced the story telling, viewer engagement and even marketing. It helps to have more accurate, cost-efficient content, saves effort and time. Data Analytics and AI technology have already made their debut in films and are going to play a big role in the film making (Datta, A., & Goswami, R,2021). The present chapter explores the various AI tools that are beneficial in film production. This chapter uses Qualitative approach. Available studies, blogs, and articles in the topic AI and Films were collected and reviewed and consolidated the following areas in which AI can be effectively integrated in film making.

Pre-Production

AI's possibilities may be explored from the preproduction stage of filmmaking. Many AI tools are there to help in content generation spanning from idea to script writing. AI technology can significantly increase the efficiency with which a film script is created; typically, it only takes one hour to write a script, allowing the creator to create his or her own script more swiftly. AI script-writing can quickly gather relevant facts and data, assisting the author in uncovering deeper plot hints and building a more compelling narrative. The science fiction short film 'Sunspring' was written with the help of an AI algorithm named 'Benjamin'. The script writers later refined and shaped the final content. The film was screened at the Sci-Fi London Film Festival in 2023 (Raj A, 2024)

Additionally, AI script writing is a novel endeavor that may inspire artists to explore more original creative concepts and produce more excellent works (Sun, P 2024). For example, Jon Finger, filmmaker created his short film D.A.N. using A.I.-generated images and video. Sora is a text-to-video generator from OpenAI. Tools like ScriptBook use natural language processing to analyze scripts, predict box office success, and offer insights into plot and character development (Sahota N, 2024).

Script analysis can also be done using AI. AI tools can analyze scripts for elements like pacing, structure, and character development, providing feedback to writers and producers. GPT-4 can create everything from story ideas, to shot lists, to breakdowns of new filmmaking techniques you want to learn, and even entire scripts.

AI can also be used in Predictive Success Modeling. AI algorithms can predict a film's potential success based on script content, cast, and historical data. Casting is another area. AI can help in talent matching. AI can match actors to roles based on factors like past performances, demographics, and even social media presence. AI can also do virtual casting. AI-driven virtual auditions allow for the creation of digital avatars to test different actors in roles without physical auditions. AI tools provide filmmakers with new creative possibilities and collaborative opportunities. The Insta360 is one such innovative device that streamlines pre-production while keeping all department heads on the same page.

Production

AI can help in the production stage from office management to special effects enhancement. Scheduling and Budgeting can be done with AI tools. AI systems optimize production schedules and budget allocation, reducing costs and improving efficiency. Virtual Cinematography is a great possibility. Creative Reality Studio offers stunning tools that can turn a photo or image of any person or character into a digital video presenter with the click of a button by combining the powers of deep-learning face animation technology, LLM-based text generation, and text-to-image capabilities. Move.ai, a company that specializes in motion capture technology, offering advanced solutions for tracking and analyzing human movement, introduced an AI feature that can capture high quality motion capture data from video in any environment using mobile phones with no need for markers, mocap suits, or studio equipment.

AI helps in pre-visualization by creating detailed digital storyboards and animatics, allowing directors to plan shots more effectively. AI can also help with tasks like camera automation for executing precise and complex camera movements, and scene optimizations for determining the best lighting conditions, composition, and camera angles (Gururaj T, 2023).

AI can be used in Special Effects and CGI. AI enhances visual effects by automating complex processes such as motion capture, rendering, and compositing. In gaming and interactive media, real-time visual effects (VFX) are becoming more essential. AI plays a key role in enabling these effects by predicting and rendering visuals based on user input and the game's environment. For instance, AI can simulate explosions, fire, or weather conditions in real time, boosting immersion and interactivity. Wrexa's AI-powered VFX solutions empower game developers to seamlessly integrate dynamic, realistic effects into their virtual worlds.

AI can also be used in music composition. AI creates music that accentuates particular moods, scenes, or plot points by analysing enormous musical datasets, learning from a variety of genres, and creating original works (Kanatt J, 2023) Beatoven is an online music generation website that will generate new songs to use in videos. Adobe Podcast helps to effortlessly record audio and podcasts with AI-powered tools that increase quality, and automatically transcribe audio so it can be edited simply by editing the text.

Post-Production

AI can be supportive in the post production works. AI-powered editing tools can sort through hours of footage to find the best takes, suggest cuts, and even assemble rough edits. Descript is an AI-powered video editing platform that allows users to edit videos by editing the text. Movavi Video Editor is being used for quick edits.

Video masking using the tool Runway is a way of modifying or overlaying the footage, often by replacing backgrounds while keeping the subject of your footage the same (Donnelly J, 2023). AI-driven color grading tools assist in achieving consistent and visually appealing color palettes throughout the film. Adobe Firefly helps to easily change the color, time of day, or season in video clips by typing, create AI generated storyboards, and even have it automatically find and add b-roll to edits. FireCut is like a personal editing assistant. It can edit long form videos by cutting out all the silence, switch between speakers and cameras for podcasts, and even add pro-level captions with a click. Imagine 3D is an AI text-to-3D model generator by Luma Labs.

Wonder Studio is a powerful AI tool that automatically animates, lights and composes CG characters into live-action scenes. Wonder Studio also automatically animates, lights and composes CG characters into live-action scenes.

Audio Enhancement may be done using AI. It improves audio post-production by automating tasks like noise reduction, dialogue replacement, and sound effects synchronization. Izotope Neutron for Audio Mixing is one popular AI tool. AI tools like Tel Aviv-based Deepdub can reduce the duration of language dubbing projects. Eleven Labs is an AI speech generator that turns text into hyper-realistic speech. Descript's text-based video editing tool helps to analyse the footage, creates a text transcript, and allows editing the video by editing the text transcript.

Distribution and Marketing

Distribution and marketing is another crucial aspect of filmmaking. Reaching the audience is very important. A thorough audience analysis can help the producers in achieving the creative and business goals. Hence audience analysis plays an important role in making any media content. AI can be used to analyse viewer data to identify target audiences and tailor marketing campaigns.

Content Personalization can be done by using AI tools. Platforms use AI to recommend films and shows to users based on their viewing habits, enhancing user engagement. For example, Warner Bros. used AI to optimize the marketing of Aquaman, leading to its box office success. Furthermore, AI-powered chatbots are used for promotional campaigns, engaging audiences in innovative ways. The chatbot for the horror movie Morgan interacted with users, creating a personalized and immersive marketing experience (Sahota N, 2024). AI can also help with Dynamic Advertising. AI creates personalized advertising content that changes based on the viewer's preferences and behavior.

Viewing Experience

Viewing experience of the films irrespective of the platforms is dynamically changing. Interactive media is well appreciated among the audience. AI enables the creation of interactive films where viewers make choices that affect the storyline, creating a unique viewing experience. Ai can provide enhanced accessibility. AI-driven subtitles, dubbing, and descriptive audio improve accessibility for diverse audiences, including those with disabilities.

Archiving and Restoration

After technological advancement archiving and restoration have been an easy and quick process. However, AI can make it more effective. AI can restore old and damaged films by removing scratches, enhancing resolution, and colorizing black-and-white footage. AI helps in digital archiving by efficient cataloguing and retrieval of film archives, making historical content more accessible. Kive.ai is an AI-powered visual reference library equipped with AI tagging.

Future Prospects

The future of film may be defined by AI-Generated Content. AI could potentially create entire short films or scenes, from script to final cut, opening new avenues for experimental and indie filmmakers. The presence of virtual actors is also possible. AI-driven virtual actors might perform alongside human actors, expanding creative possibilities while raising ethical considerations.

Challenges of Using AI in Film Making

While the use of AI tools in filmmaking presents numerous opportunities, it also brings several challenges. Relying too much on AI might lead to losing the artistic touch and make the content impersonal. Over dependence on AI may harm craftsmanship and creative problem solving. AI generates content based on already existing data and algorithms. It lacks true creativity, intuition and emotional intelligence.

The authenticity and ownership issues of the content leads to Intellectual Property Concerns. AI-generated content poses questions about ownership and copyright. The ethical and legal perspectives of the content is also under debate. Who is the actual owner of the script or music is something debatable when it comes to AI generated content. It also raises issues regarding privacy, false representation, job displacement, and the impact on traditional filmmaking roles. Another challenge is that, though AI creates content within seconds, it still requires human intervention to check its reliability. Since it does not have emotional depth, the content generated by AI still requires human touch to make it more personal and audience receptive.

The major findings are:

- AI tools are being in use in filmmaking from its pre production stage to post production
- AI tools can help in audience analysis and predict market trends and success
- AI tools can be used for distribution and marketing of films
- AI tools can help in making better viewer experience
- AI tools can be helpful in archiving and storage of data
- The scope of Ai integrated filmmaking is immense and the film industry is yet to explore it in its fullest sense.
- Use of AI cause challenges also which needs to be carefully analysed and solved

Conclusion

The integration of AI in films promises to streamline production processes, reduce costs, and open up new creative possibilities. However, it is not away from challenges or criticisms. Despite this, the use of AI in filmmaking is likely to continue growing, offering new opportunities for filmmakers to innovate. Balancing technological advances with creative integrity and ethical considerations will be crucial as AI tools become more prevalent in the industry.

References

1. Datta, A., & Goswami, R. (2021). The film industry leaps into artificial intelligence: Scope and challenges by the filmmakers. In Rising Threats in Expert Applications and Solutions: Proceedings of FICR-TEAS 2020 (pp. 665-670). Springer Singapore.
2. Donnelly J (2023), 7 AI tools for Filmmaking You Need to Know About, https://massive.io/filmmaking/6-ai-tools-for-filmmaking/
3. Gururaj T (2023) Lights, camera, action: How AI is transforming the filmmaking landscape, https://interestingengineering.com/culture/artificial-intelligence-in-filmmaking-ai-visual-effects-cgi
4. How AI video tools are changing the film industry 2023, https://www.filmmakersacademy.com/blog-how-ai-video-tools-are-changing-the-film-industry-2023/
5. Kanatt J (2023) Future of the Film Industry: 14 Ways Artificial Intelligence and Game Engines Will Shape Film industry, https://www.linkedin.com/pulse/future-film-industry-14-ways-artificial-intelligence-game-kanatt-wzcsc
6. Raj A (2024) AI in the film industry: still a long way to go, https://techwireasia.com/01/2024/ai-in-the-film-industry/
7. Sun, Peiming (2024) A Study of Artificial Intelligence in the Production of Film, SHS Web of Conferences,https://www.shsconferences.org/articles/shsconf/pdf/2024/03/shsconf_icpahd2024_03004.pdf

8. Sahota N (2024), The AI Takeover In Cinema: How Movie Studios Use Artificial Intelligence, https://www.forbes.com/sites/neilsahota/2024/03/08/the-ai-takeover-in-cinema-how-movie-studios-use-artificial-intelligence/?sh=2f2695414a3f
9. Townsend, S. (2024) Exploring the Impact of AI on Film Production in 2024, https://medium.com/@channelasaservice/exploring-the-impact-of-ai-on-film-production-in-2024f02da745af00#:~:text=AI%20is%20revolutionizing%20film%20production,create%20unique%20and%20engaging%20content.
10. The ultimate list of AI tools for filmmakers (2023), https://www.filmcrux.com/blog/ai-tools

From Automation to Innovation: AI's Impact on Contemporary Media

Dr. Tarakeswara Rao Ippili, Assistant Professor, Department of Journalism and Mass Communication, Central Tribal University of Andhra Pradesh, Vizianagaram, India. Email: ippilitarak@gmail.com

Introduction

Artificial Intelligence (AI) is an emerging technology that has brought drastic changes to several industries, among them the media industry that shifted from conventional ways of creating and sharing content (Brynjolfsson & McAfee, 2014). The application of AI in media has made it possible to produce massive satisfaction, efficiency, and creativity, how media content is created, delivered, and received. In Journalism and Media Otter.ai takes care of the interview transcriptions and in turn Google News collates the stories which allows the practitioners to concentrate on the narration and analysis (TechCrunch, 2023). It enhances user satisfaction via recommendations as recommendation systems on sites such as Netflix and Spotify's recommend content based on users' likes while adaptive learning tools such as Duolingo alters a learner's educational experience according to their needs (Harvard Business Review, 2023) AI increases people's creativity via the DALL·E and Adobe Sensei which helps create images, merch & music that are one of a kind, hence giving creators the opportunity to think outside the box (Forbes, 2023). In addition, VR and AI chatbots such as ChatGPT and Zendesk AI eliminate the time taken to resolve queries and complaints as they provide insights into users sentiments making Customer Relationship Management more effective (McKinsey, 2024) These uses prove that the influence of AI is broad and bestows changes in different fields and sectors. This technological change is not just evolutionary but revolutionary in the operation of the media system and its journalistic, advertising and public relation practices (Schwab, 2017).

As Brynjolfsson and McAfee (2014) state, "AI has the potential to revolutionize media and information interaction by introducing advanced capabilities that go beyond gradual improvements. For instance, automating complex tasks like video editing or leveraging AI-driven audience analytics for more precise targeting represents the kind of qualitative leap that is still on the horizon." It analyses how artificial intelligence technologies transform traditional media platforms and bring new approaches to content production, distribution and consumption. Some of the areas discussed in the chapter include artificial intelligence and content curation, robot journalism, artificial intelligence and influencer marketing, and algorithmic governance in media, including the question of diversity. Analysing its key components using case studies, this paper examines the opportunities and threats of adopting AI in media, with a focus on the issues of ethical concerns, legal restrictions, and concerns about the future implications. For example, the research discusses how AI can improve media accessibility; engage in dialogical narration; and transform marketing and advertising. It ends with policy implications and recommendations for policymakers, media practitioners, scientists, and scholars amid the evolving changes in the media industries due to AI.

Technologies like Machine Learning, NLP, and Computer Vision have ensured that the operations which were earlier consuming a lot of time and effort can now be automated. For example, AI can now write news articles, edit videos and produce art works which means that it has enhanced human creativity and extended the possibilities of what can be achieved in media production (Nguyen et al., 2019). Also, using AI-based analytics, the preferences and behaviours of the audience are revealed in detail, allowing media companies to create content for their viewers and readers based on their needs (Carlson, 2015; Graefe, 2016). This chapter investigates the effects of AI on the media in all its dimensions and gives appropriate guidelines on how to deal with the challenges posed by AI. The first part focuses on AI based content authoring systems, including automated news writing, video editing and personalization technologies. Afterward, the chapter looks at the moral aspects, social media at the forefront, dark patterns, algorithmic bias, disinformation and privacy issues. The third section talks about policy options, outlining possibilities to promote for creating an ethical AI in the media that would be free from these shortcomings. Collectively, these sections provide an insightful account of how the media is being transformed by the use of AI and the effects that this has on other sectors of society.

Paradigm Shifts in Media Creation and Consumption

With the development of AI, it not only helps optimize the process of media production but also challenges the conventional thinking and approach to media (McQuail, 2010). This paper examines AI-based advancements in content curation to understand how these innovations have helped media organizations to market and deliver content with a high degree of customization in response to consumers' preferences (Nguyen et al., 2019). In addition, the emerging trend of automated journalism with the help of artificial intelligence and advanced algorithms is revolutionizing news presentation, thus sparking significant concerns about the importance of quality, timeliness, and reliability of reports (Carlson, 2015; Graefe, 2016). Automatic writing practices enable the deployment of breaking news quickly while at the same time threatening usual journalistic principles. This move towards producing more content through AI also poses challenges to the reliability and legitimacy of news sources, and thus requires sound editorial control and accreditation processes to ensure the integrity of new media.

AI technologies have become integral to the media landscape, but their rapid adoption has raised significant ethical concerns that require structured examination (O'Neil, 2016). Approaching these challenges in a more integrated manner means that a comprehensive consideration of ethics should be pitched into a section that deals with matters of responsibility delegating such arrangements to revolve around three key aspects: accountability, editorial governance and transparency of the processes of accreditation. House editorial control over AI generated content is extremely important in the case where automated news writing systems or content moderation systems powered by AI could lead to biased or false coverage without the supervision of people in charge (Diakopoulos, 2019). Lacking controls, AI could ignore the accuracy of a headline and go for a more chaotic and seductive one, thus undermining the trust of audiences in media organisations (Lazer et al., 2018). Another aspect that needs to be emphasized is algorithmic transparency, because it counters the negative side of bias and false information – biased algorithms lead to biased data and biased data propagates stereotypes or divisive content and transparent development of AI provides means of detecting and practically addressing such issues (Noble, 2018). Organizations that offer AI-powered content recommendation services need to be clear in how AI recommendations are structured so that people can challenge perceived injustice (Binns, 2018). AI in the media also increases accountability through accreditation systems that set industry benchmarks for objectivity, truth and diversity, and periodic assessments will detect ethical issues and build trust (Eubanks, 2018). Addressing these concerns in a more framed manner allows then media practitioners and policy makers to analyse the social effects of AI and formulate how best to develop AI in the media while enabling new ideas to arise without sidestepping the standards of media practices.

Redefining Audience Engagement: The Rise of Virtual Influencers

The evolution of virtual influencers, or digital characters controlled solely by artificial intelligence, presents a new paradigm in marketing and customer relations (Miao et al., 2020). These entities erode the boundaries between human-made and artificial content, disputing the ideas of genuineness and power in digital media. In contrast to traditional influencers, virtual influencers do not have physical limitations, and thus, brands can spread messages across the globe. But at the same time, it poses some significant ethical concerns with regards to the genuine nature of influencer advertising. The rise of virtual influencers is a trend that requires legal regulation of AI-generated content and promotion of standards for ethical interaction to safeguard the interests of consumers and justice in the digital sphere.

Ethical and Societal Implications of AI in Media

However, the introduction of AI into the media landscape is not without its drawbacks. Concerns like algorithmic bias that reinforce stereotype and silence minority voices require post-structural and critical approaches (Noble, 2018). The general issues related to AI and media, such as privacy and fairness of algorithms, point to the necessity for proper legal regulation (Floridi et al., 2018). By shifting the control of content recommendations to AI algorithms, it becomes crucial to address issues of accuracy and fairness in the information processing and distribution to avoid degrading societal trust in media outlets. Additionally, the gathering and employing of user data for delivering AI-related preference raises data privacy and security issues and results in demands for clear data management techniques and improved methods for the protection of users in the digital world.

AI bias in regard to media continues to stir concern especially with the way algorithms discriminate and dictate the kinds of content that is present and available. One glaring instance is the depiction of women in ads. For example, in a 2019 study it was found that men were more exposed to advertisements for high paying technology jobs than women, purely by the nature of the gender neutral adverts. The problem here is that the AI algorithms in question were trained using historical data and men were considered a more viable target because they had been the predominant group in history (Lambrecht & Tucker, 2019). Such discrimination entrenches existing gender gaps in technology and entrench gender stereotypes in society's perception and in this case the perception of women.

Long-term Implications and Societal Shifts

Besides high-risk consequences, this study investigates the extended effects of AI in the media sector such as perhaps a revolution in media literacy, alteration of the audience's conduct, and new standards of medial ethicality (Sundar, 2020). It specifically explores the impact of AI on the formation of opinion, information availability, and the overall nature of communication in today's society. AI makes the media more democratic in terms of content distribution and creates new opportunities for popular audiences, but it also requires new rules to counter bad actors and to educate global audiences. Thus, AI's impact on cultural issues and particularly on cultural messages that regulate people's behaviour emphasizes the importance of presenting minorities and other non-dominant groups fairly in media products and ensuring that media content ideally contributes toward creating a cohesive society given that people are interconnected in the modern world.

Balancing Technological Advancements with Human Values

When integrating AI into media practices, evaluating its effects on human communication patterns becomes a crucial question (Van Dijck, 2013). This paper analyses the tension between technology & human values, supporting AI initiatives based on diversity and democracy (Benkler, 2006). Ethical AI development reinforces that technological advancements in media are beneficial to promoting the human rights essential to media consumption and production. Therefore, through promoting user autonomy and facilitating well-informed decisions, ethical AI contributes to the concepts of media transparency and accountability that support democracy in the digital media environments.

Theoretical Framework

Analysing the integration of Artificial Intelligence (AI) into media, some key theoretical approaches can be distinguished that describe interactions between technology, media, and society. One such framework is the Technological Determinism theory which argues that it is technology that determines social relations and culture (McLuhan 1964). This theory posits that trends of AI in media do not represent improvements on past use cases but a revolution that reinvents media content creation and distribution. Technological determinism stresses the belief that new media technologies like content personalization and automated journalism are forever changing the media industries and consumers' behaviour.

Another relevant theoretical approach is the so-called Social Construction of Technology (SCOT), suggesting that technological processes are shaped by human actions and social contexts (Bijker, Hughes, & Pinch, 1987). However, SCOT argues that it is the ways in which developers, users and regulators engage with AI that determines its deployment and experience in the media. This perspective underscores the significance of analysing the social factors and power structures that shape AI use in media. For example, the increased presence of virtual influencers and AI-driven advertising are both a symptom of the broader culture and consumer preferences, as well as a business strategy to use AI for competitive advantage adopted by media companies.

The Media Ecology theory offers a strong theoretical background to understand the systematic impact of AI in media settings. According to Postman (1970), media ecology focuses on the impact of media technologies on perception, comprehension, and communication. Applying this theory to AI in media shows how current AI algorithms and platforms are generating new media ecologies of personalized content curation and automated content creation. All of these have significant implications for media literacy, cognitive functioning, and public dialogue. Media ecology enables one to understand the environment or a landscape of AI in media where technology, content, and behaviour come together to form modern media.

Altogether, these theoretical perspectives present a multi-faceted perspective on AI and its place in modern media. They offer valuable information about how technology, culture, and systems all work together to shape the media industries and practices. Thus, anchoring this research in these theories allows understanding a multifaceted and rather fluid interaction between AI technologies and media, which is pivotal for a more profound analysis of their influence on society.

Analysis

This chapter aims at analysing the following:

1. Analyse the Impact of AI on Traditional Media Formats: Investigate how AI technologies are transforming the creation, dissemination, and consumption of media content.
2. Evaluate the Role of Automated Journalism: Explore the benefits and challenges associated with AI-generated news and reports, focusing on productivity, quality, and authenticity.
3. Investigate the Phenomenon of Virtual Influencers: Understand the advantages and ethical concerns related to the use of AI-created personas in marketing and social media.

4. Address Issues of Media Bias and Diversity: Critically examine how AI algorithms impact representation and inclusivity in media, identifying potential biases and their consequences.

This chapter uses a qualitative approach to examine the complex effects of Artificial Intelligence (AI) on modern media. Qualitative research is used because it facilitates the identification of detailed and subjective experiences from different key stakeholders who participate in media production, control, and consumption. The proposed methodology to conduct this research is based on semi-structured interviews, focus group discussions, and document review to obtain descriptive data.

Research Design and Data Collection

The qualitative study is therefore be conducted through purposive sampling of key informants including Journalists and editors from the English media in Visakhapatnam including The Hindu, The New Indian Express, The Hans India and Deccan Chronicle amongst others. These interviews are semi-constructed, aimed towards obtaining rich descriptions of participants' interactions, impressions and observations of the effects of AI on media practices, ethical considerations, and social consequences. Moreover, focus groups will enable a conversational approach to understanding the collective meanings and tensions concerning AI in media. In addition to these approaches, the research will involve a review of the literature from reports, journals, and policy documents to enrich the understanding of the context surrounding primary data sources.

Whereas, the qualitative data received from the interviews and focus group discussion and documentation review will be analysed through thematic analysis. This process is cyclical and reflects the systematic search for patterns, themes, and categories in the data, which provides grounds for constructing detailed descriptions and interpretations. Data coding and categorization will be thoroughly done in order to identify common trend and concepts most recurrent in the qualitative data to guarantee adequate coverage of issues pertaining to the effect of AI on media.

Findings

The analysis of the role that AI plays in shaping the contemporary media landscape indicates the advancements in technology as well as the concomitant focus on the ethical implications of such advancements. AI technology has evolved traditional media formats by improving the tailored content delivery to the audience and in the process improving their satisfaction levels. However, these advancements are often dogged by issues of bias in algorithmic performance and infringement on privacy, which requires proper regulation and AI accountability measures. While automated journalism has brought certain improvements in the organization of news production flow, several questions arise about the quality and standards of the created content. Likewise, the appearance of virtual influencers has elicited controversy on ethical practices involving honesty and consumer trust in marketing. It is crucial to adopt such an approach by recognising the advantages of AI and minimising its drawbacks, where AI's use has to be guided by ethical standards and should involve all stakeholders in building a media environment that is efficient and ethical at the same time.

Table 1: Impact of AI on Traditional Media Formats

Themes	Findings	Implications	Recommendations
Content Personalization	Enhanced user engagement and satisfaction through tailored content	Improved user retention	Implement robust user data privacy policies
AI Algorithms in Content	Optimization of content delivery based on user preferences and behaviour	Enhanced content relevance	Regular updates to algorithms for accuracy
Platform Adaptation	Adaptive content recommendations to improve user interaction	Increased platform usability	Monitor for algorithmic biases

Themes	Findings	Implications	Recommendations
Media Consumption Trends	Shift towards personalized content consumption and interaction	Changing audience preferences	Educate users on AI usage
Ethical Considerations	Concerns about editorial independence and homogenization of media content	Maintaining journalistic integrity	Establish transparency guidelines

The adoption of AI in the existing formats of the media as highlighted in table 1 has received mixed feelings among the media practitioners in Visakhapatnam, India especially from major media houses including Hindu, New Indian Express, Hans India and Deccan Chronicle. From the interviews conducted with these professionals, they noted that AI for content curation has greatly enhanced user interaction since the content made available to users is based on their preferences (Nguyen et al., 2019). This capability has been applauded for increasing audience engagement and their retention rates, which is in line with the growing trend of-targeted media consumption.

But they also discussed such risks as algorithmic bias and privacy violations as well as their potential impact. Journalists echoed concerns that AI might deepen existing biases in content curation resulting in marginalization of different perspectives and stereotypes (Floridi et al., 2018). Ethical considerations regarding the use of AI in media were frequently discussed, with practitioners calling for open AI systems and specific rules to prevent abuses and hold AI accountable (Benkler, 2006). One case of prevalence in AI-evaluated media is related to social media networks where content moderation systems tend to mask or suppress the voices of the minorities. Content of proponents' posts during Black Lives Matter protests was also tagged as sensitive content and hence flagged or removed by the robots (Noble, 2018). Such AI-placed discrimination stems mainly from the inadequate training data sets containing cultural or political context which diminishes the importance of critical social movements and minority parts in cyberspace. The elements of bias can also be found within the image recognition algorithms, which have resulted in and are still leading to glaring mistakes such as the case during which image recognition software confused a picture of black people for pictures of gorillas. Such an incident happened because the training datasets that designed these systems were homogenous and did not adequately capture Black individuals (Buolamwini & Gebru, 2018). Such errors not only embarrass but further paint a picture of AI systems deployed in the media as being unjust or unavailable to everyone as opposed to enhancing cultural diversity as they only reinforce the negative anthropological images.

Another form of bias evolving in artificial intelligence or AI political content curation systems is in regards to echo chambers created by the algorithm that promotes content that is in line or a user's political stance. Ribeiro et al. (2020) report that viewers of far right political content on YouTube were able to spiral further down the rabbit hole by being recommended more such radical videos which in turn became an echo of their political bias. Such a situation where the priority of interaction is at the expense of the variety of opinions promotes divides within society and makes the chances of balanced media exposure quite difficult to have. Also, tools employed to engage in content creation with voice recognition and speech analysis are known to have rampant linguistic biases as well and it relates to the way the tone is interpreted of languages like minority dialects (for example African American Vernacular or Indian English). Such tendencies develop because the training sets are constituted largely of American Standard English creating walls to content producers of a variety of languages in addition to skewing representation within the media (Koenecke et al., 2020).

Issues relating to the reconfiguration of classic media formats due to improvements in artificial intelligence were discussed. Indeed, AI increases the effectiveness and accuracy of advertisement targeting while journalists stressed the role of editorial independence and human intervention in production of the content (Schwab, 2017). They stressed the importance of continuous conversation between the media professionals, technologists, and regulators to understand how to use AI in media responsibly and safely. Besides helping media companies improve user interaction with content,

AI technologies have radically changed the internal processes of traditional media formats in Visakhapatnam. Qualitative interviews with media practitioners also identified aspects of AI in news production, not just as a tool of audience management but also as a means to improve efficiency and manage resources within news organisations. With the help of AI, journalists are able to spend more time on investigative reports as many monotonous tasks are handled by AI systems, including data analysis and content selection (Carlson, 2015; Graefe, 2016). Such efficiency not only shortens the time for producing news but also allows the media organizations to better plan and respond to changing audience demands and habits.

But as with most operational efficiencies, questions about systemic control of AI algorithms over editorial discretion and content pluralism remain pertinent. Journalists highlighted the significance of human intervention in decision-making, especially when working on certain and specific news topics, for which ethical concerns are critical (O'Neil, 2016). Another important concern is the ability of AI algorithms to perpetuate bias and prejudice, and that remains a major concern today, and there should be constant monitoring and prevention strategies to make sure that AI content does not favour inaccurate or discriminating preferences (Noble, 2018).

The change of traditional media formats by the help of AI and the related new approaches would raise more general questions on the ethicality of media and the general impact on society. Various journalists and media workers underlined that it is still ethically questionable to use AI in journalism; they should set specific rules and explain how they will be held responsible to ensure independence in their work (Floridi et al., 2018). It is also worth noting that as AI's development progresses, more discussions focus on how to properly implement them in Media practices while addressing the various potential ethical issues and considering the collective education of all stakeholders to achieve the best results of AI in Media actions.

While AI has undoubtedly changed the way information is presented to the audience by providing personalized encounters, its effect and use are not consistent throughout the world's geography, particularly among less intelligible economies. In advanced economies which have adequate technological infrastructure, AI-enabled systems can collect data, tailor content, and improve interaction with the audience in an effective manner. However, the situation is quite the opposite in many emerging economies, where nuances such as lower availability of advanced systems and inadequate web connectivity restrict AI's capacity. For example, the absence of high-speed internet or access to last-generation hardware limits the capacity of AI to collect and analyse data intended for content's personalization. This gap in infrastructure leaves a very wide gap in the level of digitalization, meaning that more developed region users are more likely to see less generic content while audiences from less advanced regions still receive media that is intended to be generic and appeal to many people.

Ensuring multilingual content delivery using AI in developing areas is a challenge on its own as language barrier affects the intended application. Owing to their very small population, many languages do not feature in AI models as AI development emphasizes languages with a larger user base like English, Chinese, or Spanish. This trend can be detrimental as the potential of AI media to serve many people from different indigenous or regional languages gets compromised, rendering them cut off. This is visible in India with its vast linguistic diversity where AI applications have limitations of deploying localized content catering for the users and their respected region. Addressing these regional issues will require technological innovation as well as the consideration of an all-embracing strategy in AI development as well as the idea of global media AI systems design that cater for regional infrastructure, linguistic, and cultural diversity.

Table 2: Evaluation of Automated Journalism

Themes	Findings	Implications	Recommendations
Productivity Benefits	Increased news production efficiency and cost-effectiveness	Faster news dissemination	Ensure human oversight in critical news
Quality vs. Authenticity	Challenges in maintaining editorial standards and authenticity	Risk of misinformation	Implement fact-checking protocols

Themes	Findings	Implications	Recommendations
Bias and Accuracy	Risks of bias in AI-generated news and the need for transparency	Potential credibility issues	Regular audits of AI algorithms
Impact on Journalistic Ethics	Discussions on maintaining journalistic integrity amidst automation	Ethical implications	Train journalists in AI ethics
Future Directions	Recommendations for balancing efficiency with ethical journalism standards	Sustainable journalism practices	Collaborate with AI developers

Introducing AI in automation is a great idea as per the English journalist media in Visakhapatnam as this provides the unparalleled speed and scalability of news distribution to cope up with demand of digital QToday's audience (Carlson, 2015; Graefe, 2016). This capability has been of great helpful in breaking news coverage and data driven disruption of newsrooms to depicting timely information of different populace.

This led to discussion on the quality and authenticity aspect of the content that is developed with AI's help. Some journalists raised concerns over the subject of AI algorithms acting as sole editors concerning news articles due to circumstances where the algorithms may not consider the need to provide a detailed background or moral issues involved in an event (O'Neil, 2016). Many of them emphasized the qualitative aspect of the job and insisted that human intervention in writing articles and selecting materials was paramount to keeping the standard of journalism high and to prevent distortion of the truth in delicate and complicated stories.

The ethical aspects were included in their assessments, and these concerns were shared most importantly regarding the issue of AI's transparency. Newspaper professionals stressed that the journalists and the audiences should be informed of the role and apportion of AI in the news reporting and called for the ethical principles of AI. Future steps, they advocated for continuous joint initiatives to disseminate ethical standards into AI development to make automated journalism as ethical as possible. The advent of automated journalism has led to many discussions among media professionals in Visakhapatnam regarding the effects of the new technology. It is for this reason that despite highlighting the strengths of AI-driven systems in providing the breaking news or data-based reports in a timely manner, questions arise as to the recognition of professional journalism principles. Buyers singled out the complexity of the context and possible ethical issues in journalism, which AI can possibly fail to understand or determine as important (O'Neil, 2016). This poses pertinent questions on how institutions of editorial control ensure the credibility and accuracy of the news content especially when dealing with such topics or in making a follow-up check on information.

Automated journalism has without a question improved newsroom efficiency and cost-cutting allowing the media firms to produce content faster and in bulk. However, it also brings great worries concerning the originality and the authenticity of the content. The problem for the news organisations is how to get their automation economies while ensuring that their editors and journalists' practices are not compromised. To achieve this equilibrium some media outlets have sought to integrate AI assistance and content moderation. For example, the AP (Associated Press) has generated earnings reports and basic data-driven articles through AI based applications. The AP, however, makes sure that all such automatic reports are verified and examined by qualified reporters to prevent factual distortions and binary content. This AI-led approach of producing content with subsequent human edit review protects the stories' trustworthiness and still reaps the benefits of automation.

Other institutions including Reuters are now adopting AI within their operations, particularly citing limited areas such as writing about sporting events that need a fast turnaround. However, Reuters believes in the editorial checking of AI generated materials by resource persons before the material is made available for the general public. In this sense, automated journalism is viewed as providing assistance to the human journalists and not fully eliminating them. Furthermore, some institutions have formed codes of conduct to govern the employment of AI such as the provision of explanation regarding the AI based materials and the attribution of the reports done by AI and reporters (Froelich, 2021). These case studies show that automation can enhance the output of media houses, but on the other hand, editorial control and clear communication of the purpose of the news should be maintained to enhance the quality of the news. This hybrid model allows news publishers to use AI tools but still preserves the level of journalism as it ought to be, therefore illustrating the relationship between automation and the values of the editorial department.

The media professionals declared the necessity of joint efforts to implement ethical guidelines to the AI processes successfully. This anticipative approach seeks to reduce possible vices emanating from algorithmic bias and fake news so that automated journalism will not go against societal norms and ethical values (Floridi et al., 2018). Through engagement of technologists, journalists, and regulatory bodies, stakeholders can align themselves towards improving AI's in comparison to the New York Times, and improving the newsroom efficiencies without compromising journalists' ethics and sans the dilution of public's trust in editorials.

Table 3: Phenomenon of Virtual Influencers

Themes	Findings	Implications	Recommendations
Audience Engagement	Enhanced audience interaction and message consistency through virtual influencers	Increased brand awareness	Monitor for ethical guidelines
Authenticity Concerns	Ethical dilemmas regarding transparency and authenticity in digital marketing	Consumer trust	Disclosure of virtual status

Themes	Findings	Implications	Recommendations
Brand Influence	Redefining marketing strategies with AI-generated personas	Targeted advertising	Develop AI content policies
Regulatory Considerations	Calls for clear guidelines to ensure ethical marketing practices	Legal compliance	Advocate for industry standards

The emergence of virtual influencers has begun to pose questions about ethical, social, and legal concerns while also shifting the paradigms of marketing and digital communication. In Visakhapatnam, media professionals seem to be divided on how these influenced AI personas are being used and their consequences, while being rational on how attributing they could lead to improved communication practices, trust degeneration and social issues as well.

Opportunities in Marketing

The virtual influencers seem to be a game-changer for the businesses that want to cut across their messages and increase the level of interaction with the consumers. It is said that their capability to integrate with the company's image makes it possible to recruit them for campaigns that rely on maximum targeting precision. Some of the media professionals based in the city Visakhapatnam noted that virtual influencers are effective in cutting chances of mistakes during brand communication since they are able to provide consistency and control. There are no scandals, no timetable clashes, and no personal opinions to contend with as is the case when working with human influencers which is likely why many brands are looking for a more secure alternative.

Their use gives marketers the opportunity to generate and build characters who appeal to various age groups whose attention may be targeted in the bid to further personalize a campaign. For example, a virtual influencer that incorporates more of a brand's vision can be attached to its social reinforcement, cultural trend, or even expectation – all of which makes sense when it comes down to targeted advertising (Miao et al, 2020).

Ethical Concerns and Transparency Issues

Many professionals raised concerns about the deception involved, saying that people could easily believe that these avatars are actual people. While AI-enabled characters enable businesses to communicate with a wider audience, they also pose a threat to the integrity of websites. This, in turn, reduces the level of trust that consumers have in brands.

Of utmost concern to me are issues of trust, norms and the embedded values, which influence the endorsement of such deception, and potentials such as Consumer Trust. For instance, such deception undermines the reality of the created digital content as well as consumer trust in business. For instance, it is otherwise alarming that the consumers lack understanding when it comes to the broader message that such AI- generated characters present, a factor that may in turn breed doubt over any authenticity for the brand.

Societal and Cultural Implications

As such, advertisements require a measure of ethical conduct since content affects audience perception, hence, lower advertising credibility. A further concern that emerges in this case is ensuring that consumers are able to navigate through much of the content found online without being misled. However, AI generates characters that are able to reach people in more complex ways than advertisements, thus altering the ideals, trends, and the purchasing decision.

An example can be seen with AI avatars whereby Ai avatars or virtual influencers can create consumers with particular beauty or lifestyle aspirations that are not realistic. This could add to the already existing problems like self-esteem issues, materialism, or cultural assimilation. Those working in Visakhapatnam were worried about how these factors would affect culture particularly in places like Andhra Pradesh that have a rich history and differing cultures.

Legal and Regulatory Challenges

These concerns, with their ethical dimensions, and their societal bases, are made worse by the lack of firm rules and guidelines regarding the application of virtual influencers. Media personnel have suggested that there should be guidelines adopted by the industry as-a-whole which would regulate the practice. These regulations could address several critical areas:

1. Transparency Requirements: Mandating the disclosure of AI-generated content to prevent deceptive practices.
2. Consumer Protection: Safeguarding audiences from manipulative marketing tactics and ensuring informed decision-making.
3. Competition Ethics: Preventing unfair advantages in digital marketing that could marginalize traditional influencers or smaller brands.

While Cuolry and Hepp (2016) say that AI personas should be regulated to avoid their excess, and point out that a proper regulation policy is the most effective in creating a fair AI marketplace. Hepp also suggests that the AI marketplace would benefit from clear guidelines as to conduct.

Balancing Innovation and Accountability

For all the advantages that virtual influencers open up for companies, there are some ethical issues and some societal issues that must be taken into consideration. Companies and advertisers have to be responsible in this changing world, weighing the benefits of AI technologies against ethical ideas and transparency.

The rise of virtual influencers has both advantages and disadvantages. With society and ethical values remaining intact, the media and marketing industries stand to benefit from these AI powered personas through being transparent, building consumers trust, and supporting suitable legislation. An advocacy that balances these two considerations will guarantee that the virtual influencers benefit the digital ecosystem without undermining public trust or cultural variety.

Table 4: Issues of Media Bias and Diversity

Themes	Findings	Implications	Recommendations
Algorithmic Bias	Risks of perpetuating stereotypes and marginalizing underrepresented groups	Social inequality	Diversify AI development teams
Diversity in AI Development	Importance of diverse AI development teams for mitigating bias	Improved AI fairness	Implement bias detection tools
Ethical Implications	Addressing privacy concerns and ensuring equitable representation	User trust	Establish AI ethics committees
Societal Impact	Influence on public discourse and societal norms	Cultural perceptions	Promote inclusive media content

The implementation of AI technologies challenged the reconsideration of content representation and viewers' perceptions (Noble, 2018). There were concerns raised by journalists that potentially bias algorithms could prejudice stereotyping and under-representation of minorities, which was anathema to the media industry that prides in diversity and equal representation. Matters regarding transparency and accountability of algorithms were key issues of their discourse. Media professionals recommended that AI should be developed with diversity in the team; there should be strict methods of identifying prejudice when implementing recommendation systems (Floridi et al., 2018). It underlined the importance of the freedom of the media in the representation of various views and the access to information by all, calling for more ethical approaches to the integration of AI technology into societies. Furthermore, ethical aspects related to the media content creation through the use of Artificial Intelligence led to the demand for changes in the legislation and the development of specific guidelines. There was a call by various journalists to eliminate or at least redress algorithmic biases, and prevent programmes and scripts from being biased and develop algorithmic accountability that features transparency, accuracy and diversity of the media (Gillespie, 2018). They underlined further research and cooperation in creating the AI technologies which would bring more content diversity and representation to marginalised people, make the voice of everyone heard and help build a more diverse media environment.

Some media professionals interviewed in Visakhapatnam stressed the importance of creating a set of measures to respond to the algorithmic prejudices and for transparency in the development of the algorithm media content (Gillespie, 2018). It is for this reason that they called for more transparency regarding AI practices in media to promote fairness, accuracy, and diversity. Journalists urged for better bias detection and the more diverse AI development teams to avoid discrimination tendencies of content recommendation systems (Floridi et al., 2018). Such initiatives are important to ensure that AI technologies improve inclusiveness and help amplify the voices of underrepresented communities in the media landscape. Some of the key points that emerged from the discussion concerned the importance of constant research and cooperation to improve AI tools and integrate them with moral values that would ensure equal distribution of information and its positive effects on society.

Conclusion

The emerging technologies in AI have been discussed as to how they reallocate the conventional media forms, affect the journalism, transform the role of marketing with virtual influencers, and put forward various issues of biasness and diversity. Thus, the information obtained from the media professionals in Visakhapatnam shows the ways in which technological innovations complement and sometimes challenge societal processes.

Technology adoption, especially AI, has expanded content personalization, increasing consumer engagement and satisfaction (Nguyen et al., 2019). This capability enables media platforms to better reach target audiences and improve retention rates in the digital age. There are still doubts about the algorithm's unbiased nature and fair use of people's data; therefore, stringent regulations and organizations that oversee AI use and development are required.

While Automated journalism has brought shifts in news production, new challenges related to the content quality and authenticity still persists (Carlson 2015; Graefe 2016). Although the AI systems perform well in timely delivery of the news and evidence-based reporting, the human intervention and decision-making regarding the ethical practices of journalism cannot be overemphasized (O'Neil, 2016). This duality comes in a request for what can be termed as harmonized human-machine incorporation where the AI offers a supplement to the human talent, a request for a media that balances efficiency and ethics.

Virtual influencers have recently come into the limelight through controversies surrounding their efficiency as promoters and their place in ethical dilemmas in new media. Despite the benefits that virtual influencers can bring to brands in terms of marketing opportunities, the issue of transparency and consumer trust highlights the need for ethical marketing approaches and AI-generated content labelling. Media professionals call for standardization of the truth that digital advertising cares for and supports the light of reality by becoming ethical ambassadors in consumption promotion strategies.

Discriminatory media bias and diversity furthered by AI algorithms to require analysis and intervention (Noble, 2018; Gillespie, 2018). It implies that restricted accessibility and preference for certain classes of media content by biased algorithms could impact negatively on achieving the goal of equality and eliminating prejudice in present day's society. Bias is recommended to be detected using strict measures and media organizations and policymaking bodies need to encourage diverse AI development teams to overcome these risks. In general, algorithmic transparency and its regulation lead to the creation of new opportunities and approaches in the media industry that contribute to the institution of equality and the appearance of fair and objective information.

In this respect, it can be acknowledged that the development of AI technologies and their further application as tools that redefine the media environment primarily disclosed by their innovative powers, while at the same time, posing serious ethical questions and dilemmas. These findings stress the need for careful AI implementation, regulatory monitoring, and continuous discussions among all the interested parties to leverage the potential of AI while minimizing risks. In the next step, one needs to apply a more careful and harmonized approach that will continue incorporating technological development but will pay more attention to the ethical issues so that a fair and open media environment is formed.

References

1. Benkler, Y. (2006). The Wealth of Networks: How Social Production Transforms Markets and Freedom. Yale University Press.
2. Bijker, W. E., Hughes, T. P., & Pinch, T. J. (1987). The Social Construction of Technological Systems: New Directions in the Sociology and History of Technology. MIT Press.
3. Binns, R. (2018). On the ethical implications of artificial intelligence. *Journal of AI Ethics*, 1(1), 3-14.
4. Brynjolfsson, E., & McAfee, A. (2014). The Second Machine Age: Work, Progress, and Prosperity in a Time of Brilliant Technologies. W.W. Norton & Company.
5. Buolamwini, J., & Gebru, T. (2018). Gender Shades: Intersectional Accuracy Disparities in Commercial Gender Classification. *Proceedings of Machine Learning Research*, 81, 1-15.
6. Carlson, M. (2015). Automating the News: How Algorithms Are Rewriting the Media. Columbia University Press.
7. Carlson, M., & Zenger, T. (2015). Do paywalls work? A natural experiment from 1,000 US newspapers. *Journal of Marketing Research, 52*(3), 378-396. doi:10.1509/jmr.14.0101

8. Couldry, N., & Hepp, A. (2016). The Mediated Construction of Reality. Polity Press.
9. Diakopoulos, N. (2019). Automating the news: How algorithms are rewriting the media. Harvard University Press.
10. Eubanks, V. (2018). Automating inequality: How high-tech tools profile, police, and punish the poor. St. Martin's Press.
11. Floridi, L., Cowls, J., Beltrametti, M., Chatila, R., Chazerand, P., Dignum, V., & Vayena, E. (2018). AI4People-An Ethical Framework for a Good AI Society: Opportunities, Risks, Principles, and Recommendations. Minds and Machines, 28(4), 689-707.
12. Forbes. (2023, August 15). How AI is transforming creativity in art, design, and music. Forbes. Retrieved from
13. https://www.forbes.com/sites/forbestechcouncil/2023/08/15/how-ai-is-transforming-creativity-in-art-design-and-music/
14. Froelich, M. (2021). Artificial intelligence in journalism: Ethics, guidelines, and automation. *Media Ethics Journal*, 3(2), 45-60.
15. Gillespie, T. (2018). Custodians of the Internet: Platforms, Content Moderation, and the Hidden Decisions That Shape Social Media. Yale University Press.
16. Graefe, A. (2016). Guide to Automated Journalism. Tow Center for Digital Journalism.
17. Harvard Business Review. (2023, June 10). Personalization at scale: How AI is enhancing user experiences. Harvard Business Review. Retrieved from https://hbr.org/2023/06/personalization-at-scale-how-ai-is-enhancing-user-experiences
18. Koenecke, A., Nam, A., Lake, E., Nudell, J., Quartey, M., Mengesha, Z., ... & Goel, S. (2020). Racial disparities in automated speech recognition. *Proceedings of the National Academy of Sciences*, 117(14), 7684-7689.
19. Lambrecht, A., & Tucker, C. (2019). Algorithmic Bias? An Empirical Study of Apparent Gender-Based Discrimination in the Display of STEM Career Ads. *Management Science*, 65(7), 2966-2981.

20. Lazer, D. M., et al. (2018). The science of fake news. *Science*, 359(6380), 1094-1096.

21. McKinsey & Company. (2024, January 5). The future of customer service: AI-driven solutions for enhanced support. McKinsey Insights. Retrieved from https://www.mckinsey.com/business-functions/mckinsey-digital/our-insights/the-future-of-customer-service-ai-driven-solutions

22. McLuhan, M. (1964). Understanding Media: The Extensions of Man. McGraw-Hill.

23. McQuail, D. (2010). McQuail's Mass Communication Theory (6th ed.). Sage Publications.

24. Miao, M., Wei, W., & Wang, J. (2020). Virtual influencer marketing: Exploring the concept and its implications. *Journal of Business Research, 117*, 614-625. doi:10.1016/j.jbusres.2020.08.013

25. Miao, W., Cao, J., Wang, Z., & Li, Y. (2020). The rise of virtual influencers: A study of their persuasive effects on consumers. *Journal of Interactive Advertising, 20*(2), 108-119. doi:10.1080/15252019.2020.1756322

26. Nguyen, T. T., Hui, P.-M., Harper, F. M., Terveen, L., & Konstan, J. A. (2019). Exploring the Filter Bubble: The Effect of Using Recommender Systems on Content Diversity. Proceedings of the 18th ACM Conference on Computer-Supported Cooperative Work & Social Computing, 677-686.

27. Nguyen, T., Kietzmann, J., & Pitafi, A. H. (2019). The impact of artificial intelligence on media content personalization: A conceptual framework and research agenda. *International Journal of Information Management,* 46, 266-276. doi:10.1016/j.ijinfomgt.2018.11.002

28. Noble, S. U. (2018). Algorithms of Oppression: How Search Engines Reinforce Racism. NYU Press.

29. O'Neil, C. (2016). Weapons of Math Destruction: How Big Data Increases Inequality and Threatens Democracy. Crown Publishing Group.

30. Parker, A. (2019). The role of artificial intelligence in newsrooms: A case study of the Associated Press. *Journalism Studies Review*, 5(1), 19-33.

31. Postman, N. (1970). The Reformed English Curriculum. In A.C. Eurich (Ed.), High School 1980: The Shape of the Future in American Secondary Education. Pitman Publishing Corporation.

32. Ribeiro, M. H., Ottoni, R., West, R., Almeida, V. A. F., & Meira Jr, W. (2020). Auditing radicalization pathways on YouTube. *Proceedings of the 2020 Conference on Fairness, Accountability, and Transparency*, 131-141.

33. Schwab, K. (2017). The Fourth Industrial Revolution. Crown Business.

34. Sundar, S. S. (2020). The MAIN Model: A Heuristic Approach to Understanding Technology Effects on Credibility. In M. B. Oliver, A. A. Raney, & J. Bryant (Eds.), Media Effects: Advances in Theory and Research (4th ed., pp. 407-424), Routledge.

35. TechCrunch. (2023, September 20). AI tools revolutionizing journalism and media workflows. TechCrunch. Retrieved from https://techcrunch.com/2023/09/20/ai-tools-revolutionizing-journalism-and-media-workflows/

36. Van Dijck, J. (2013). The Culture of Connectivity: A Critical History of Social Media. Oxford University Press.

Building Safer Online Communities: The Role of AI in Cyberbullying Prevention

Ms.D. Simona, Assistant Professor, Department of Psychology, The American College, Madurai. Email: simona@americancollege.edu.in

Ms.K. S. Amritha, Assistant Professor, Department of Psychology, The American College, Madurai. Email: sekaramritha97@gmail.com

Mr.Daniel B, Lecturer, Department of Psychology, The American college, Madurai. Email: danielb@americancollege.edu.in

Introduction

The rising incidence of cyberbullying calls for more effective detection and intervention strategies, particularly through advanced technologies. This chapter examines the potential of artificial intelligence (AI), including machine learning algorithms, natural language processing (NLP), and multimodal analysis, in enhancing cyberbullying prevention. Traditional methods, such as manual monitoring and reporting systems, often fall short due to delays and difficulties in identifying nuanced instances of harassment. AI technologies offer significant advancements in cyberbullying detection by enabling real-time analysis and intervention capabilities. However, it is essential to acknowledge that these technologies may struggle with accurately detecting nuanced forms of cyberbullying, such as sarcasm or cultural references. Their deployment raises ethical concerns, including privacy issues such as unauthorized data access and algorithmic biases that could lead to unfair treatment of certain user groups, as evidenced by instances where algorithms misidentified non-abusive content due to cultural or linguistic variances.

Artificial Intelligence (AI) offers promising solutions for creating safer online communities by preventing and mitigating the impacts of cyberbullying, a pervasive issue with severe emotional and psychological consequences for victims (Patchin & Hinduja, 2018). AI technologies use Natural Language Processing (NLP) to analyze text for abusive language. They also employ advanced algorithms to detect nuanced forms of bullying, such as sarcasm and coded language (Chatzakou et al., 2017). Additionally, AI can analyze images and videos to identify harmful content, providing real-time monitoring and alerting moderators or users about potential cyberbullying incidents (Zhong et al., 2016). Preventive measures include content filtering, which blocks offensive messages, and user education, which encourages positive interactions (Dinakar et al., 2012). Effective user education programs, such as the 'Be Internet Awesome' initiative by Google, have demonstrated success in teaching digital literacy and safe online behavior. These programs incorporate interactive modules and real-world scenarios to equip users with the tools to identify and respond to cyberbullying. For intervention and support, AI-driven tools facilitate the reporting of cyberbullying, streamline evidence collection, and offer emotional support through chatbots and virtual assistants (Saha et al., 2021). AI aids community management by flagging harmful content for human moderators and ensuring consistent enforcement of community guidelines (Chen et al., 2020). However, the implementation of AI in cyberbullying prevention raises ethical concerns regarding privacy, data security, and potential biases in algorithms, necessitating a balance between effective monitoring and user privacy (Dwork et al., 2012). Collaboration among AI developers, policymakers, and online platforms is essential for developing transparent, fair, and inclusive AI systems that enhance the safety and positivity of digital environments for all users.

Cyberbullying

Cyberbullying is a form of bullying that occurs through digital devices such as computers, smartphones, and tablets. It involves the use of electronic communication to bully a person, typically by sending messages of an intimidating or threatening nature. Cyberbullying can take place on various platforms, including social media, text messages, emails, and online gaming communities. The anonymity and wide reach of the internet amplify the potential harm caused by cyberbullying, making it a significant concern in today's digital age (Patchin & Hinduja, 2018).

Prevalence of Cyberbullying

Cyberbullying has become a pervasive issue in the digital age, affecting individuals across various age groups and platforms. The prevalence of cyberbullying differs in different cultures and countries. The following statistics aid in shedding light on the same. According to Patchin and Hinduja (2019), approximately 36.5% of students aged 12-17 in the United States, have experienced cyberbullying. This statistic highlights the widespread nature of the problem among American youth. The Global Kids Online study conducted by Livingstone et al. (2016) found that one in three children aged 9-17 years in Europe had experienced cyberbullying. This study underscores the prevalence of cyberbullying across different European countries.

Prevalence rates of cyberbullying can vary significantly depending on the study's methodology, definitions, and sample populations. Kowalski et al. (2014) reviewed multiple studies and found that cyberbullying rates ranged from 10% to 40% among youth populations. These variations highlight the complexity of accurately measuring the prevalence of cyberbullying due to differing operational definitions and reporting practices.

Various Forms of Cyberbullying

- **Harassment:** Harassment involves repeatedly sending offensive, rude, and insulting messages to an individual. This can include threats, derogatory remarks, and hate speech. The repetitive nature of harassment makes it particularly distressing for victims (Smith et al., 2008).
- **Flaming:** Flaming refers to online fights or heated arguments where participants exchange hostile and vulgar messages. This type of cyberbullying often occurs in public forums or comment sections, where the aggressive interactions are visible to a broader audience (Kowalski et al., 2014).
- **Exclusion:** Exclusion involves deliberately excluding someone from an online group, chat, or game. This form of cyberbullying can make the victim feel isolated and rejected, significantly impacting their self-esteem and sense of belonging (Tokunaga, 2010).

- **Outing and Doxxing:** Outing refers to publicly sharing someone's private, sensitive, or embarrassing information without their consent. Doxxing involves revealing personal information, such as home addresses or phone numbers, with malicious intent. Both practices can lead to severe emotional distress and real-world consequences for the victims (Hinduja & Patchin, 2009).
- **Masquerading:** Masquerading involves creating fake identities or impersonating someone else to deceive or harass a victim. This can include hacking into someone's account to send harmful messages or create damaging posts. The anonymity provided by fake accounts makes it challenging to identify and stop the perpetrator (Willard, 2007).
- **Cyberstalking:** Cyberstalking is the use of the internet to stalk or harass an individual, often involving monitoring the victim's online activities, sending threatening messages, and spreading false information. Cyberstalking can escalate into real-world stalking and poses significant risks to the victim's safety (Bocij & McFarlane, 2003).
- **Trolling:** Trolling involves deliberately provoking and upsetting people online to elicit emotional responses. Trolls often post inflammatory or off-topic messages in online communities, disrupting discussions and causing distress to participants (Buckels et al., 2014).

Thus, understanding the various forms of cyberbullying, as discussed above, is crucial for developing effective prevention and intervention strategies. Each type of cyberbullying presents unique challenges and requires tailored approaches to address the specific behaviors and impacts involved. By recognizing the diverse manifestations of cyberbullying, stakeholders, including educators, parents, and policymakers, can better protect individuals from online harassment and create safer digital environments.

Impact of Cyberbullying

I. Psychological Impact

The psychological impact of cyberbullying on victims is profound and multifaceted, often leading to long-term mental health issues. Studies indicate that victims may develop chronic anxiety, depression, and trust issues, which can affect personal relationships and professional success.

Anxiety and Depression: Victims of cyberbullying frequently experience heightened levels of anxiety and depression. Hinduja and Patchin (2018) reported that individuals subjected to cyberbullying exhibited increased feelings of sadness and hopelessness compared to their peers. The persistent and invasive nature of cyberbullying contributes to chronic stress, which can exacerbate pre-existing mental health conditions or lead to the development of new psychological issues (Van Geel et al., 2014).

Low Self-Esteem and Suicidal Ideation: Cyberbullying significantly impacts victims' self-esteem, often resulting in feelings of worthlessness and diminished self-worth. The constant negative feedback and personal attacks can erode an individual's confidence and self-perception (Ortega et al., 2012). In severe cases, the psychological distress caused by cyberbullying can lead to suicidal thoughts and behaviors. Studies have shown a strong correlation between cyberbullying victimization and an increased risk of suicide among adolescents (Van Geel et al., 2014).

II. Emotional Impact

The emotional toll of cyberbullying can be severe, affecting victims' overall emotional well-being and stability.

Emotional Trauma: Victims often experience significant emotional trauma, including feelings of fear, anger, and helplessness. The relentless nature of cyberbullying can lead to a constant state of emotional distress (Kowalski et al., 2014). The anonymity and 24/7 nature of online harassment amplify the emotional impact, as victims can be targeted at any time and place, making it difficult to find respite from the abuse (Ortega et al., 2012).

Isolation and Loneliness: Cyberbullying can lead to social withdrawal and isolation as victims may avoid online interactions to escape further harassment. This isolation can result in loneliness and a lack of social support, which are critical for emotional health (Perren et al., 2010). The fear of judgment and further bullying can prevent victims from seeking help, exacerbating their feelings of isolation and loneliness (Tokunaga, 2010).

III. Social Impact

The social repercussions of cyberbullying extend beyond the individual, affecting relationships and community dynamics.

Disrupted Relationships: Victims of cyberbullying often struggle to maintain healthy relationships, both online and offline. The fear of becoming a target can lead to trust issues and difficulties in forming new friendships (Perren et al., 2010). Existing relationships may also suffer as victims withdraw from social activities and interactions to avoid bullying, leading to a breakdown in social connections (Slonje et al., 2013).

Academic and Extracurricular Decline: The stress and distraction caused by cyberbullying can negatively impact academic performance and participation in extracurricular activities. Victims may find it challenging to concentrate on schoolwork or feel motivated to engage in activities they once enjoyed (Hinduja & Patchin, 2018). The decline in academic and extracurricular involvement can further isolate victims and limit their opportunities for positive social interactions and personal growth (Kowalski et al., 2014).

IV. Community Impact

On a broader scale, cyberbullying contributes to a toxic online environment, undermining trust and safety in digital communities. The pervasive fear of being bullied can deter individuals from participating in online platforms and forums, reducing the overall quality of digital interactions (Slonje et al., 2013). It also alters community dynamics by discouraging participation in digital spaces and fostering a culture of hostility. This highlights the need for interventions that address both individual behaviors and systemic issues within online platforms. The impact of cyberbullying on community dynamics highlights the need for comprehensive strategies to address and prevent online harassment, fostering a more inclusive and supportive digital culture (Livingstone et al., 2016).

This study is justified by the urgent need to address the rising prevalence of cyberbullying, which affects a significant portion of the youth population, with approximately 37% of U.S. teenagers reporting such experiences (Cyberbullying Research Center, 2023). Traditional prevention methods, including manual monitoring and reporting systems, have proven inadequate due to their inefficiency in real-time detection and response (Tokunaga, 2010). The integration of advanced AI technologies, such as machine learning and natural language processing, offers a promising alternative by enhancing the accuracy and immediacy of cyberbullying detection and intervention (Gao et al., 2021; Devlin et al., 2018). However, the deployment of AI in this context raises critical ethical considerations, including privacy, free speech, and algorithmic bias, which must be addressed to ensure fair and effective implementation (Binns et al., 2018). This study aims to explore these technological advancements and their potential to transform cyberbullying prevention, providing valuable insights for developing comprehensive strategies and policies to create safer online environments (Sweeney et al., 2019).

Methodology

Literature Search Strategy

Information Sources: To ensure a comprehensive review of the existing literature on the role of AI in cyberbullying prevention, we utilized multiple databases, including PubMed, IEEE Xplore, ACM Digital Library, Google Scholar, and PsycINFO. The search was conducted from inception to July 2024.

Search Terms: The following search terms and their combinations were used: "cyberbullying," "artificial intelligence," "machine learning," "natural language processing," "multimodal analysis," "cyberbullying detection," "cyberbullying prevention," "online harassment," and "AI ethics."

Inclusion and Exclusion Criteria

Inclusion Criteria:

1. Type of Studies: Empirical studies, reviews, theoretical papers, and conference papers.

2. Language: Articles published in English.
3. Focus: Studies that focus on the application of AI technologies such as machine learning algorithms, NLP, and multimodal analysis in cyberbullying detection and prevention.
4. Population: Studies involving participants of any age group affected by cyberbullying.
5. Date Range: Studies published from January 2000 to July 2024.

Exclusion Criteria

1. Non-Peer-Reviewed Sources: Articles that are not peer-reviewed, such as opinion pieces, news articles, and editorials.
2. Irrelevant Focus: Studies that do not specifically address the use of AI in cyberbullying prevention or detection.
3. Insufficient Data: Studies with insufficient methodological detail or incomplete data.

Study Selection

Screening Process: The initial search yielded 3,287 articles. After removing duplicates, 2,563 articles remained. Titles and abstracts were screened and irrelevant articles were excluded. This process resulted in 456 articles being selected for full-text review.

Full-Text Review: The full-text articles were reviewed for eligibility based on the inclusion and exclusion criteria. Discrepancies were resolved through discussion. This process resulted in 123 articles being included in the final analysis.

Data Extraction: A standardized data extraction form was used to collect relevant information from each study. The following data were extracted:

- Study details: authors, publication year, journal/conference
- Study design: empirical study, review, theoretical paper
- AI technology used: machine learning algorithms, NLP techniques, multimodal analysis

- ○ Key findings: effectiveness of AI in cyberbullying detection/prevention, ethical considerations, limitations

Data Synthesis

Qualitative Synthesis: A thematic analysis was conducted to identify key themes and patterns across the included studies. This involved coding the extracted data and organizing it into themes such as "effectiveness of AI technologies," "ethical challenges," and "integration with existing frameworks."

Quantitative Synthesis: Where possible, a meta-analysis was conducted to quantitatively synthesize the results from empirical studies. Effect sizes were calculated using standardized mean differences for continuous outcomes and odds ratios for categorical outcomes. Heterogeneity was assessed using the I^2 statistic, and random-effects models were applied to account for variability among studies.

Reporting and Transparency

PRISMA Guidelines: The methodology and findings of this literature review are reported in accordance with the Preferred Reporting Items for Systematic Reviews and Meta-Analyses (PRISMA) guidelines. A PRISMA flow diagram is provided to illustrate the study selection process, and a PRISMA checklist is included to ensure comprehensive reporting.

Phase	**Number of Records**
Identification	
Records identified through database searching (PubMed, IEEE Xplore, ACM Digital Library, Google Scholar, PsycINFO)	3,287
Additional records identified through other sources	0
Screening	
Records after duplicates removed	2,563
Records screened	2,563

Phase	Number of Records
Records excluded	2,107
Eligibility	
Full-text articles assessed for eligibility	456
Full-text articles excluded (with reasons)	333
Included	
Studies included in qualitative synthesis	123

By adhering to these rigorous methodological steps, this literature review aims to provide a comprehensive and unbiased synthesis of the role of AI in cyberbullying prevention, highlighting both the potential benefits and ethical considerations associated with these technologies.

Current Challenges in Cyberbullying Prevention

Traditional approaches to cyberbullying prevention face several significant challenges, particularly concerning manual monitoring, reporting systems, and delayed responses. Manual monitoring and reporting systems, though foundational, have notable shortcomings:

Volume and Scale: The vast amount of online content generated daily makes comprehensive manual monitoring impractical. The sheer scale of interactions across social media platforms, messaging apps, and forums far exceeds the capacity of human moderators to effectively review and address all instances of cyberbullying (Gillespie, 2006). For example, Facebook's content moderation system, despite employing thousands of moderators, still struggles to keep up with the volume of user-generated content (Ponce, 2019).

Subjectivity and Inconsistency: The interpretation of what constitutes cyberbullying can vary widely among moderators. This subjectivity often results in inconsistent enforcement of anti-bullying policies. Research indicates that different moderators might have different thresholds for what is considered harmful or abusive, leading to variability in the handling of reported incidents (O'Keeffe & Clarke-Pearson, 2011). This inconsistency undermines the effectiveness of traditional reporting systems.

Underreporting by Victims: Victims often do not report cyberbullying incidents due to concerns about retaliation, a lack of trust in the reporting process, or embarrassment. This underreporting limits the effectiveness of manual systems, as a significant proportion of bullying incidents go unreported and, therefore, unaddressed (Livingstone et al., 2011). For instance, a study by the Cyberbullying Research Center found that less than 40% of victims reported the incidents to authorities (Patchin & Hinduja, 2018).

Delay in Response and Intervention

The effectiveness of traditional methods is further compromised by delays in response and intervention:

Time Lag: The time required to detect, report, and respond to cyberbullying incidents can result in significant delays. This lag can lead to prolonged victim suffering and escalation of the bullying behavior. Patchin and Hinduja (2015) highlighted that the average time from reporting to resolution can vary widely, often leaving victims in distressing situations for extended periods.

Resource Constraints: Many institutions and online platforms lack the resources needed for prompt and effective intervention. Schools and smaller platforms, in particular, may face constraints related to staff, funding, and technological support, which can delay their ability to address reported incidents effectively (Shariff, 2008). Resource limitations often result in inadequate support for victims and insufficient measures to deter perpetrators.

Legal and Bureaucratic Hurdles: Navigating legal and bureaucratic frameworks adds complexity and delays to the response process. Compliance with privacy laws, the need for permissions, and coordination among various stakeholders can slow down intervention efforts. Hinduja and Patchin (2013) noted that the bureaucratic nature of handling cyberbullying cases can impede timely action and resolution.

Concerns regarding Cyberbullying

Identifying and addressing cyberbullying presents its own set of challenges, particularly concerning the detection of subtle or context-specific behaviors and the difficulties faced by platforms and educators. Cyberbullying often involves nuanced and context-specific behaviors that are challenging to detect:

Evolving Language and Behaviors: Cyberbullying often involves coded language, slang, and memes that evolve rapidly. Automated systems and human moderators may struggle to keep up with these changes, resulting in missed instances of bullying. Dinakar et al. (2012) emphasized that the dynamic nature of online communication necessitates constant updates to detection algorithms to effectively identify and address cyberbullying.

Context and Intent: Accurate detection of cyberbullying requires understanding the context and intent behind online interactions. Automated systems often struggle with this nuance, leading to potential false positives or negatives. Cheng et al. (2017) highlighted that context-sensitive detection is critical, as the same phrase or behavior can be interpreted differently depending on the situation and relationships involved.

Private and Encrypted Communications: Many instances of cyberbullying occur in private messages or through encrypted channels, which are challenging for both human moderators and automated systems to access. Boyd (2014) discussed the difficulties in monitoring private communications while respecting user privacy, which complicates efforts to detect and address cyberbullying.

Challenges Faced by Platforms and Educators

Platforms and educators face several specific challenges in their efforts to prevent and address cyberbullying:

Resource Allocation: Effective cyberbullying prevention requires significant resources, including technological tools, staff training, and support services. Smaller platforms and educational institutions often struggle to allocate sufficient resources, impacting their ability to effectively monitor and address bullying (Kowalski et al., 2014).

Training and Awareness: Educators and platform moderators may lack comprehensive training in identifying and responding to cyberbullying. Ongoing professional development is crucial to equip them with the necessary skills and knowledge. Cassidy et al. (2013) stressed the importance of training programs to enhance the ability of educators and moderators to handle cyberbullying incidents effectively.

Policy Implementation: Developing and enforcing anti-cyberbullying policies is complex. Effective policies must be clearly defined, consistently applied, and communicated to all stakeholders. Hinduja and Patchin (2015) noted that creating and maintaining comprehensive policies requires continuous effort and coordination among various parties involved.

Balancing Freedom of Speech: Platforms must navigate the delicate balance between preventing cyberbullying and protecting freedom of speech. Overly restrictive measures can stifle legitimate expression, while lenient policies can fail to address harmful behavior. Citron (2014) discussed the challenges of finding this balance, emphasizing the need for policies that protect users while preserving their rights to free expression.

AI Technologies in Cyberbullying Detection and Prevention

Machine Learning Algorithms

Machine learning (ML) algorithms play a pivotal role in the detection and prevention of cyberbullying by automating the analysis of large volumes of data to identify abusive language and behavior. These algorithms utilize various techniques to discern patterns indicative of cyberbullying:

Classification Models: Classification algorithms, such as support vector machines (SVMs) and decision trees, are commonly used to categorize text into predefined classes such as "abusive" or "non-abusive." These models are trained on labeled datasets of known cyberbullying incidents and learn to predict the likelihood of new instances being abusive (Yang et al., 2019). For example, SVMs can be particularly effective due to their ability to handle high-dimensional data and classify text based on complex feature spaces (Joachims, 1998).

Deep Learning Techniques: More advanced ML models, such as deep neural networks (DNNs) and recurrent neural networks (RNNs), have shown promising results in detecting cyberbullying. DNNs, including convolutional neural networks (CNNs) and Long Short-Term Memory networks (LSTMs), are adept at capturing intricate patterns in text data and learning from vast amounts of input. For instance, LSTMs are particularly useful for understanding sequences in text, allowing them to capture context and nuances in language (Hochreiter & Schmidhuber, 1997).

Ensemble Methods: Ensemble techniques, which combine the predictions of multiple models, can enhance the accuracy of cyberbullying detection. Methods such as random forests and gradient boosting aggregate predictions from various base models to improve performance and robustness (Breiman, 2001). These methods help address the challenge of variability in user-generated content by leveraging multiple perspectives on the data.

Natural Language Processing (NLP)

Natural Language Processing (NLP) is critical for understanding the context and intent behind online interactions, which is essential for accurate cyberbullying detection:

Contextual Analysis: NLP techniques enable the analysis of contextual information within text, which helps distinguish between harmless and harmful interactions. Techniques such as sentiment analysis, named entity recognition (NER), and semantic role labeling are employed to understand the context in which certain terms or phrases are used (Manning et al., 2014). For example, sentiment analysis can help identify negative emotions associated with text, which may be indicative of bullying behavior.

Intent Detection: Understanding the intent behind a message is crucial for effective cyberbullying detection. Advanced NLP models, such as those based on transformer architectures (e.g., BERT, GPT-3), leverage contextual embeddings to capture the subtle nuances of language and intent. These models can analyze complex sentence structures and infer meanings based on surrounding text (Devlin et al., 2018). For instance, BERT's bidirectional context understanding enables it to identify subtle cues that may indicate abusive intent.

Contextual Embeddings: Contextual embeddings, generated by models like BERT, provide a nuanced representation of words based on their usage in specific contexts. This approach allows NLP systems to better understand ambiguous terms and phrases that might otherwise be misclassified as non-abusive (Peters et al., 2018). For example, the term "hate" may be benign in some contexts but harmful in others, and contextual embeddings help differentiate between these scenarios.

Image and Video Recognition

AI technologies extend beyond text to include image and video recognition, which is increasingly used to detect visual forms of cyberbullying:

Image Analysis: Machine learning models are trained to identify harmful imagery associated with cyberbullying. Techniques such as convolutional neural networks (CNNs) are employed to analyze visual content, detecting inappropriate or abusive images. CNNs can classify images based on learned features, such as explicit content or visual harassment (Krizhevsky et al., 2012). For instance, CNNs can be used to identify and flag images containing hate symbols or offensive gestures.

Video Analysis: Video recognition technologies analyze moving images to detect instances of cyberbullying. Recurrent neural networks (RNNs) and temporal convolutional networks (TCNs) are used to process video sequences and identify abusive behavior over time (Donahue et al., 2015). These models can detect patterns of aggression, such as bullying gestures or physical harassment, in video content.

Multimodal Approaches: Combining text, image, and video analysis enhances the ability to detect and address cyberbullying comprehensively. Multimodal AI systems integrate information from multiple sources to improve detection accuracy. For example, combining text analysis with image recognition can help identify instances where harmful language is paired with offensive images, providing a more complete picture of the bullying behavior (Wu et al., 2019).

Ethical Considerations in Using AI

Privacy and Data Protection

The application of AI in cyberbullying detection and prevention raises significant concerns regarding privacy and data protection. Ensuring the responsible use of AI technologies involves addressing these concerns comprehensively:

Ensuring User Privacy: Protecting user privacy is paramount when implementing AI systems for cyberbullying detection. AI technologies often require access to sensitive user data, including personal messages, images, and videos. To mitigate privacy risks, it is essential to implement robust data protection measures, such as anonymization and encryption. Anonymization techniques, like data masking and pseudonymization, help ensure that personal identifiers are not exposed (Garfinkel et al., 2012). Encryption, both at rest and in transit, safeguards data from unauthorized access and breaches (Anderson, 2020).

Compliance with Data Protection Laws: Adhering to data protection regulations, such as the General Data Protection Regulation (GDPR) in the European Union and the California Consumer Privacy Act (CCPA) in the United States, is crucial for AI applications. These laws mandate strict requirements for data collection, storage, and processing. For instance, GDPR emphasizes the importance of obtaining informed consent from users before collecting personal data and provides individuals with the right to access, rectify, and delete their data (Voigt & von dem Bussche, 2017). Compliance with these regulations helps protect user rights and builds trust in AI systems.

Transparency and Accountability: AI systems should operate with transparency, allowing users to understand how their data is being used. Implementing transparency measures, such as clear privacy policies and user notifications, is critical for maintaining accountability. Additionally, organizations should conduct regular audits of AI systems to ensure compliance with data protection standards and address any potential vulnerabilities (Dastin, 2021).

Balancing Intervention and Free Speech

Navigating the balance between moderating content and preserving free speech is a complex ethical issue in AI-based cyberbullying prevention:

Moderating Content: AI systems must be designed to identify and address harmful content without overly censoring legitimate expression. Developing effective moderation policies involves defining clear criteria for what constitutes cyberbullying and ensuring that AI systems are calibrated to enforce these criteria consistently. For instance, content moderation policies should differentiate between harmful behavior and benign speech to avoid stifling free expression (Gillespie, 2018).

Preserving Free Speech: Ensuring that AI systems do not infringe on users' freedom of speech is essential. Overzealous moderation can lead to the suppression of legitimate discourse and the chilling of free expression. Striking a balance involves setting thresholds for intervention that respect both user rights and community standards. For example, platforms can implement appeal processes allowing users to contest moderation decisions and ensure that content removal decisions are subject to review (Citron, 2014).

Ethical Frameworks: Applying ethical frameworks, such as the principle of proportionality, can guide AI systems in balancing intervention and free speech. The principle of proportionality ensures that interventions are appropriate to the severity of the behavior and that any restrictions on speech are justified and minimal (Binns et al., 2018).

Bias and Fairness

Addressing biases in AI algorithms is critical for ensuring fairness and inclusivity in cyberbullying detection systems:

Bias in AI Algorithms: AI systems can inadvertently perpetuate biases present in training data. For example, if training datasets contain biased representations of certain groups, the AI algorithms may produce skewed results that disproportionately affect these groups. Research has shown that biased datasets can lead to discriminatory outcomes, such as higher false positive rates for certain demographic groups (Buolamwini & Gebru, 2018).

Addressing these biases requires careful dataset curation and algorithmic adjustments.

Fairness and Inclusivity: Ensuring fairness in AI systems involves implementing techniques to detect and mitigate biases. Techniques such as fairness-aware machine learning, which adjusts algorithms to reduce disparities in outcomes across different groups, can help achieve more equitable results (Kamiran & Calders, 2012). Additionally, involving diverse teams in the development and evaluation of AI systems can provide multiple perspectives and help identify potential biases (Raji & Buolamwini, 2019).

Transparency and Accountability in AI: Transparency in AI development and deployment processes is essential for addressing biases and ensuring fairness. Providing clear documentation of algorithmic decisions, including the rationale for specific outcomes, helps stakeholders understand and scrutinize the system's behavior. Regular audits and evaluations of AI systems for fairness and bias are crucial for maintaining accountability and improving the system over time (Suresh & Guttag, 2019).

Role of Social Media Platforms

Policies and Tools

Major social media platforms have adopted a variety of policies and tools to combat cyberbullying. These measures include:

Content Moderation Policies: Platforms like Facebook, Twitter, and Instagram have established comprehensive content moderation policies designed to address cyberbullying. These policies outline prohibited behaviors and content, including harassment, threats, and hate speech. For instance, Facebook's Community Standards prohibit harassment and hate speech, and the platform uses both automated and human review processes to enforce these rules (Facebook, 2023). Twitter has similar policies that address abusive behavior and provides users with options to report, block, or mute accounts engaging in harassment (Twitter, 2023).

Automated Detection Tools: To enhance the efficiency of content moderation, social media platforms have implemented automated detection tools. These tools utilize machine learning algorithms and natural language processing (NLP) to identify potentially harmful content. For example, Instagram's AI-powered systems are designed to detect and remove offensive comments and images, helping to reduce the prevalence of cyberbullying on the platform (Instagram, 2023). These tools are continually updated to improve accuracy and adapt to evolving patterns of abusive behavior.

User Reporting and Blocking Features: Social media platforms offer users tools to report and block individuals who engage in cyberbullying. Reporting features allow users to flag abusive content or behavior for review, while blocking features enable users to prevent specific individuals from interacting with them. These features empower users to take control of their online experiences and reduce exposure to harmful content (YouTube, 2023).

Educational Resources: Many platforms provide educational resources and guidelines to help users understand and address cyberbullying. For instance, Facebook's Safety Center offers information on recognizing and dealing with cyberbullying, as well as tips for maintaining a positive online environment (Facebook, 2023). These resources aim to raise awareness and equip users with tools to protect themselves and others from cyberbullying.

Collaboration and Partnerships

Social media platforms are increasingly collaborating with AI developers, researchers, and policymakers to enhance their efforts in combating cyberbullying:

AI Developers and Researchers: Platforms partner with AI developers and researchers to advance the development of sophisticated detection and moderation tools. Collaborations focus on I;mproving the accuracy of AI algorithms and reducing false positives and negatives. For example, Facebook has worked with researchers to develop and refine machine learning models for detecting hate speech and harassment (Facebook, 2022). Similarly, Twitter has collaborated with academic institutions to research the impact of automated moderation on user experience and effectiveness (Twitter, 2022).

Policymakers and Advocacy Groups: Social media platforms engage with policymakers and advocacy groups to develop and implement effective regulations and standards for cyberbullying prevention. These collaborations aim to align platform policies with legal and ethical standards and to advocate for laws that address cyberbullying and online harassment. For example, platforms have supported initiatives such as the European Union's Digital Services Act (DSA), which seeks to establish a safer online environment by regulating harmful content and enhancing transparency (European Commission, 2022).

Public-Private Partnerships: Platforms also participate in public-private partnerships to tackle cyberbullying on a broader scale. These partnerships bring together stakeholders from various sectors, including technology companies, educational institutions, and non-profit organizations, to address cyberbullying through joint initiatives and research. For instance, the Global Internet Forum to Counter Terrorism (GIFCT), which includes major tech companies, works collaboratively to combat online abuse and misinformation (GIFCT, 2023).

Legal and Regulatory Frameworks

Existing Laws and Regulations

Various jurisdictions have established legal frameworks to address cyberbullying, each tailored to its legal and cultural context.

United States: In the U.S., the legal landscape for cyberbullying is shaped by a combination of federal and state laws. While there is no specific federal law targeting cyberbullying, several states have enacted legislation that includes provisions for online harassment:

- **California:** The California Cyberbullying Prevention Act (Cal. Penal Code § 653.2, 2020) criminalizes the use of electronic communication to cause harm or fear. The law provides for penalties for those who engage in online harassment that causes significant emotional distress.
- **New York:** The Dignity for All Students Act (DASA) (New York State Education Law § 13, 2012) addresses bullying and

harassment, including cyberbullying, in schools. DASA mandates that schools create a safe environment and provides guidelines for addressing and preventing bullying behaviors.

United Kingdom: The UK addresses cyberbullying through multiple legal provisions:

- **Malicious Communications Act 1988:** This Act criminalizes the sending of malicious, threatening, or offensive messages through electronic communication (Malicious Communications Act 1988). It provides for penalties for individuals who use electronic communications to cause distress or alarm.
- **Communications Act 2003:** This Act includes provisions against sending offensive messages through electronic communication (Communications Act 2003). The Act is used to address online harassment and abusive behavior.
- **Online Safety Bill:** Proposed legislation, the Online Safety Bill, aims to establish a comprehensive regulatory framework for online platforms to tackle harmful content, including cyberbullying (UK Government, 2023).

European Union: The EU has introduced several regulations to address online safety and cyberbullying:

- **General Data Protection Regulation (GDPR):** Enforced since 2018, GDPR regulates the processing of personal data and includes provisions for data protection and privacy, which are relevant for cases of online harassment (European Parliament & Council, 2016).
- **Digital Services Act (DSA):** The DSA aims to create a safer online environment by imposing obligations on digital platforms to manage harmful content, including cyberbullying (European Commission, 2022). It mandates transparency and accountability measures for online platforms.

Australia: The Enhancing Online Safety Act 2015 provides a framework for dealing with cyberbullying, particularly among children and teenagers. The Act establishes the Office of the eSafety Commissioner, which is empowered to issue removal notices and work with online platforms to address harmful content (Enhancing Online Safety Act 2015).

India: India's approach to cyberbullying is shaped by various laws addressing online harassment and abuse:

- **Information Technology Act, 2000:** The IT Act includes provisions for addressing cybercrime and online harassment. Section 66A (repealed in 2015) previously dealt with sending offensive messages through communication devices. Section 66E criminalizes the transmission of private images without consent, and Section 67 covers the transmission of obscene material (Information Technology Act, 2000).
- **Indian Penal Code (IPC):** Several sections of the IPC address online harassment, including Section 354D, which deals with stalking, and Section 509, which addresses insulting the modesty of a woman (Indian Penal Code, 1860). These sections can be applied to cases involving online harassment and threats.
- **The Protection of Children from Sexual Offences (POCSO) Act, 2012:** This Act provides protection against sexual offenses, including those committed online (POCSO Act, 2012). It includes provisions for addressing online exploitation and abuse of minors.

Supporting Legal Enforcement with AI

AI technologies play a pivotal role in supporting legal actions related to cyberbullying by enhancing evidence collection and analysis.

Evidence Collection: AI tools facilitate the efficient collection and organization of digital evidence. Automated data scraping technologies can aggregate relevant information from social media platforms and online communications. For example, AI-driven web scraping tools can systematically collect data related to harassment incidents, providing comprehensive evidence for legal cases (Gao et al., 2018).

Text and Sentiment Analysis: Natural Language Processing (NLP) techniques are employed to analyze and classify text data related to cyberbullying. AI systems can detect and categorize abusive language and identify patterns of harassment. Sentiment analysis models can assess the emotional tone of messages to determine if they are harmful or threatening (Peters et al., 2018). These capabilities are crucial for generating evidence and supporting legal claims.

Image and Video Analysis: AI technologies also extend to visual content analysis. Image recognition algorithms can identify and flag inappropriate or abusive visual content, such as explicit images used in harassment. For example, AI systems can analyze images and videos to detect signs of abuse, helping to build a case for legal action (Krizhevsky et al., 2012).

Legal Analytics: AI-powered legal analytics tools assist legal professionals by providing insights into case law and predicting legal outcomes. These tools use data from past cases and legal documents to support strategy development and decision-making in cyberbullying cases (Susskind, 2019).

Community and Educational Initiatives

Awareness and Education Programs

Awareness and education programs are crucial in combating cyberbullying by informing users about its impact and providing strategies for prevention and intervention. These initiatives often target children, teenagers, and the broader community.

Online Safety Campaigns: Various organizations and government bodies run online safety campaigns to raise awareness about cyberbullying. For example, the UK's "Be Smart Online" campaign provides resources and information to help individuals understand and deal with cyberbullying (UK Safer Internet Centre, 2021). Similarly, the U.S. Federal Trade Commission's "OnGuardOnline" initiative offers tips and educational materials about online safety, including how to handle cyberbullying (Federal Trade Commission, 2023).

Educational Workshops and Programs: Schools and community organizations often conduct workshops and educational programs focusing on digital citizenship and online behavior. Programs such as "Digital Citizenship Curriculum" by Common Sense Education provide lessons on responsible online behavior, including recognizing and responding to cyberbullying (Common Sense Media, 2023). These programs are designed to teach students about internet safety, the impact of cyberbullying, and strategies for protecting themselves and others.

Public Service Announcements (PSAs): PSAs are used to spread awareness about cyberbullying through various media channels, including television, radio, and social media. Campaigns like "Stop Bullying" by the U.S. Department of Health and Human Services use PSAs to educate the public about the signs of cyberbullying and how to seek help (StopBullying.gov, 2023).

Collaborations with Tech Companies: Technology companies often partner with educational institutions and non-profits to develop and promote educational resources. For instance, Google's "Be Internet Awesome" program includes interactive lessons and games designed to teach children about internet safety and responsible online behavior (Google, 2023).

Role of Schools and Parents

Schools and parents play a pivotal role in preventing and addressing cyberbullying through collaborative efforts and proactive strategies.

School-Based Programs: Schools are implementing comprehensive programs to address cyberbullying. These programs include anti-bullying policies, curriculum integration, and student support services. For example, the "Olweus Bullying Prevention Program" used in schools worldwide includes components specifically addressing cyberbullying and involves students, teachers, and parents in creating a positive school climate (Olweus & Limber, 2018). Schools may also offer counseling services and establish reporting systems to support victims and address incidents of cyberbullying.

Parent-Teacher Associations (PTAs): PTAs and other parent organizations play a role in raising awareness about cyberbullying and supporting school-based initiatives. By organizing workshops and discussions, PTAs help parents understand the signs of cyberbullying and how to support their children (Harrison & Weiner, 2021). These associations also advocate for effective anti-cyberbullying policies and practices within schools.

Parental Involvement and Education: Parents are crucial in preventing cyberbullying by educating their children about online safety and maintaining open lines of communication. Programs such as "Parent's Guide to Cyberbullying" by the Cyberbullying Research Center offer resources and guidance for parents to understand and address cyberbullying (Cyberbullying Research Center, 2023). Effective parental involvement includes monitoring online activity, setting rules for internet use, and discussing the potential risks associated with digital communication.

Community Engagement: Community organizations, such as non-profits and local advocacy groups, work to promote awareness and support for cyberbullying prevention. These organizations often collaborate with schools and parents to organize community events, educational sessions, and support networks for affected individuals. Initiatives like the "Cyberbullying Helpline" provide support and resources for both victims and their families (National Bullying Prevention Center, 2023).

Future Directions and Innovations

Emerging AI Technologies

The field of artificial intelligence is rapidly evolving, with emerging technologies poised to revolutionize cyberbullying detection and prevention. Key advancements include:

Advanced Machine Learning Models: New machine learning models, particularly those leveraging deep learning techniques, are enhancing the ability to detect and analyze cyberbullying. Recent developments in transformer-based models, such as GPT-4 and its successors, improve contextual understanding and can better identify nuanced instances of online harassment (Brown et al., 2020). These models are capable of analyzing large volumes of text and recognizing subtle patterns indicative of bullying.

Emotion Recognition and Sentiment Analysis: Emerging AI technologies are improving emotion recognition and sentiment analysis. AI systems that analyze tone, sentiment, and emotional content in text are becoming more sophisticated. These systems use advanced natural language processing (NLP) techniques to detect emotional cues and intent behind communications, thereby identifying potentially harmful interactions more accurately (Devlin et al., 2018).

Behavioral Pattern Recognition: AI is also advancing in the realm of behavioral pattern recognition. Machine learning algorithms are increasingly effective at recognizing patterns of behavior associated with cyberbullying, such as repeated targeting or harassment. Techniques such as anomaly detection can identify deviations from normal online behavior, flagging potential cases of cyberbullying for further review (Cheng et al., 2019).

Multimodal Analysis: The integration of text, image, and video analysis into a unified AI framework is an emerging trend. Multimodal AI systems are capable of analyzing various types of content simultaneously, providing a comprehensive approach to detecting cyberbullying across different formats. For instance, combining text-based analysis with image recognition allows for the detection of abusive language in conjunction with harmful visual content (Krizhevsky et al., 2012).

Creating a Safer Online Environment

The future of online safety is likely to be shaped by increasingly sophisticated AI technologies designed to create safer digital spaces. Key aspects of this vision include:

Proactive Moderation and Real-Time Interventions: AI-driven systems are expected to enhance proactive moderation by identifying and addressing cyberbullying in real-time. Advanced algorithms can monitor online interactions continuously, providing immediate alerts to moderators when potentially harmful behavior is detected. This proactive approach aims to prevent the escalation of cyberbullying incidents before they reach a critical stage (Gao et al., 2021).

Personalized Safety Measures: Future AI systems may offer personalized safety measures tailored to individual users' needs. Machine learning models could analyze users' interaction patterns and customize safety settings based on their behavior and preferences. For example, AI could adjust content filters and notifications to suit different users' sensitivities and experiences (Yin et al., 2020).

Enhanced User Education and Empowerment: AI technologies will likely play a role in enhancing user education and empowerment. AI-driven educational tools could provide interactive training on recognizing and responding to cyberbullying. These tools may use simulations and real-life scenarios to teach users how to handle online harassment effectively (Reddy et al., 2022).

Ethical and Transparent AI Systems: The development of AI systems for online safety will need to address ethical considerations, including transparency and fairness. Future AI solutions are expected to include features that ensure transparency in how algorithms make decisions and provide users with insights into moderation processes. Ensuring fairness and minimizing biases will be critical to maintaining trust and effectiveness in AI-driven safety measures (Binns et al., 2018).

Collaborative AI Ecosystems: The future may also see the development of collaborative AI ecosystems where multiple stakeholders, including tech companies, policymakers, and researchers, work together to create integrated safety solutions. Such ecosystems could involve sharing data and insights to improve AI models and develop comprehensive strategies for tackling cyberbullying across different platforms (Sweeney et al., 2019).

Suggestions

To enhance cyberbullying prevention, it is essential to integrate advanced AI technologies such as machine learning and natural language processing for real-time detection and intervention, while addressing ethical concerns including privacy, bias, and the balance between moderation and free speech. Developing comprehensive frameworks that combine AI with existing legal and educational strategies is crucial, as is promoting user education on recognizing and reporting cyberbullying and understanding AI's role in online safety. Additionally, fostering collaboration among tech developers, researchers, and community stakeholders will drive innovation and refinement in prevention methods. Regular monitoring and evaluation of AI systems are necessary to assess their effectiveness and adapt to evolving trends in online harassment.

This chapter highlights these challenges and proposes integrating AI with existing legal and educational frameworks to develop a comprehensive approach. The chapter suggests that while AI-driven solutions hold promise for more effective cyberbullying prevention, addressing ethical considerations is crucial to ensure fairness and respect for user rights. The study also underscores the importance of user education and collaboration among technology developers, policymakers, and educators. Future research should focus on ongoing innovation in AI technologies, their application in prevention strategies, and rigorous monitoring and evaluation to adapt to evolving online behaviors.

Reference

1. Anderson, M. (2018, September 27). *A majority of teens have experienced some form of cyberbullying*. Pew Research Center. https://www.pewresearch.org/internet/2018/09/27/a-majority-of-teens-have-experienced-some-form-of-cyberbullying/

2. Bocij, P., & McFarlane, L. (2003). Cyberstalking: The Technology of Hate. *The Police Journal: Theory, Practice and Principles*, *76*(3), 204–221. https://doi.org/10.1350/pojo.76.3.204.19442

3. Cassidy, W., Faucher, C., & Jackson, M. (2013). Cyberbullying among youth: A comprehensive review of current international research and its implications and application to policy and Practice. *School Psychology International*, *34*(6), 575–612. https://doi.org/10.1177/0143034313479697

4. Chatzakou, D., Kourtellis, N., Blackburn, J., De Cristofaro, E., Stringhini, G., & Vakali, A. (2017). Detecting aggressors and bullies on Twitter. *Proceedings of the 26th International Conference on World Wide Web Companion - WWW '17 Companion.* https://doi.org/10.1145/3041021.3054211

5. Citron, D. K. (2016). *Hate crimes in cyberspace*. Harvard Univ Press. *Data Protection Impact Assessments (dpias)*. ICO. (n.d.). https://ico.

org.uk/for-organisations/uk- gdpr-guidance-and-resources/accountability-and-governance/data-protection-impact-assessments-dpias/

6. Department for Science, I. and T. (2023, June 30). *Online safety bill.* GOV.UK. https://www.gov.uk/government/collections/online-safety-bill

7. *Digcit Landing Page*. Common Sense Education. (n.d.). https://www. [illegible]

8. Health Resources and Services Administration (HRSA). (2024, March 21). *Stop bullying home page.* StopBullying.gov. https://www.stopbullying.gov/

9. Hinduja, S., & Patchin, J. W. (2010). Bullying, cyberbullying, and suicide. *Archives of Suicide Research*, *14*(3), 206–221. https://doi.org/10.1080/13811118.2010.494133

10. Hinduja, S., & Patchin, J. W. (2018). Connecting adolescent suicide to the severity of bullying and cyberbullying. *Journal of School Violence*, *18*(3), 333–346. https://doi.org/10.1080/15388220.2018.1492417

11. Insight - Amazon scraps secret AI recruiting tool that showed bias against women | reuters. (n.d.). https://www.reuters.com/article/us-amazon-com-jobs-automation-insight- idUSKCN1MK08G/

12. Kamiran, F., & Calders, T. (2011). Data preprocessing techniques for classification without discrimination. *Knowledge and Information Systems*, *33*(1), 1–33. https://doi.org/10.1007/s10115-011-0463-8

13. Kochan, M. (2024, June 7). *Parent's guide to cyberbullying*. ConnectSafely. https://connectsafely.org/cyberbullying/

14. Kowalski, R. M., Limber, S. P., & Agatston, P. W. (2008). *Cyber Bullying*. https://doi.org/10.1002/9780470694176

15. Machine learning with legal texts. (2017). *Artificial Intelligence and Legal Analytics*, 234–258. https://doi.org/10.1017/9781316761380.008

16. Molenda, Z. A., Marchlewska, M., Rogoza, M., Michalski, P., Górska, P., Szczepańska, D., & Cislak, A. (n.d.). Cyberpsychology. https://cyberpsychology.eu/article/view/15360

17. *Pacer's National Bullying Prevention Center*. PACER's National Bullying Prevention Center. (n.d.). https://www.pacer.org/BULLYING/

18. *Parents and carers*. UK Safer Internet Centre. (2021, November 24). https://www.saferinternet.org.uk/advice-centre/parents-and-carers

19. *The Digital Services Act Package*. Shaping Europe's digital future. (n.d.). https://digital-strategy.ec.europa.eu/en/policies/digital-services-act-package

20. Tokunaga, R. S. (2010). Following you home from school: A critical review and synthesis of research on cyberbullying victimization. *Computers in Human Behavior, 26*(3), 277–287. https://doi.org/10.1016/j.chb.2009.11.014

21. Tressler, C., Heras, G. de las, Miller, T., Puig, A., & Kreidler, J. (2024, July 16). *Online privacy and security*. Consumer Advice. https://consumer.ftc.gov/identity-theft-and-online-security/online-privacy-and-security

22. Van Geel, M., Vedder, P., & Tanilon, J. (2014). Relationship between peer victimization, cyberbullying, and suicide in children and adolescents. *JAMA Pediatrics, 168*(5), 435. https://doi.org/10.1001/jamapediatrics.2013.4143

The Impact of Artificial Intelligence on Media and Journalism

Mr B. Mohan Sachin, Undergraduate Student, Department of Visual Communication, The American College, Madurai. Email: 2004mohansachin@gmail.com

Mr Abishieke R, Undergraduate Law Student, Amity Law School, Amity University, Noida, Uttar Pradesh. Email: abishiekeramachandran@gmail.com

Introduction

Artificial Intelligence (AI) is constantly discussed for its importance in the current scenario. Amazon's Alexa can understand and follow human commands, which can be considered one of the first introductions of AI to the consumer. It establishes that AI can have machines perform tasks with human-like dexterity. A lending machine's ability to make decisions without human assistance sets it apart from a well-designed service. In simple words, devices can make decisions without explicitly being programmed. Since the beginning of human development, intelligence has only been associated with humans. From the brain, the most vital organ to humans claiming to be the most intelligent organisms on the planet, we have claimed the top spot in possessing and exercising the prime intellect. However, we pride ourselves on this prime intellect because humans can communicate more volumes of information than any other animal on earth. Since the invention of the printing press, media and technology have been knotted, evolving together to shape communication as we know it. As technology advanced over the centuries, so did the channels and methods of media. With the rise of digital media, our reliance on technology increased. This paper deals with how digital media has evolved under the aegis of artificial intelligence and automation and what we need to understand about their relationship. It also examines the effects of artificial intelligence on newsrooms and broadcasting.

Moreover, we can make one's voice or words reach millions, an unparalleled communication ratio. Furthermore, we can save, print and distribute information, which makes it possible to preserve information for the future. Communication occurs because of our ability to understand, from deciphering to visualising. It is an outcome of intellectual ability, which psychologist *Robert Sternberg* defined as *"cognitive activity directed toward the purposeful adaptation to, selection of, and structuring of one's real-world environments."* The same intellect is now attributed to machines, giving way to AI technology. Undoubtedly, AI can save time, energy, and money in all sectors, but that is a narrow evaluation of its potential contribution to human development. Machine Learning which was introduced during the period of 1950s, is one of AI's earliest and most widespread implementations, is ubiquitous in our lives as AI allows machines to improve and learn from experience without being explicitly programmed. Like, Computer Vision in Facial Recognition and Natural Language Processing in auto text completion and Recommendation Systems in digital marketing.

Development of AI

John McCarthy, an American computer science leader and innovator, first used the phrase *"artificial intelligence"* in a presentation he wrote in 1955 for the Dartmouth Conference, 1956. According to John McCarthy, Artificial intelligence is the science and also engineering of creating intelligent machines, especially intelligent computer programs and also it can help to improve the efficiency of production process in the media industry. He asserted that, in theory, every facet of learning and intelligence could be characterised precisely enough for a device to be built to imitate it. In October 1981, Japan unveiled a nationwide project called Fifth Generation Computer Systems to create cutting-edge computer networks for the 2020s. Japan was the first country to take such an initiative. Other prominent pursuits include 'Project Elvi' by Great Britain and the European Union's 'Esprit Program'.

With the advent of steam-powered mechanisation, we witnessed a massive reduction in manual production, ushering in the first industrial revolution. We then entered a period of fast scientific advancement, standardisation, mass manufacturing, and industrialisation known as the Second Industrial Revolution or the Technical Enlightenment. Now, the third industrial revolution is Artificial Intelligence and Machine Learning. It has dramatically reduced human labour, improved the quality of life and expanded human capability. AI and machine learning replace human cognitive labour for specific works like medicine, media, and marketing. With the combination of AI and machines replacing humans mentally and physically, a new problem begins. The UN Committee on Human Rights has found some issues dealing with discrimination against humans. In 2016 book *"Weapons of Math Destruction"*, *Cathy O'Neil* argues how algorithms are not predicting but simply classifying. An example would be the models used to predict recidivism in individuals convicted of a crime, which can unfairly burden people, typically people of colour, who are poor, live in the wrong neighbourhood, or have untreated mental health problems. This limitation stems from the strategy by which a machine-learning model learns, which is solely data-based. It is as if one communicates in fluent Japanese solely using English-to-Japanese and Japanese-to-English dictionaries. Computer scientist and UC Berkeley professor *Alexei Efros* believes that almost all contemporary AI systems rely too much on labels created by humans. *Alexei Efros* reported that students do not pay attention or try to learn the information in class. We are bringing up a new generation of algorithms, like college students who slacked off all semester and then tried to cram for the final exam the evening prior.

AI and Media Learning in Media and Communication

Media, a mass communication tool, has helped empower people with information. Journalists collect news and publish it for society. Journalists are divided into reporters and editors based on the nature of their work. People who spread information among others are called communicators. Several people work as communicators, but they are not considered professional journalists. AI is now vital in both the communication and journalism industries. Here are some areas where AI is being used in media and communication purview:

○ Social Media and Digital Promotion

The information flow on social media platforms like Facebook and X (then Twitter) is easily manipulated. Tweets and posts with specific criteria or agendas can be critical on social media. In other words, the topics of significant importance on social media are decided in advance. Bots (on X) are robotic accounts that can be programmed to respond like a human being. It can generate a message, retweet message, and support message. Bots can support any information or oppose any fact. Spam bots are a kind of X account involved in deceptive, harmful, or damaging activities. X, a means of communication, is a medium of political brand signalling. The machine-operated X accounts or bots spread misinformation during the 2016 US election. It was a significant actor who could change, shape political opinion, and influence political thought-artificial intelligence in excellently promoting digital marketing. India passed the *IT Act* in 2000 to control web-based crime and misconduct. Now, we need to introduce a new law for social media because of stalking, bullying, morphing, and other social media cheating methods. These misconducts of social media are changing their face day by day. Even new *IT Regulations, 2021* are insufficient to control current social media-related issues.

○ AI in Content Creation

AI-generated content is becoming increasingly popular in the media industry. With the ability to analyse the data and create content based on trends and user preferences, AI generated content that can save the time and money of the media companies while still delivering higher quality content.

For example, news organisations can now use generative AI to create articles from the data sets, including sports scores, financial reports and weather forecasts. Namely, The Associated Press which was founded in the year 1846 uses machine learning to gather, produce, and distribute the news which includes reporting, distribution, AP stylebook, AP polls and photography. Tools that help automate journalism can help organisations scale article production and leverage data to inform their content and increase quality in guiding AI more effectively.

AI does not just help organisations or companies create written content. However, it also effectively impacts both audio and video.

AI-powered video editing tools are already helping automate tedious tasks such as audio syncing, colour corrections and text animation; this helps save time and enables the teams to focus on their efforts elsewhere to scale their creation and stay on top of new trends in consumption. Image recognition is another section in which AI effectively impacts the media. With the ability to analyse and recognise objects and people and even emotions in images and videos, AI is helping media companies better understand and engage with their audiences. For example, image recognition technology can track how many people are in a particular shot, like what they are reacting to and where they are looking; all of that could be used in the accelerating content search. AI is also used to create jumpstart mastering and musical compositions. AI-generated music composition services use algorithms that create original music based on user input, such as genre, tempo, and mood. AI-powered tools can analyse audio tracks and optimise them for the best sound quality to a certain degree. These use cases only show how this technology can change the media industry. It will also impact how organisations personalise their content towards their audiences.

- **AI in Broadcasting**

Real-time streaming works for the news and entertainment broadcasters and those who watch. AI can help customise, package, and send audio-visual content in real-time, improving the experience for the audience. It can also help increase ad sales by putting ads in the right places. The digital billboard replacement services brought in more money from advertising during live sports. AI is enhancing the newsroom in many ways. BBC has introduced an AI-based news processing technology called BBC's Juicer. It is a news aggregation and content extraction API that works on the beta web interface. BBB's Juicer scraps the article and rewrites it as per the RSS and searchable content. It is called BBC's news labs. It takes articles from BBC and from other news sites and it automatically parses them and tags them with related DPpedia entities and these entities are grouped under four categories such as people, places, organisations and things.

Predictive Analytics

Analytics of popular media content can be utilised to find out what people like to see. When changing content, promotional strategies, promotions, and supply chains, it is essential to have advanced analytics skills. It has the potential to show people the right content and figure out which content makes money.

AI in Media Analysis and Decision-Making

AI could analyse and identify trends and patterns in an audience's behaviour, allowing teams to make informed decisions about their content. With sentiment analysis and audience insights, creators can refine their work by measuring audience reactions to the content. For example, AI can analyse social media activity and identify popular topics or keywords that can be incorporated into the content to improve visibility and engagement. AI can also help creators understand their audience's emotions and opinions, enabling them to tailor their content accordingly. Today, AI technology is already used in broadcasts to measure the performance of advertisements with the target audience. It also helps to track the content, indexing it to make airchecks easier to pull, reuse content, and repurpose content for other channels such as social media.

We will see predictive analytics continue to improve and help forecast content performance, guide strategic decisions, and improve visibility. This information can guide strategic decisions and help the creators to optimise their content for maximum reach and engagement.

AI in Newsroom

The most popular international news agency, Reuter, uses AI-based technology to track breaking news. After adopting this technology, journalists do not need to work hard to track news. Reuters made semantic technology company Graphiq a technology partner. Graphiq provides various free data visualisations in entertainment, sports, and the news sectors. Data is automatically updated on the publisher's website in real time. American media house, The Washington Post is also using AI in the form of automated news writing, also known as 'robot journalism' or simply 'automated journalism.' The post is using Heliograf software. The Rio Olympic Games have been covered with the help of automated journalism. British newspaper, The Guardian introduced the AI-based tool Chatbot. It was initially launched with Facebook. It saves time searching news stories in different segments based on time, country, language, etc. American news agency, The New York Times has also adopted an AI-based editor application. The 'Editor' is part of The New York Times research and development lab.

The Future of AI Media

The future of AI in media is promising, with the potential for AI-powered virtual and augmented reality experiences to transform media consumption. These technologies offer interactive and immersive experiences that can significantly enhance user engagement. AI can also help ensure a safe environment by modulating social media content by identifying and removing harmful content.

However, as mentioned above, privacy concerns and personalisation of AI content must be balanced to prevent potential harm and misinformation. Ethical AI implementation is typically crucial, and collaboration between industry leaders, AI experts and policymakers can be instrumental in shaping the future of AI in the media. Despite those challenges, AI is effectively changing the media industry. From content personalisation to AI-assisted editing, media-related companies are finding innovative and new ways to use AI to improve their processes and for better engagement with their audiences. As technology advances, it will be more exciting to see what new possibilities AI will bring to the media world.

Conclusion

AI and automation are integral to the media and the communication sector. Media cannot survive without the support of technology. AI has started a new age of journalism, and news can be produced and circulated with AI. By automating routine tasks and analysing audience behaviour, AI enables newsrooms to focus on quality journalism while creating content to meet evolving consumer demands.

AI can track the news circulation and attention users give to digital media. Media monitoring is possible and easy with the support of AI technology. Popular media organisations are using newer advanced technology to reach their respective audience, leveraging AI to expand their reach and personalise user experiences, thus building stronger connections with their audiences.

While AI is an effective tool for the media, its use must be ethical and accountable. Encouraging transparency and accountability in automated processes is essential as AI will continue to influence journalism's future. By finding the balance, AI can improve the media's contribution to society by empowering communities with timely, accurate, and relevant information and encouraging an informed public.

References

1. Aissani, Rahima & Abdallah, Rania & Taha, Sawsan & Al Adwan, Muhammad Noor. (2023). Artificial Intelligence Tools in Media and Journalism: Roles and Concerns. 19-26. 10.1109/MCNA59361.2023.10185738.
2. Noain-Sánchez, Amaya. (2022). Addressing the Impact of Artificial Intelligence on Journalism: the perception of experts, journalists and academics. Communication & Society. 35. 105-121. 10.15581/003.35.3.105-121.
3. https://www.presscouncil.nic.in/Pdf/Topic2023.pdf
4. https://www.forbes.com/sites/nelsongranados/2024/05/31/how-artificial-intelligence-is-shaping-the-new-media-and-entertainment-economy/
5. https://www.leewayhertz.com/ai-in-media-and-entertainment/
6. https://www.veritone.com/blog/transforming-the-future-of-media-with-ai/

7. https://www.globallogic.com/insights/blogs/ai-is-the-future-of-media/
8. https://www.infosysbpm.com/blogs/media-entertainment/use-of-ai-in-media-entertainment-industry.html
9. https://www.plattform-lernende-systeme.de/files/Downloads/Publikationen_EN/AG3_WP_ES_AI_in_Journalism.pdf
10. https://www.diva-portal.org/smash/get/diva2:1815699/FULLTEXT02.pdf

Artificial Intelligence and Cyber Terrorism

Thenmozhi Pandian, PhD Research Scholar, Department of Media Sciences, CEG—Anna University, Chennai - 600025. Email: thenmozhi.dms@gmail.com

Introduction

Artificial Intelligence (AI) is fundamentally reshaping industries by providing innovative solutions to complex challenges. In healthcare, AI supports diagnostic precision and personalized treatments, while in finance, it enhances fraud detection and trading strategies. In transportation, AI drives advancements in autonomous vehicles and logistics optimization. These transformative capabilities reflect the immense potential of AI in modern society.

However, these developments come with risks, particularly in the realm of cybersecurity. AI's evolution has opened new opportunities for cybercriminals and terrorists to exploit technology for malicious purposes. Cyber terrorism, distinct from conventional cybercrime, involves the use of digital technologies to instill fear, cause harm, or disrupt critical systems for ideological, political, or religious motivations. Unlike financially motivated cybercrime, which targets individual or organizational wealth, cyber terrorism aims for broader societal impacts, such as destabilizing governments or undermining public trust.

This chapter explores the dual role of AI in the context of cyber terrorism. On one hand, AI can be weaponized by cyber terrorists to conduct precise, large-scale attacks. On the other, it provides advanced tools for cybersecurity professionals to identify and neutralize these threats. Understanding this dynamic is crucial for developing effective strategies to mitigate risks associated with AI-driven threats while harnessing its defensive potential.

Defining Cyber Terrorism and Differentiating It from Cybercrime

Cyber terrorism is often conflated with cybercrime due to their shared use of digital platforms for malicious purposes. However, the two differ significantly in their objectives and impacts. Cyber terrorism is driven by ideological, political, or religious motives. Its primary goal is to disrupt societal stability, instill fear, and challenge national security. For instance, a cyber terrorist might target a nation's power grid, causing widespread outages that disrupt daily life, cripple infrastructure, and undermine public confidence in governmental systems.

Cybercrime, by contrast, is financially motivated. It focuses on exploiting individuals or organizations for monetary gain through activities like ransomware attacks, identity theft, or phishing schemes. While cybercrime can have significant consequences, its impact is typically localized and lacks the broader societal implications of cyber terrorism. Recognizing this distinction is essential for framing AI's role in these domains and addressing the unique challenges posed by each.

The Capabilities of AI in Cyber Terrorism

AI's capacity to analyze vast amounts of data, recognize patterns, and automate processes makes it a powerful tool in cyber operations. Cyber terrorists leverage AI to enhance the scale, precision, and adaptability of their attacks, creating a new frontier of threats. One area of concern is AI-driven malware. Unlike traditional malware, which relies on pre-programmed behavior, AI-powered malware can learn from its environment, adapting to circumvent security measures in real time. For example, AI algorithms can identify vulnerabilities in a system and modify their behavior to exploit those weaknesses, making them harder to detect and neutralize.

Another significant threat is the use of AI in phishing attacks. Traditional phishing schemes often rely on generic, poorly constructed messages that can be easily identified by vigilant users. AI-powered phishing, however, employs natural language processing to craft highly convincing, personalized emails that mimic legitimate communications. Such messages are not only difficult to identify but also increase the likelihood of victims falling prey to scams.

Deepfake technology further exemplifies the weaponization of AI in cyber terrorism. By creating realistic but entirely fabricated audio or video content, cyber terrorists can manipulate public opinion, spread misinformation, or impersonate individuals to deceive targets. For instance, a deepfake video of a government official delivering a fabricated speech could incite panic or erode public trust.

The ability of AI to automate these processes exponentially increases the scale of potential attacks. Cyber terrorists can target multiple systems simultaneously, exploiting vulnerabilities with precision and efficiency. This highlights the urgent need for robust defenses against AI-enabled cyber threats.

Defensive Capabilities of AI in Cybersecurity

While AI poses significant threats when weaponized, it also offers formidable tools for defending against cyber terrorism. AI-driven cybersecurity systems are revolutionizing how organizations detect, respond to, and mitigate threats. One such application is in intrusion detection systems (IDS). Traditional IDS often struggle to identify complex or evolving threats due to their reliance on static rules. AI-powered IDS, on the other hand, leverage machine learning algorithms to analyze network traffic and detect anomalies in real time. These systems improve over time, adapting to new threat patterns and reducing false positives.

Threat intelligence platforms are another critical application of AI in defensive cybersecurity. By analyzing historical data, these platforms can predict emerging threats and identify system vulnerabilities. For example, by studying trends in ransomware attacks, AI systems can recommend proactive measures to secure critical infrastructure before an attack occurs.

AI also enhances incident response capabilities. Automating responses to cyber threats, such as isolating affected systems or deploying patches, significantly reduces response times. This not only minimizes the damage caused by attacks but also allows human cybersecurity experts to focus on more complex tasks. These defensive applications underscore the importance of integrating AI into cybersecurity strategies to counter the growing sophistication of cyber terrorism.

Ethical and Policy Considerations

The integration of AI into cybersecurity raises critical ethical and policy challenges. One of the foremost concerns is privacy. Defensive AI systems often rely on extensive data collection to identify potential threats. While this enhances their effectiveness, it also raises questions about the balance between security and individual privacy. Ensuring that these systems operate within legal and ethical boundaries is essential to maintaining public trust.

Another issue is accountability. Autonomous AI systems in cybersecurity operate with minimal human intervention, making it difficult to attribute responsibility for unintended consequences. For example, if an AI-driven defensive system mistakenly identifies a legitimate user as a threat and restricts their access, who should be held accountable?

The weaponization of AI by cyber terrorists adds another layer of complexity. International agreements and regulations are needed to prevent the misuse of AI technologies. Without such measures, the risk of AI being exploited for malicious purposes will continue to grow.

Transparency is equally important. Organizations must clearly communicate how AI technologies are used and their implications for privacy and security. Transparent practices not only foster public trust but also ensure ethical compliance in the deployment of AI systems.

Addressing AI-Driven Cyber Terrorism: Recommendations

To combat AI-driven cyber terrorism effectively, a multifaceted approach is required. Collaboration between governments, academia, and the private sector is essential for pooling knowledge and resources. Public-private partnerships can facilitate the sharing of threat intelligence and the development of innovative defensive technologies.

Investment in research and development is also crucial. Advancing AI-powered cybersecurity tools will enable organizations to stay ahead of emerging threats. This includes improving threat detection systems, enhancing predictive analytics, and automating response mechanisms.

International cooperation is vital for addressing cross-border cyber threats. Cyber terrorism does not recognize national boundaries, making a unified global approach essential. Countries must work together to establish regulatory frameworks that govern the ethical use of AI in cybersecurity.

Education and training programs are equally important. Raising awareness about AI-driven threats and equipping individuals and organizations with the skills to mitigate them can significantly reduce vulnerabilities. Such initiatives ensure that all stakeholders are prepared to navigate the evolving landscape of cyber terrorism.

Conclusion

AI's role in cyber terrorism highlights its dual potential as both a tool for attack and a mechanism for defense. While cyber terrorists exploit AI to conduct sophisticated and large-scale attacks, AI-driven cybersecurity systems offer powerful solutions to counter these threats. Addressing the challenges posed by AI-driven cyber terrorism requires a proactive approach that includes collaboration, research, international cooperation, and ethical compliance.

By understanding AI's capabilities and limitations, stakeholders can develop strategies to mitigate its risks and harness its potential for good. As AI continues to evolve, vigilance and innovation will be key to ensuring its responsible and beneficial use in the fight against cyber terrorism.

References

1. Jiang, F., Jiang, Y., Zhi, H., Dong, Y., Li, H., Ma, S., &; Wang, Y. (2017). Artificial intelligence in healthcare: past, present and future. Stroke and vascular neurology, 2(4).
2. Abduljabbar, R., Dia, H., Liyanage, S., &; Bagloee, S. A. (2019). Applications of artificial intelligence in transport: An overview. Sustainability, 11(1), 189.

3. Bianchi, S., Mancuso, M., Paternoster, C., Kalpakis, G., Tsikrika, T., Vrochidis, S.,&; Jaeger, B. (2023, May). Artificial Intelligence to Counter Cyber-Terrorism. In International Conference on Cybersecurity and Cybercrime (Vol. 10, pp. 12-20).

4. Brenner, S. W. (2006). Cybercrime, cyberterrorism and cyberwarfare. Revue internationale de droit pénal, 77(3), 453-471.

5. Yamin, M. M., Ullah, M., Ullah, H., &; Katt, B. (2021). Weaponized AI for cyber attacks. Journal of Information Security and Applications, 57, 102722.

6. Guembe, B., Azeta, A., Misra, S., Osamor, V. C., Fernandez-Sanz, L., &; Pospelova, V. (2022). The emerging threat of ai-driven cyber attacks: A review. Applied Artificial Intelligence, 36(1), 2037254.

7. Basit, A., Zafar, M., Liu, X., Javed, A. R., Jalil, Z., &; Kifayat, K. (2021). A comprehensive survey of AI-enabled phishing attacks detection techniques. Telecommunication Systems, 76, 139-154.

8. Westerlund, M. (2019). The emergence of deepfake technology: A review. Technology innovation management review, 9(11).

9. Enoch, S. Y., Huang, Z., Moon, C. Y., Lee, D., Ahn, M. K., &; Kim, D. S. (2020). HARMer: Cyber-attacks automation and evaluation. IEEE Access, 8, 129397-129414.

10. Bace, R. G., &; Mell, P. (2001). Intrusion detection systems.

11. Dutta, A., &; Kant, S. (2020). An overview of cyber threat intelligence platform and role of artificial intelligence and machine learning. In Information Systems Security: 16th International Conference, ICISS 2020, Jammu, India, December 16–20, 2020, Proceedings 16 (pp. 81-86). Springer International Publishing.

12. Dunsin, D., Ghanem, M. C., & Quazzane, K. (2022). The use of artificial intelligence in digital forensics and incident response in a constrained environment. International Journal of Information and Communication Engineering, 16(8), 280-285.

13. Vashishth, T. K., Sharma, V., Samania, B., Sharma, R., Singh, S., &; Jajoria, P. (2025). Ethical and Legal Implications of AI in Cybersecurity.

In Machine Intelligence Applications in Cyber-Risk Management (pp. 387-414). IGI Global Scientific Publishing.

14. Bignami, F. (2022). Artificial intelligence accountability of public administration. The American Journal of Comparative Law, 70(Supplement_1), i312-i346.

15. Burton, J., &; Soare, S. R. (2019, May). Understanding the strategic implications of the weaponization of artificial intelligence. In 2019 11th international conference on Cyber Conflict (CyCon) (Vol. 900, pp. 1-17). IEEE.

16. Khan, F. A., Li, G., Khan, A. N., Khan, Q. W., Hadjouni, M., &; Elmannai, H. (2023). AI- Driven Counter-Terrorism: Enhancing Global Security Through Advanced Predictive Analytics. IEEE Access, 11, 135864-135879.

17. Chatzis, P., &; Stavrou, E. (2022). Cyber-threat landscape of border control infrastructures. International Journal of Critical Infrastructure Protection, 36, 100503.

18. Prince, N. U., Faheem, M. A., Khan, O. U., Hossain, K., Alkhayyat, A., Hamdache, A., &; Elmouki, I. (2024). AI-powered data-driven cybersecurity techniques: Boosting threat identification and reaction. Nanotechnology Perceptions, 20, 332-353.

19. Olatunji, A. P., Ajibola, O. S., &; Agunbiade, N. O. (2024). Leveraging AI-driven training programs for enhanced organizational security awareness. International Journal of Science and Research Archive, 13(1), 301-311.

20. Theodorio, A. O. (2024). Understanding cyber threats in an era of digitally connected classrooms: Lessons for the Nigerian higher education system and society.

www.ingramcontent.com/pod-product-compliance
Ingram Content Group UK Ltd.
Pitfield, Milton Keynes, MK11 3LW, UK
UKHW060117010826
14089UKWH00004B/34

9 798899 299520